TOWN PLANNING IN LONDON

St. George's, Bloomsbury, and houses in
Hart Street (now Bloomsbury Way), 1799

TOWN PLANNING IN LONDON

THE EIGHTEENTH & NINETEENTH CENTURIES

Second Edition

DONALD J. OLSEN

Yale University Press · New Haven & London

Printed in Great Britain by Butler & Tanner Ltd, Frome and London.

Library of Congress catalog card number: 64-20929.

ISBN 0 300 02914-4 (cloth).
0 300 02915-2 (paper).

TO MY FATHER AND MOTHER

CONTENTS

LIST OF ILLUSTRATIONS

ABBREVIATIONS

In the notes the Parliamentary Papers are cited in the manner recommended by P. Ford and G. Ford, *Select List of British Parliamentary Papers, 1833–1899* (Oxford, 1953). The page number is that of the report, not of the volume. The number in the parenthesis after the year is the command number, followed, in small roman numerals, by the volume in which the report appears. The minutes of evidence of the Royal Commission on the Housing of the Working Classes are abbreviated HWC (see Chapter 1, note 19). The several volumes of the minutes of evidence of the Select Committee on Town Holdings are abbreviated TH (see Chapter 2, note 5). The Reports of the Royal Commission and Select Committee, together with all references to other Parliamentary Papers, are cited in full.

Unless otherwise indicated, all manuscripts referred to in connection with the Bedford estate are in the Bedford Office in London. Similarly, except for the minute books of the General Court, which are to be found in the London office of the Captain Coram Foundation (formerly the Foundling Hospital), all manuscript sources cited in connection with the Foundling Hospital estate are deposited in the London County Record Office in County Hall.

Spelling and punctuation in quotations have been modernized throughout.

PREFACE TO SECOND EDITION

In 1964, when *Town Planning in London* first appeared, Europe and America were buoyantly optimistic about the prospects for revitalizing their cities: embarking on massive projects of comprehensive redevelopment; harnessing the resources produced by high rates of economic growth, the white heat of modern technology, and the impressive body of theory being produced by social scientists, and of designs by architects. In the United States the Model Cities program of the Johnson administration was beginning to put to the test Sigfried Giedion's prescription for urban regeneration: to save our cities by first destroying them. Britain was going forward with expensive schemes for new towns, high-rise housing estates, and motorway boxes. Piccadilly Circus and Covent Garden were to be demolished and replaced by futuristic complexes, complete with elevated walkways and new brutalist towers. In France, Paris was pushing through the Right Bank motorway and preparing to transform the site of Les Halles into an expression of all that was best in modern technology and urban design. Outside the capital, Sarcelles and La Défense were to demonstrate how planners, unconstrained by historical fact and historical forms, could create healthier and more beautiful cities, nurturing environments for human growth and creativity.

In such a climate of opinion it is not surprising that few of the reviews of *Town Planning in London* noticed its subversive message: that the experience of the great landed estates of London provided little cause for optimism that any town planning scheme, no matter how carefully thought out, how vigorously executed, how tirelessly enforced, could achieve its goal in more than a limited and temporary way. True, Jane Jacobs had, in *The Death and Life of Great American Cities* (London: Jonathan Cape, 1962), already questioned the most fundamental assumptions of the planners of the 1960s, but the dominant mood remained confident as to the possibilities for recreating our cities, and thereby effecting a significant improvement in the quality of the lives lived in them. Even critics of individual schemes retained their faith in planning as such, accounting for particular failures by particular weaknesses in the original design, by insufficiently rigorous controls on the greed of private developers, by there having been too little planning rather than too much.

How different are the expectations of 1982! If twenty years ago the sheer intractability of market forces and their resistance to governmental controls were wildly underestimated, today, in Britain and the United States, market forces are being hailed as not only powerful, but beneficent. Nor can the disillusionment with planning as perceived in the 1960s be seen simply as an expression of a resurgent conservatism. Preservation, "recycling", conservation, and environmentalism are the watchwords of the left as well. A broad consensus among all groups—save for a few outposts of planners and architects holding fast to their original beliefs—has abandoned not only its faith in the efficacy of the techniques of town planning but its desire to see them succeed. We have seen the future—in the shape of windswept, vandalized tower blocks, decayed and crime-ridden pedestrian precincts, and express highways blighting whole neighborhoods—and concluded that not only does it not work, but that we wouldn't like it if it did. We are sadly convinced that any new building we erect will be worse than the one it replaces: uglier, less convenient, more wasteful of scarce resources. So, with diminished expectations, we dismantle programs of governmental control, we patch and mend, and hope that the free market will succeed where planning boards and public agencies have failed.

If in the 1960s we believed town planners could do anything they set out to do, today we think they can achieve nothing, except perhaps exacerbate the problems they try to solve. In such a mood I fear that the other conclusion I reached in *Town Planning in London*—that the policies of the Bedford Office and the Foundling Hospital produced results that, if more limited and less permanent than their creators wished, still made *some* difference—will be as much ignored as was the more pessimistic message in 1964.

Certainly the published scholarship in urban history in the past two decades has de-emphasized the scope of both the intentions and the success of urban landlords in directing the development of their estates. Outside London C. W. Chalklin found little evidence of planning by ground landlords or anyone else in *The Provincial Towns of Georgian England: A Study of the Building Process, 1740–1820* (London: Edward Arnold, 1974). Within London Hermione Hobhouse showed, in *Thomas Cubitt, Master Builder* (London: Macmillan, 1971), how much more important the large building contractor was than the landowner in creating Belgravia and Pimlico. F. M. L. Thompson in *Hampstead: Building a Borough, 1650–1964* (London: Routledge & Kegan Paul, 1974) has pointed out how little the landlords, large and small, of that parish were able to deflect the operation of anonymous market forces. In *The Fields Beneath* (London: Maurice Temple Smith, 1977), Gillian Tindall found the landowners of Kentish Town even less able to exert direct control over the fortunes of that neighborhood. In "House upon House: Estate Development in London and Sheffield", H. J. Dyos and Michael Wolff, eds., *The Victorian City* (London: Routledge & Kegan Paul, 1973), vol. I, I argued that Eton College and the Duke of Norfolk took generally passive roles in the development, respectively, of the Chalcots estate north of Regent's Park and in the latter's vast working-class and industrial properties in Sheffield. And while the Greater London Council's *Survey of London*, vol. XXXIX, *The Grosvenor Estate in Mayfair*, Part I (London: Athlone Press, 1977) indicates that after the succession of the second Marquess of Westminster in 1845, the Grosvenor estate came to take an active and creative role in northern Mayfair, before then it had responded to the pressures of builders and tenants more than it initiated change.

The most probing and comprehensive treatment of urban leasehold estate management is David Cannadine, *Lords and Landlords: the Aristocracy and the Towns, 1774–1967* (Leicester: Leicester University Press, 1980). Cannadine ultimately finds the diversity of practice and experience of urban ground landlords so great as to make any clearcut generalizations impossible. In answer to the question whether the existence of large leasehold estates makes very much difference to the course of urban history, he concludes, in effect, no, except when it does. Ordinarily, he decides, whatever alterations in detail a landlord may impose, neighborhoods establish themselves, grow, and decay as topographical, demographic, economic, and other forces dictate, with successful estate plans being those that happen to accord with such external causes. Yet it was not the inexorable push of History, he finds, but the Dukes of Devonshire, who made Eastbourne. I would agree both with his cautious generalizations and his willingness to admit exceptions, and suggest that Bloomsbury and Covent Garden, if less spectacular achievements than Eastbourne, also represent triumphs by the landowner over the environment.

A developer with the resources and vision of Thomas Cubitt might well have embarked on a scheme as spacious and generous as in fact emerged in northern Bloomsbury even if there had been no Bedford estate. Yet it is unlikely that builders like William Scott, Robert Grews, James Burton, Henry Scrimshaw, and James Sims would have had either the will or the means to provide a comparably elegant and unified layout for southern Bloomsbury without the support and supervision of the Bedford Office. The physical survival of Bloomsbury, to the extent that it has survived—and it was London University, not the Bedford Office, that destroyed Torrington and Woburn squares—would have been inconceivable without the tireless, apparently quixotic efforts of the ground landlord to resist the forces of geography, economics, and fashion. It is hard to imagine what saved the Bedford estate from the far greater decay and deterioration of immediately adjacent streets apart from the policies of the Duke's agents. Poverty can protect a district from the depredations of the redeveloper, but it cannot secure the maintenance and repair of its physical fabric the way well-drafted and conscientiously enforced leasehold covenants can.

On the other side of New Oxford Street the events of the past few years have done even more to vindicate in retrospect the policies of the Bedford estate in the years before the sale of 1914. The economic and aesthetic success of the transformation of Covent Garden into London's newest tourist mecca depends on nearly three centuries of estate management, doggedly preserving and maintaining streets and buildings in the face of the best contemporary architectural, social, and economic opinion.

In 1964 I thought the activities of the Bedford Office and the Foundling Hospital representative of what urban ground landlords in general did. Since then it has become increasingly clear that the practices of the two estates are instead an indication of what ground landlords could do if they tried. Far from being typical, the Bedford estate may well have been the best managed urban estate in England. The difference in the quality of planning and direction that the Foundling Hospital exercised over its property from that of the Provost and Fellows of Eton is both immense and greatly to the credit of the former. The question emerges: why did the Dukes of Bedford and the Foundling Hospital try so much harder than most, or even all, other ground landlords?

One part of the answer, as far as the Bedford estate is concerned, may be the particular virtues of the Duke's servants, virtues transmitted from the seventeenth century to the present as a tradition of good management. David Spring devotes much of *The English Landed Estate in the Nineteenth Century: its Administration* (Baltimore: The Johns Hopkins Press, 1963) to the reforms which the seventh Duke and his agent Christopher Haedy introduced in 1839, but those reforms would have been ineffective without a pre-existing body of devoted professionals in the ducal employ, and of administrative machinery at once independently efficient and responsive to changing wishes from above. The Bedford Office, as an institution, would seem to conform to G. R. Elton's definition of "bureaucratic government" as opposed to "household government", which he set forth in *The Tudor Revolution in Government* (Cambridge: Cambridge University Press, 1953). In brief a bureaucratic government, while obedient to the commands of individual kings (or prime ministers, or dukes), is able to act forcefully and effectively in the absence of continual direction from higher authority; household government is subject to the vagaries of a succession of "strong" and "weak" kings (or conscientious and uninterested landlords). The fact that the Bedford estate was managed by a body of full-time employees and not, like the Grosvenor estate, by professionals combining their services to the Duke of Westminster with those to other clients, gave it a degree of attention otherwise unattainable. The many years of service that the auditors, stewards, and surveyors ordinarily performed gave them ample opportunity to imbibe the values and techniques of their predecessors and to pass them on, modified by their own experience, to their successors. They were well paid and their accomplishments justified their salaries.

A tradition of high competence and devotion to the business of the estate goes back at least as far as the early seventeenth century. Volume XXXVI of the *Survey of London, The Parish of St. Paul Covent Garden* (London: Athlone Press, 1970) shows the estate, as early as the 1630s, following policies that differed not at all in kind from those of two and three centuries later. While the influence of Charles I and Inigo Jones on the conception and layout of Covent Garden is evident, equally so are the skill and imagination with which the fourth Earl of Bedford and his servants responded to the royal challenge to use the physical expansion of London as an occasion for embellishing the metropolis. Restrictive covenants that first anticipated and later surpassed in stringency those of the post-Fire Building Acts, prohibitions of offensive trades, provision for paving, sewers, and water conduits, requirements for the landlord's approval of plans and elevations, sanctions against unauthorized alterations, all characterized the original leases for Covent Garden as they did the eighteenth and nineteenth-century ones for Bloomsbury and Figs Mead. Even the deliberate difficulties of communication with less fashionable surrounding districts—no longer evident because of estate-financed street improvements in the nineteenth century—anticipate the efforts in the 1820s and 1830s to insulate Bloomsbury and Figs Mead from Somers Town and other unsavory surroundings through gates and an avoidance of through streets.

No other estate that has yet been studied approaches the Bedford estate in continuity of endeavor—maintaining policies it was convinced were right irrespective of passing fashions—or in its patient determination as it formulated, imposed, maintained, and modified coherent plans for its portion of London. That, time and again, it had ultimately to retreat before forces stronger than itself in no way detracts from its achievement. The Bedford estate has suffered so much uninformed and spiteful criticism from the press, particularly in the late nineteenth century, that justice demands that its unusual virtues be emphasized.

The adjacent Foundling estate, given its far smaller financial resources and even less favorable location, had almost as much cause for pride in what it accomplished. Sold by the Hospital when it moved to Berkhamstead in 1926, and since damaged by bombing and defaced by postwar excrescences like the Brunswick Centre, the Foundling estate has to be judged less by its present appearance than by its character when it housed John and Isabella Knightley and the envious friends of the Sedley family, themselves so grandly established in nearby Russell Square. The minutes of the Building Committee and the General Committee during the period of development—1790 to 1823—are a record of continuous, detailed, conscientious efforts to achieve the best possible urban environment. The Bedford estate to the west as an obvious model for emulation, their good fortunes in attracting a builder of the resourcefulness of James Burton, and a supervising architect of the calibre of Samuel Pepys Cockerell explain some, but not all, of their success. More important was excellence of the administration of all the business of the charity. As Ruth K. McClure has shown in *Coram's Children: the London Foundling Hospital in the Eighteenth Century* (London and New Haven: Yale University Press, 1981), it attracted not only a large and fashionable body of Governors, but a small and devoted core that worked with zeal and intelligence for the interests of the institution and the children who depended on it. Unusually sensitive to the possibility of public criticism, it sought to polish the image as well as enhance the real effectiveness of the Hospital. Eton College felt rich and secure enough to ignore the possibilities for urban design and environmental control in Chalcots, out of sight in distant London; for the Foundling Hospital its estate, directly impinging on its buildings and grounds, had to be made into a worthy setting and a stable source of income for itself and its charges.

The very strength of the efforts of the two estates makes the present situation of Bloomsbury all the more poignant. When I wrote *Town Planning in London* I could speak of the Georgian terraces in Torrington and Woburn squares in the present tense, while James Burton's houses, in however dilapidated a state, still lined the west side of Brunswick Square. All these, and much more, are now gone. The Bloomsbury of the 1930s, so evocatively described by Steen Eiler Rasmussen in *London: the Unique City* (London: Jonathan Cape, 1937), seems as distant as the Bloomsbury of Christopher Haedy. Yet the virtues it retains even today can in large measure be attributed to the operations of the Bedford Office, still functioning in its nineteenth-century quarters in Montague Street, on what had been the grounds of eighteenth-century Bedford House. And Marchmont Street, if not quite what the Governors and Guardians of the Foundling Hospital had in mind, is today a lively and attractive shopping street that shows how well small Georgian houses can be adapted to provide pleasure for another and very different age.

The text remains as it was in 1964. Were I to attempt to rewrite it today I might be tempted to remove one or two youthful rhetorical flights, and certainly the occasional snide remark about Victorian taste, but on the whole I stand by what follows. If I had to hazard a generalization today, it would be something like this: Planning, whether by landlord and private developer, or by state and municipality, is unlikely to succeed in its aims without the support of market forces and other broad historical determinants; but in certain situations, in certain periods, under certain circumstances, it can achieve something. If not a particularly stirring manifesto, this is one intended to encourage the urban historian searching, not for universal laws, but for instances of the perplexing but delightful diversity that characterizes human creation and experience.

Poughkeepsie, New York   Donald J. Olsen
April 1982

PREFACE TO FIRST EDITION

Town planning as a consciously separate art and profession is a product of our own time. The first use of the expression noted by the *Oxford English Dictionary* was in 1906.[1] Yet in fact town planning is as ancient as the town. A village might just happen, but the establishment of a town or city necessarily involves some governing intelligence. Walls, roadways, public open spaces, temples, water supply, and drainage require a minimum of planning and foresight. Babylon, Alexandria, and Peking show or showed at least as much conscious direction of their layout and development as Amsterdam or St. Petersburg or Washington.

The following pages will examine the kind of town planning which the ground landlords of London tried—from the seventeenth to the nineteenth centuries—to put into effect on their estates, how they went about doing it, and how successful their attempts were. They suggest certain ways in which the conscious practices of a number of ground landlords have been responsible for some of the qualities that distinguish London from the other great cities of the world.

Historians of town planning have long admired the spacious and symmetrical layout of many of the estates west of the City of London, commending the low density of housing, the large proportion of space devoted to garden squares, and the high standard of domestic architecture to be found on all but the more recently developed estates. Lewis Mumford has argued that the concentrated ownership of urban land "would have advantages, if the owners of such land were as socially and architecturally enlightened as the great ground landlords who built up Bloomsbury, Mayfair, and Belgravia . . . between the seventeenth and the nineteenth centuries."[2] Sir John Summerson, Steen Eiler Rasmussen, and

1. The phrases "town-building plan" and "town-extension plans" date from 1904. "Street-planning" was used as early as 1851. John Weale, *London Exhibited in 1851* (London, 1851), p. 770.

2. Lewis Mumford, *City Development* (London, Secker and Warburg, 1947), p. 79.

William Ashworth have all described the kind of planning to be found on London's great estates, and the influence which the system of leasehold tenure has had on the pattern of growth of the metropolis.[3] H. J. Dyos in his study of nineteenth-century Camberwell has shown how the interaction of the practices of leasehold estates and other social and economic forces determined the character of a typical south London suburb.[4] But no one has yet analyzed in any detail the planning that actually took place in the estate offices of the great landlords, nor exactly how they went about putting their plans into effect. Such work as has been done concentrates almost wholly on the first stages of planning, which came to an end once the streets had been laid out, the gardens planted, and the houses built. But the remarkable thing about the London leasehold system is that it enabled the freeholder of a big estate to retain control over the use and maintenance of his property while it was on lease, and to engage in schemes of redevelopment and rehabilitation once the leases expired. Admirably conceived building plans on a large scale can be found in many European and American cities. Only in certain towns in the British Isles, notably London, has the system of land tenure permitted the continuing, centralized control of a neighborhood that is necessary if the aims of the original plan are to be maintained, and if the plan is to be sensibly adapted to the changing needs of succeeding generations.

Sir John Summerson has remarked on the comparatively recent public awareness "that a city is a living creature which must be controlled and which, to be controlled, must be understood."[5] It is hard today to appreciate the state of mind which, prior to the formation of the London County Council in 1889, and even more before the creation of the Metropolitan Board of Works in 1855, could allow the metropolis to be governed as if it were a collection of separate and autonomous villages. In 1855 Sir Benjamin Hall estimated that London was governed by no fewer than three hundred different authorities.[6] The confused and overlapping jurisdictions, together with the ineffectiveness or corruption of many of the governing bodies, explain how, with "no government and no ideal," early Victorian London "drifted just as events directed, into a cholera epidemic, into a chaos which was too stupid and serious to be allowed to go on . . ."[7]

---

3. Sir John Summerson, *Georgian London* (Baltimore, Penguin Books, 1962). Steen Eiler Rasmussen, *London: The Unique City* (London, Cape, 1948). William Ashworth, *The Genesis of Modern British Town Planning* (London, Routledge and Kegan Paul, 1954).

4. H. J. Dyos, *Victorian Suburb* (Leicester, Leicester University Press, 1961).

5. *Georgian London*, p. 24.

6. Sir George Laurence Gomme, *London in the Reign of Victoria* (Chicago, 1898), p. 51.

7. Ibid., p. 67.

Yet the mid-nineteenth century, which Sir George Laurence Gomme saw as the dawn of a new era of rational, centralized planning, seems today from an aesthetic point of view the beginning of a Dark Age from which we have yet to emerge. For while we must admit that with respect to water supply, sewers, paving, lighting, garbage disposal, and the physical comforts in general, the worst speculative housing estate of the 1930s was immensely superior to Bedford Square in the 1770s, the student of town planning is far more likely to pay pilgrimages to Bloomsbury than to Beckenham, and as likely to admire Belgravia as Lansbury. And however deficient some Georgian and Victorian planned estates may be in meeting the demands of the mid-twentieth century, they did fulfill admirably the requirements of their own times, and have not proved wholly incapable of adaptation to those of later periods. Nobody would suggest that this came about by accident. But it is too easy to attribute the virtues of Georgian London to bloodless abstractions, such as the Spirit of the Age, Eighteenth-Century Taste, or the Dominance of the Classical Tradition. Even to agree with Rasmussen's thesis that the system of building leases in itself was in large measure responsible for the spaciousness—which its detractors call "sprawl"—of London's layout, is not to deny the importance of conscious planning in achieving the form and outline which such spacious development took.

The greater part of the following study is based on the manuscript records of two of London's estates, that of the Foundling Hospital and that of the Dukes of Bedford. The minutes of evidence of the Royal Commission on the Housing of the Working Classes (1884–85) and the Select Committee on Town Holdings (1886–90) provide further examples to support or modify conclusions based originally on the Bedford and Foundling archives. The material from the Parliamentary Papers allows these findings to be put in the broader perspective of the contemporary practices of the Portman, Westminster, Portland Marylebone, and Northampton estates.

The organization is not chronological, but topical. The study will concern itself not with the historical development of the different estates but with determining how they dealt with certain recurring situations. Inevitably a disproportionate amount of the evidence comes from the nineteenth century and, in Chapters 4 and 5, from the latter part of that century. There is little to suggest, however, that either the attitudes or the methods of urban estate management had changed in essentials from what they were in earlier, less well documented periods. The scope of the activities of an estate office might be widened, its workings more efficient, and its officers more articulate, but its fundamental aims remained the same, as did the basic weapons with which it fought.

Unrestricted access to the relevant documents in the Bedford Office was granted to me by the kind permission of the late Duke of Bedford; I am indebted to the Trustees of the Bedford Settled Estates for enabling me to publish the results of my findings. I should like in addition to thank Viscount Portman for permission to study the material in his estate office, and Mr. H. H. Nichols and Mr. W. Brown, former and present secretaries of the Foundling Hospital (now the Captain Coram Foundation), for permission to make use of the minute books of that institution. I wish also to thank Harcourt Brace and World, Inc. and Martin Secker and Warburg, Ltd., for permission to reprint the extracts from Lewis Mumford, *City Development;* and the Cresset Press, Ltd., for permission to include the quotations from Sir John Summerson, *Georgian London.*

I am most grateful for the generous assistance given me in my research by the staffs of the three offices, as well as that of the London County Record Office, in which much of the material relating to the Foundling estate is now deposited. I wish to mention in particular Mr. F. L. A. Gover, head of the legal department of the Portman Office, and Mr. P. R. Stansfield in the same office; Miss E. M. Brooks, chief clerk of the Foundling Hospital office; and at the Bedford Office Mr. L. A. Ayling, steward of the London estate, and Mr. W. Corbett, secretary of the London and Devon Estates Company.

In addition I am indebted to Miss E. Bright Ashford of the London Society for information about the garden enclosures of the metropolis. Miss Hermione Hobhouse was kind enough to let me read a portion of her forthcoming biography of Thomas Cubitt. The staffs of the United States Educational Commission in the United Kingdom, the Institute of Historical Research, the British Museum, and the libraries of the University of London, Yale University, and Vassar College were of great help at various stages of the research.

A Fulbright scholarship for study in England in 1951–52, made possible the commencement of this study, and a Vassar Faculty Fellowship for the year 1959–60 made possible its completion.

For assistance in proofreading, I should like to thank my colleagues Rhoda Rappaport and Hsi Huey Liang, my student assistant Peggy Dye, and my mother Mrs. Anna M. Olsen (who also helped with the index), together with Virgil M. Beall and John C. Sutherland. Miss Eleanor Rogers and Mrs. Ruth Ashman were responsible for the typing. For the gathering of a large proportion of the illustrations, under great pressure of time, I am indebted to Mrs. Ruth Rubinstein. Mr. John Gere of the Department of Prints and Drawings of the British Museum and Mr. Nicholas Cooper of the National Buildings Record were particularly helpful in this connection.

I should like to express my gratitude to David Horne, editor of the Yale Historical Publications, Edward T. McClellan, arts editor, and Sally Hargrove, designer, for making the process of publication such a painless experience.

Professor Mildred Campbell of Vassar College, Professor Rosalie Colie of the State University of Iowa, and Miss Gladys Scott Thomson were kind enough to read and criticize my manuscript in different stages of completion. For continuing advice and encouragement, from the time when the study was no more than a collection of unanswered questions until the present, I am indebted to Lewis P. Curtis of Yale University and T. F. Reddaway of the University of London.

Poughkeepsie, New York   D. J. O.
February 1964

I *INTRODUCTION*

1 London and the Great Estates

It is no wonder that London, in proportion to its size and its advantages of site . . . should be the least beautiful city in the world. Nor is it only thus wanting in beauty, but also in convenience, through the deficiency of those arteries of main communication which are not only indispensable to the traffic of a town of its size, but an important element of aesthetic grandeur.—The Saturday Review (1856)

In 1766 John Gwynn described London as "inconvenient, inelegant, and without the least pretension to magnificence or grandeur . . ."[1] And while the London that grew up in the sixty or seventy years following Gwynn's attack might at its best have satisfied his desire for convenience and elegance, it would not have satisfied his desire for magnificence and grandeur. Even today the visitor will search in vain for the great public buildings, the dramatic vistas, or the striking monuments of Rome, Paris, or Washington. Even Edinburgh has far more splendor. There is much in London that will please, but little that will astonish. And—the British Travel Association to the contrary—it isn't even quaint.

London rarely attempts to look like a great city, being content to be one. Until its recent discovery of the skyscraper, London, despite Somerset House and the Shell-Mex Building, usually avoided both the impressive and the merely big. Its passion for understatement sometimes makes it appear mean and shabby but has enabled it to escape the sort of grandeur represented by the Victor Emmanuel Monument.

A travel book published in 1851 regretted that, with what it thought the exception of the recent developments in Bayswater, "we have no instance of that studied symmetry and variety in street-planning which the classic taste of Wren and Evelyn vainly endeavoured to introduce into the city after the fire, and for which the size of the suburban estates, and vast scale of the operations on them,

1. *London and Westminster Improved* (London, 1766), p. 5.

might be supposed to present opportunities unequalled in modern times."[2]

London's attempts at monumentality are indeed pale and insipid in comparison with Continental equivalents. The most patriotic Englishman who compares Trafalgar Square with the Place de la Concorde, Buckingham Palace with the Louvre, or Shaftesbury Avenue with the meanest boulevard in Paris must admit that the English are amateurs at the grand manner. The failure of Baroque architecture ever to attain real popularity in England supports the theory that the English, where they must choose, prefer comfort to luxury, convenience to display.[3] Where they have sought luxury and display, they have done so not in town but in the country. The country house is the great architectural symbol of post-Reformation English culture. The town house was by comparison a machine for living which people used when they had to be in London.

Since London has few buildings of the first importance, and since those few are often poorly situated, it is easy to conclude that the metropolis is badly planned and architecturally insignificant. The ordinary Londoner is certain that his is an unplanned city. For many it is a source of pride to reflect on the haphazard nature of London, which seems a concrete symbol of English pragmatism, of "muddling through," of the "absence of mind" theory of the Empire. Depending on one's point of view, London can serve as an object lesson of the deplorable results when planning and foresight are not used, or of the happy result of natural, organic adaptation to historical change.

The planning that has in fact taken place is not the kind that immediately impresses itself upon the beholder. The main thoroughfares twist and turn, widening and narrowing themselves at irregular intervals. The architectural face of Knightsbridge or Bond Street or the Strand is one of unrestricted free competition, each building trying either to shout its neighbor down or to withdraw smugly, contemplating its own superior uniqueness. Occasional pockets of aesthetic delight burst upon the observer as happy accidents, scattered hap-

---

2. Weale, *London Exhibited in 1851*, p. 770.

3. "To live within his own family, free from interruption, contest, or intrusion; to have apartments that are clean and warm, adapted to their several purposes, and in every respect convenient, is the Englishman's delight; and to effect all these, the architect exerts his utmost skill. Even in the mansions of rank and opulence, grandeur is seldom more than a secondary object. . . . whatever vanity or magnificence (be it real or imaginary) may boast, there is no city on earth the inhabitants of which enjoy so many of the accommodations which architecture can afford as those of London. Nations that prefer the parade of pomp to the enjoyment of social comforts, and the convenient performance of social duties, must include the buildings of London among its greatest defects; truth and common sense will esteem them to be one of its characteristic blessings." [John Feltham], *The Picture of London, for 1815* (London, 1815), p. 70.

hazardly about as if to compensate for the general visual squalor. But good planning can be found by those who know where to look.

Those who accuse London of having no plan usually contrast it with Paris. Actually London and Paris are both planned, but their plans differ completely in aim and character. London is a collection of autonomous villages, many of which have been carefully planned within themselves but with little reference to the adjoining villages. Paris is a dense forest that grew up initially with no plan whatsoever, through which a system of magnificent avenues has been cut. The real Paris remains an unplanned jungle, hidden behind the elegant façades of Haussmann's boulevards. The French tradition of landscape gardening is closely connected with the French tradition of town planning. Both involve geometrical patterns cut through a dense substance, shrubbery in the one and buildings in the other. Both aim chiefly for dramatic visual effect. Both are seen to best advantage from a distance.

The plan of London, or of those parts that are planned, is of a more basic but less obvious nature. Everything that one can see in a typical Bloomsbury street and much that one cannot—the dimensions of the houses, the width of the street, the ornaments on the façades, the color of the paint on the wood and stucco, the brass plates on the doors, the sort of people who live inside, the state of repair of the premises—can be understood only in relation to the conscious policies of the Bedford Office. Bloomsbury was planned from the outset, Paris only as an afterthought.

London has some examples of planning of the Parisian type, too, mostly resulting from the metropolitan improvements of the nineteenth century. Beginning with Regent Street, the Office of Woods and Forests, and later the Metropolitan Board of Works and London County Council began to cut wide paths through an older London. Trafalgar Square, New Oxford Street, Shaftesbury Avenue, Charing Cross Road, Kingsway, and the Aldwych are some of the results. But the main thoroughfares of London, unlike the boulevards in Paris, are almost invariably ugly; to see good architecture and good planning one must go behind them. Behind Oxford Street—a typically undistinguished thoroughfare—one finds elegant eighteenth-century squares and Regency terraces. Behind the rue de Rivoli and the rue de la Paix one finds the untamed forest. The streets behind the boulevards in Paris are usually, admittedly, charming and delightful, but they show planning in neither the English nor the French sense.

From the seventeenth century onward countless town planners (who would never have called themselves that) were engaged in imposing rationally conceived patterns of growth and development on London. For the most part they were not associated with any political body but were connected with one or another of the ground landlords or building speculators who were ultimately responsible for the face which London presents to the world.

Before the formation of the Metropolitan Board of Works in 1855, and to a great extent thereafter, the primary planning unit in London was the landed estate. London differs significantly from cities outside the British Isles in its pattern of landownership, being divided not into tiny freeholds, but into great estates. The concentration of landownership in the hands of a few families and corporate bodies has enabled them to exert an immense control over the fortunes of the metropolis.

London, thought the writer of an article in the *Saturday Review* in 1856, was "the result of a gigantic accident. London . . . is what it is from the fortuitous conditions of the various properties over which it has rambled." After lamenting the failure of the City to adopt Wren's plan for rebuilding after the fire, he deplored the fact that "the *rationale* of the . . . growth of the largest town in the world is to be found in the attorney's office and the builder's counting-house. It was," he thought, "the simple unchecked competition of rival estates sent into the market to hustle against each other."[4]

It was estimated in 1887 that there were seven times as many buildings in London held on leasehold tenure as there were standing on freehold land.[5] Death duties and other circumstances have since reduced the proportion of London that belongs to one or another of the great estates, but for most of its history London outside the City itself has been controlled by a comparatively small group of landowners. (See Figure 1 for a map, made in the late 1880s, of the location of the principal estates; Figure 2 shows the precise boundaries of the estates in the parishes of Paddington, St. Pancras, and St. Marylebone in the 1830s.)

Before the reign of Henry VIII the lands extending from the boundaries of the City westward to Hyde Park and Westminster had belonged for the most part to religious institutions, notably the Abbey of Westminster, St. Giles's Hospital, and the London Charterhouse. The Mercers' Company and the City of London also held considerable properties. Except for their proximity to the capital, to which they supplied food, the estates were indistinguishable from any other part of the southern English countryside.

---

4. "London and Paris Improvements, I," *Saturday Review, 1* (1856), 295.

5. *Town Holdings: A Digest of Evidence* (London, 1888), p. 153. Yet Dyos, *Victorian Sub-*

urb, p. 90, estimates that "freehold may have comprised about a third of residential property in London in the last quarter of the nineteenth century . . ."

In 1536 Henry VIII acquired by purchase or expropriation most of the land that today comprises the West End. He was especially eager to control the property, since it provided the water supply for his new palace at Whitehall. In later years he and his successors leased or sold chunks of the land, either to acquire funds or to reward court favorites. By the seventeenth century the freehold of most of the area was in private hands.

At the accession of James I London and Westminster still formed two distinct cities, connected by a thin row of houses, chiefly great mansions along the Strand, with clusters of less substantial buildings to the north. During the early seventeenth century other houses, chiefly of wooden construction, began to appear west of the City, in defiance of a number of royal proclamations. Alarmed at London's rapid growth, and fearing the spread of the plague and disorder in the new, unregulated suburbs, the Stuarts tried vainly to check the spread of the town. While unable to stop the expansion, they did succeed in regulating it by forcing the landowners to abide by the stipulations of the building licenses which they granted. These invariably called for brick or stone construction and required that the developments be such as would embellish the metropolis.

The Earl of Bedford was responsible for the first of the great developments, laying out Covent Garden and the adjacent streets in the 1630s. Thereafter London moved westward in a succession of irregular spurts. Building booms were succeeded by periods of little or no new construction. The first boom came in the 1660s, stimulated by the exodus from the City that followed the great fire and plague. In this period the Earl of St. Albans developed St. James's Square and its neighborhood, and the Earl of Southampton began to grant building leases on his Bloomsbury estate. The next building mania began shortly before the Treaty of Utrecht and lasted until around 1730. Hanover, Cavendish, and Grosvenor squares appeared during this period (see Figs. 3–5). Toward the close of the Seven Years' War there was much new construction, especially in the fields north of Oxford Street. Portman and Manchester squares date from this time. The period of the French Revolution saw the beginnings of even greater expansion, particularly in Bloomsbury. In 1811 the Crown began to develop its lands around Regent's Park, to the benefit of adjacent estates. The rest of the nineteenth and twentieth centuries has witnessed a succession of still bigger booms as London moved outward to cover whole counties.[6]

Any town planner would envy the power the great landowners of London had

6. Summerson, *Georgian London,* esp. pp. 17–26 is the best account of the building history of London from the seventeenth to the nineteenth centuries.

1. Map of central London showing approximate locations of principal estates, 1890

2. Southern portion of John Britton's map of St. Marylebone (1837), showing the boundaries of the different estates in the parishes of St. Marylebone, Paddington, and St. Pancras

3. Hanover Square, 1800

4. Cavendish Square, 1800

5. Grosvenor Square, 1800

6. Seventeenth-century houses in Great Queen Street, 1843

within the boundaries of their own estates. Instead of selling their freehold interest or building on their property themselves, they ordinarily disposed of it on
long building leases, of up to ninety-nine years. The leaseholders erected the
buildings and kept them in repair, according to the terms of their agreements
and leases. When the leases expired, the land and the houses on it reverted to the
ground landlord. He could then either relet the property on repairing leases—
twenty-one years came to be a standard term—or have the old buildings demolished and the sites let on new building leases. It was customary to insert provisions which limited severely the freedom of the lessee to introduce structural
or occupational changes in the premises. Before the building lease could be
granted in the first place, the builder would have to show that he had constructed the house according to a precise set of specifications in a building agreement. Before a repairing lease could be granted, the new lessee would have to
carry out a set of specified repairs and improvements. If at any time during the
course of a lease the lessee failed to abide by any of its provisions, the ground
landlord could legally eject him and regain absolute ownership of the property.

All this is, of course, true of any leasehold property, and is not in itself necessarily conducive to enlightened town planning. What has given the ground
landlords of London and other cities in the British Isles their particular power
and responsibility has been the enormous size of their holdings. The freeholder
of two or three lots or even two or three streets may have some discretion as to
the sort of houses his lessees erect; but he can hardly aspire to anything worthy
of the name of planning. The Duke of Westminster, in contrast, had the whole
of northern Mayfair together with what is now Belgravia and Pimlico to work
with. Lord Portman and the Duke of Portland had nearly the whole of Marylebone between them. The Duke of Bedford had Bloomsbury and Covent Garden. The Marquis of Northampton had Clerkenwell and Islington. The whole
character—social, architectural, and economic—of a neighborhood could be determined by the kind of street plan the landlord chose to impose, the kind of
leases he chose to grant, and the kind of control he chose to exercise over his tenants. And when the original leases fell in, he was at liberty to start anew and
create an entirely different kind of neighborhood. Or at least so it seems in
theory.

The fact that most of the important landowners of London have been either
men of great wealth and high social position or public bodies or charitable
institutions has enabled them to plan without continual preoccupation with immediate financial returns. They could afford to ignore immediate profits and
concentrate instead on enhancing the long-range value of their estate. This gave

them greater freedom of choice, greater scope for imaginative planning, greater chance to make their self-interest coincide with that of the community at large. At the same time, of course, the extent of their holdings and of their economic power gave them equally great possibilities for evil. In theory, the partial land-holding monopoly of one of the big London freeholders gave him unsurpassed possibilities for exploiting his tenants. A big landowner could presumably grind down the faces of the poor with far more thoroughness and efficiency than a small one.

In recent years historians have been placing less emphasis than they once did on the differences between public and private ownership. The separation of ownership and management in limited companies has made it harder to assume that the profit motive always acts with classical directness in a capitalistic econ-omy. Since 1945 Conservatives and Socialists alike have been surprised to dis-cover how small an effect nationalization in itself has had on the industries affected. It is therefore more common today to stress the steady increase of state intervention in hitherto private affairs, whether or not it involved an actual transfer of ownership. It is easy to trace the continuity of development linking the early factory acts and the 1834 poor law with Disraeli's sanitary reforms, the Lloyd George budget of 1909, and the legislative program of the Attlee Govern-ment. Yet such a development might best be seen in the context of something more fundamental: the steadily increasing size and complexity of organizations and institutions, whether political or economic, public or private.

The transfer of duties and responsibilities from the parish vestries to the borough and county councils, and from them to a centralized national authority, could be included in the same category as the movement toward consolidation and monopoly in industry and trade. If today the Organization Man has more in common with the Civil Servant than either would like to admit, it may simply mean that bigness in itself creates a recognizable pattern of personality and behavior.

Whatever the validity of such an approach to recent economic and adminis-trative history as a whole, it does seem to apply to London in the eighteenth and nineteenth centuries. There, at least, the difference between a large estate and a small freehold was more than quantitative, while similarities in function and attitude between large estates and political units of comparable size were often remarkably great. In this context a "large" estate would be one big enough in area to permit a coherent plan, with an owner able to care more about long-run capital gains than short-term profits. As a working hypothesis, it might be suggested that if an estate exceeds a certain size, and if the greater part of the financial gain for its owner is pushed far enough into the future, its policies and practices come to resemble those of a public administrative body.

H. J. Dyos has shown in his study of Camberwell the difference between the policies of the vast estate of Dulwich College and the multitude of small properties in the northern part of the parish. The leases granted by the governors of the College "translated into practical terms their precise social requirements of an exclusive, spacious suburb of expensive homes and prosperous tenants," while the "unsophisticated letting" of the much smaller Bowyer-Smijth estates, at the other extreme, "allowed at least one of them to experience the full declension of meadow to slum in a single generation."[7]

Describing a great rural estate in the eighteenth century, A. S. Turberville writes that "as the estates were as a rule very extensive, and the landlord was responsible for the lives of his tenants, their housing, their industry, and their welfare, he performed several of the functions which in the national economy of the twentieth century are performed by more than one government department."[8] One might go further and say that a landowner was for most purposes sovereign over his estates. He had absolute authority in all those areas where the formal organs of government did not choose to interfere, and before the late nineteenth century those areas embraced most human activities. He could, for instance, provide his own ministries of agriculture, welfare, health, local government, housing, and town and country planning; he was his own Arts Council, his own Local Authority. The comprehensive scope of his activities makes it doubtful that his tenants enjoyed any of the laissez-faire which supposedly characterized the eighteenth and nineteenth centuries.

Any account of the system of landed estates in London must ask how far the landlord carried over such paternalism, benevolent or otherwise, from his country to his town properties. What use did he make of the enormous power the possession of a great tract of urban land gave him? How aware was he of his ability to control and regulate the growth and development of his part of London? Of what did his plans consist, and to what ends were they directed?

In brief: what were the ground landlords trying to achieve on their estates? how did they go about doing it? how successful were they?

There are three separate stages of town planning, each with its own peculiar problems and its own ways of meeting those problems. Not every "planned town" is planned in all three stages; the great estates of London, for the most part, were.

7. Dyos, *Victorian Suburb*, p. 84.　　　　　8. *A History of Welbeck Abbey and Its Owners* (London, Faber and Faber, 1938–39), 2, 53.

The first stage is the creation of a town where none had existed before: a Greek colony in Sicily, a Roman city in provincial Britain, a medieval *ville neuve,* a Letchworth, a Radburn, a Crawley. Into this category would also come a planned suburban development on the outskirts of an existing town: a Becontree or a St. Helier in the twentieth century, a Covent Garden or a Bloomsbury in the seventeenth. Here the planner has the greatest freedom of choice: while limited by the geographical nature of the site, the kind of resident he hopes to attract, and the financial resources at his disposal, he does not have to worry about superimposing his scheme on an already existing town.

Many towns and neighborhoods have been admirably planned in the first instance, but left to develop without supervision from then on. Sometimes the result has been good: organic adaptation to changing circumstances, or at worst picturesque decay. Sometimes the result has been less good, and the absence of a controlling intelligence to guide and direct the town or neighborhood painfully obvious. It is the rare town whose requirements remain indefinitely what they were when it was founded. Growth or diminution of population, changing economic circumstances, technological alterations, shifts in the class structure, new aesthetic values—all demand conscious planning if the physical structure of the town is to adapt itself properly to the changing needs of its inhabitants. The second stage also involves the preservation of the essentials of the original plan by protecting it from the ravages of age, decay, and indifference.

If it is decided that external requirements have changed so much as to demand the replacement of the old plan by a new one, the third stage, that of redevelopment, comes into existence. Often, indeed, it is made necessary by the absence of planning either in the first or the second stage, or by an inadequate earlier plan. The County of London Plan of 1944 is an excellent example.

The three stages—building, preservation, and rebuilding—often overlapped. This was notably true on the Bedford estate, where at any given time from the mid-seventeenth to the mid-nineteenth century some parts would be undergoing their original transformation from country to town, others would be on building leases, while still others would be in process of being replanned and rebuilt. Although the specific techniques of planning would vary according to such circumstances, the fundamental ends which those techniques were designed to serve remained remarkably constant.

2 *The Heavenly City*

The technical and economic studies that have engrossed city planners to the exclusion of every other element in life, must in the coming era take second place to primary studies of the needs of persons and groups. Subordinate questions—the spatial separation of industry and domestic life, or the number of houses per acre—cannot be settled intelligently until more fundamental problems are answered: What sort of personality do we seek to foster and nurture? What kind of common life? What is the order of preference in our life-needs?—Mumford, City Development *(1947)*

The town planning of any period will vary according to the kind of town the age wants, what it thinks a town ought to contribute to the good life, and its view of what the good life is. The planner will inevitably shape his schemes to promote the kind of life he thinks ought to be pursued. Every town plan is designed to meet the needs, real or supposed, of the society for which it is formulated. If the needs are thought to be chiefly military and defensive, the result will be Palma Nuova or Carcassonne. If the needs are thought to be the glorification of an absolute prince, the result will be Versailles or Karlsruhe.

There are two main approaches to town planning, the aesthetic and the functional. The first aims chiefly at the creation of a visually pleasing composition, and regards town planning as a logical extension of architecture. Planners of this school regard their task as one of providing proper settings for buildings, so that their façades will appear to the most striking effect: a town to them is essentially a vast stage setting. Another kind of planner is more interested in achieving some functional end: defense against siege or revolution, the speedy flow of traffic, a lower mortality rate, or simply the good life, however defined.

Such classification is, of course, far too facile. One need not necessarily believe that form follows function to admit that town planners of the first school are not indifferent to problems of traffic or sanitation, and that no one of the second school would deliberately create an ugly city. Obviously any town plan tries to be both practical and beautiful: the wide avenues of Washington and Paris were designed both for military purposes and as dramatic settings for impressive architecture. Beauty is not necessarily incompatible with utility; but neither are the two identical, and while any town plan will try to achieve both, it will often have to sacrifice one in order to get the other.

It is an historical commonplace that ideas of beauty vary with the age. So do ideas of utility. To an absolute monarch, visual magnificence was an eminently useful way of enhancing his power: Louis XIV knew what he was doing when he chose to put fountains in the gardens at Versailles rather than bathrooms in the palace. To the prospective occupant of an eighteenth-century town house, a decent, regular façade was as much a practical necessity as a chimney that didn't smoke or a roof that didn't leak.

The whole complex of techniques and practices that go into the town planning of any age will depend on the scale of values then held by the landlord and the householder. A secluded, detached suburban villa would have seemed a less desirable residence before the days of gas lighting and the Metropolitan Police than after. Similarly, a style of architecture which emphasized the uniqueness and individuality of each house would have seemed highly improper to most eighteenth-century town dwellers.

Yet bearing in mind the revolutionary changes that shook English life and economy from the early seventeenth to the late nineteenth century, what is remarkable is not so much that the town planning which took place in London changed, but that it changed so little. Ladbroke Grove and Addison Road are recognizable products of the tradition established by the Piazza in Covent Garden and Great Queen Street (see Figs. 6–14). The qualities which make a London street or square easily recognizable as such derive in part from the nature of the local bricks and stone available, and from the requirements of the London building acts. But in large measure they also suggest the existence of a set of practical and aesthetic values commonly accepted by the great landlords who controlled and guided the building history of the greater part of the metropolis.

It is foolhardy to pretend to know the real motives either of individuals or of groups. The agents and stewards and surveyors of the great London estates were not given to putting down on paper the innermost secrets of their hearts for the instruction of future historians. Yet in the wording of building agreements, leases, and licenses, and in the reports which they made for their employers, there appear certain recurring phrases, embodying certain unquestioned assumptions, certain accepted principles of behavior. The ways in which the representatives of the estates defended themselves against criticisms made before the Royal Commission on the Housing of the Working Classes and the Select Committee on Town Holdings are equally revealing—if not of what they themselves thought they were doing, at least what they wanted others to believe.

London itself, or at least those parts of it which have been under the management of great landed proprietors, is the best source for what the estates did in fact accomplish. But in order to decide how successfully the town planners in the estate offices put their plans into effect, we must know what those plans were. What sort of heavenly city were the ground landlords trying to build? What were the pure ideas of which Bloomsbury and Marylebone and South Kensington are the pale material reflections? Toward what final cause were the estates of Stuart, Georgian, and Victorian London striving?

That the estates did engage in conscious planning there can be no doubt. The planning of an urban estate was not an elegant luxury like the planning of a landscaped park, but an obvious economic necessity. So at least the ground landlords and their agents believed. Only careful planning, they thought, could ensure the success of a building scheme. By preserving the reversionary value of the property, enlightened planning could mean the difference between moderate wealth and immense affluence for their great-great grandchildren.

From the perspective of the mid-twentieth century, it seems obvious that the owner of a fairly large block of land in the London area would, so long as he resisted the temptation to sell, have found it difficult to avoid making a fortune, if only for his heirs. The steady growth in size and wealth of the metropolis has consistently provided both freeholders and leaseholders with a handsome "unearned increment." But no landowner at any period could have known this pleasing truth.

It is for one thing necessary to distinguish between the growth of the population of greater London and the increase in its physical size. Great building booms sometimes accompanied a period of relative stability in population, while population growth did not in itself build houses. The really startling growth in its population did not come until the first half of the nineteenth century. Cheap gin helped to keep the population stable from 1700 to 1750, at less than 700,000.[1] By the first census in 1801 it had risen to 864,845. In 1851 it was 2,362,236, and in 1901, 6,581,402.[2]

As important as what was actually happening to London was what contemporaries thought was happening. The men responsible for the County of London Plan of 1944 were not the first to be alarmed at its outward growth. The Tudors and Stuarts did all that legislation and proclamation could to bring it

---

1. M. C. Buer, *Health, Wealth, and Population* (London, Routledge & Sons, 1926), p. 272, estimates the population in 1700 to have been 674,000, and no more than 676,000 in 1750.

2. T. F. Reddaway, "London in the Nineteenth Century, I," *Nineteenth Century and After, 145* (1949), 366.

to a halt. In 1766 John Gwynn in an otherwise highly perceptive work wrote that his "principal intention" was "to advise . . . that proper bounds may be set to that fury which seems to possess the fraternity of builders, and to prevent them from extending the town in the enormous manner they have done and still continue to do . . ." He was confident that London could be kept permanently from expanding west of Park Lane or north of the New Road (today the Euston and Marylebone roads) if only the proper controls were imposed.[3]

Even those who did not deplore the growth of London had no way of knowing that such growth was more than a temporary aberration. The uncertainty as to how long the expansion could continue made each new housing development seem a gamble. The specter of possible failure was never absent from building speculation. Neither the landowner nor the builder had any guarantee that anyone would buy or rent the new houses once they were built. The supply in particular of the more expensive type of house did usually exceed the demand. And even if respectable tenants moved into a neighborhood, there was no certainty that they would remain there. The competition of newer houses in other parts of the town and the unpredictable movements of fashion have kept house property from being a wholly secure investment. No landlord ever had a monopoly of land, no builder a monopoly of houses. The business cycle created further uncertainties. London's physical growth was neither steady nor continuous but, as Summerson has pointed out, a series of disconnected spurts of building separated by periods of inactivity.[4] Any builder who tried to develop a housing estate during an economic depression was likely to end in bankruptcy. Many of them did for just that reason.

The builder ran most of the risks. But if the landowner rarely contemplated bankruptcy, he still had every economic incentive to encourage the initial success and continuing prosperity of a building development. In order to ensure the success of his New Town, the landlord felt obliged to plan its every detail, leaving nothing to chance. The layout of the great estates in the West End can only be understood as attempts by the various landowners to make their developments as attractive as possible, both to the speculative builder and to the prospective tenant. Even when the landowner had achieved a satisfactory building plan and found contractors to put it into effect, the planning had only begun. From then on, he had to supervise and control first the builders, to see that they carried out his plan correctly, and then the tenants, to keep the estate from deteriorating. Ultimately replanning and rebuilding would become necessary, and the whole process would repeat itself.

3. *London and Westminster Improved*, p. 16.   4. *Georgian London*, p. 24.

The initial transformation of an estate from one of pastures, swamps, and market gardens to one of streets, houses, and plane trees was a long and complicated process, in which the landowner and his officers played a role scarcely less important than that of the actual builders. It consisted of two phases: the formulation of the building plan, and its execution.

It is difficult to assign the responsibility for most building plans. Sometimes a building contractor would present a development scheme to an estate for its approval; sometimes the ground landlord's surveyor would draw up a plan for the builders to carry out. Sometimes the estate would set forth the layout of the streets and the general character of the houses, and allow the builders to fill in the details. In the course of negotiations between freeholder and builder, modifications would inevitably be made in the original scheme. The precise procedure varied from estate to estate and from development to development on the same estate.

But although in many instances the estates did not initiate the building plan, but contented themselves with approving, rejecting, or modifying the plans of speculative builders, they nonetheless possessed a set of standards by which to judge such plans. For the character of the resulting New Town would have to be such as would not cast discredit on the freeholder.

"Owners of a large estate," remarked Edward Bailey, trustee of the Portland Marylebone estate, "take a pride in it, just as a nobleman does in his country estate."[5] The street names themselves of much of London, reflecting as they do the family names, titles, and country seats of its landlords, would indicate that the freeholders hoped that their estates would shed luster on themselves and their families. The ideal estate would serve both to ornament the metropolis and to remind its inhabitants of the splendor of the House of Russell or Grosvenor, or the dignity of the Foundling Hospital or the Church of England. In proposing that two garden squares be placed on either side of the Foundling Hospital, its surveyor, Samuel Pepys Cockerell, argued that such a layout would maintain the Hospital's conspicuous character, by exposing it "as much as possible to the public view . . ." The houses on the estate would have to be "so respectable as rather to raise than depress the character of the Hospital itself as an object of national munificence."[6]

Today we admire the planning of the Georgian estates chiefly for their aesthetic qualities, for the coherence, order, and symmetry which characterize what remains of eighteenth- and early nineteenth-century London. But although far

5. TH, p. 444; 1887 (260) xiii.
6. Foundling Hospital, Building Committee

Minutes, *1*, 8–9 (27 December 1790). Hereafter cited as Building Committee.

from indifferent to aesthetic considerations, the conscious planning of the estate offices was more often directed toward functional than toward visual ends. The Earl of Bedford, with his Piazza in Covent Garden, indulged in architectural innovation, and provided London with a new kind of town plan; but for the most part later ground landlords were content to maintain existing standards of taste.

The architectural values of the estate office and of the speculative builder remained neoclassical long after such standards had ceased to be fashionable. They retained a belief in the desirability of uniformity and balance when more sophisticated circles were proclaiming the desirability of variety, intricacy, and surprise. As late as 1887 John Dunn, the surveyor of the Norfolk estate, warned that breaking up the estates would result in unrestricted competition and consequent aesthetic disorder: "One person would build a classic house; another would build a Queen Anne; another would put up a gothic, and so on . . . but if the whole is in one person's hand we can get a uniformity that would not be otherwise attainable."[7] Building agreements ordinarily imposed such uniformity, either by including precise elevations to be followed or by requiring that the external dimensions correspond with those of adjoining houses.

Of course the qualities of uniformity and the subordination of the individual house to an over-all design were not confined to the great estates. The rigid requirements of the successive London building acts severely limited the possible variations on the standard terrace house until well into the reign of Victoria.[8] The estate or the building contractor had chiefly to decide whether the houses in a particular street should be of the first, second, third, or fourth "rate of building," the first being the largest; the building acts provided a separate set of specifications for each rate of house. Eighteenth- and early nineteenth-century London houses of the same rate of building of any one period differ but slightly from one another, so that a certain uniformity can be seen in almost any Georgian street.

An estate surveyor could go further and impose still more rigid requirements, setting forth standard dimensions for the several stories of the houses in a given street, so that they would range in a uniform line. In the more important streets and squares the estates and the builders often imposed on the whole a definite pattern, so that the whole range of houses would appear to form one large building. This was particularly common from the late eighteenth century onward. Bedford Square, begun in 1776, was the first entire square in London to be so

7. TH, p. 624; 1887 (260) xiii.
8. See Summerson, *Georgian London*, pp. 125–

29, for a description of the Building Act of 1774, and a discussion of its architectural implications.

arranged (see Figs. 18–20), but there are earlier examples elsewhere, notably the Royal Crescent and Circus at Bath.[9] Bedford Square set the pattern for later squares in London, which from that time were virtually all built to a single uniform and symmetrical design.[10]

Dignity and uniformity characterize eighteenth-century architecture throughout the western world. The distinguishing quality of town planning in the British Isles is its combination of neoclassical façades with a profusion of semiformal open spaces: "the great principle, as I consider it, of large squares and short streets connecting them."[11]

A guide book of 1851, while lamenting that London, unlike other European cities, was "unfortunately composed chiefly of large undivided estates, and the supply of houses and streets by the hundred a matter of wholesale speculation," admitted that such circumstances did promote the building of squares. "Of course the quantity of ground appropriated to these ventilators is merely calculated so that the increased rental of houses enjoying the sight of a tree, may compensate for the loss of ground from the immediate purposes of the speculator," it pointed out, "and hence the proportion these gardens bear to the whole area in any district is a measure of the value there set on this privilege." Still, it could not wholly regret that the "same misfortune," the existence of the great estates, "which banishes from our urban architecture the attributes of durability and beauty, and nearly forbids any advance in that of salubrity, ensures us, however, the advantage of more of these openings than could be expected where the ground is minutely divided; and also affords a chance of more regular and extensively designed arrangements of streets."[12]

The justification for the wide streets and the garden squares was less aesthetic than sanitary. Ventilation, both outdoors and in, was regarded as essential to a healthy life. "Squares are an excellent feature," the same guidebook remarked, "peculiar to the large towns of England, but more particularly to London, being

9. The north and east sides of the Piazza in Covent Garden and the original east side of Grosvenor Square are earlier examples in London itself, but Bedford Square was the first to have all four sides uniform.

10. "It has been contended by the admirers of this system of letting large tracts of land on building leases, that, whilst the old parts of London as well as most old towns, seem to have been produced more by accident, whim, or caprice than from any regard to individual convenience or grandeur of appearance; by this new system many of our streets and squares are formed with all possible attention to strict regularity. This may be true, but then it must be remembered that by this very regularity we have exchanged the grand effects of architecture for disgusting insipidity and tiresome monotony." Sir John Soane, *Lectures on Architecture* [1809–1836], ed. A. T. Bolton (London, Sir John Soane's Museum, 1929), p. 156.

11. George B. Gregory, treasurer of the Foundling Hospital. TH, p. 174; 1887 (260) xiii.

12. Weale, *London Exhibited in 1851*, p. 770.

distinguished from the *Piazze, Plazas, Places,* etc., of continental cities, by having originated in a sacrifice of building ground, not to the purposes of ornament and architectural beauty, but to the pure necessity of ventilation." The garden enclosure enhanced the therapeutic value of the circulating air: "A garden enclosed by open railing . . . though occupying some of the space, hardly impedes the circulation of air, but, according to modern chemists, actually helps to renew its vital principle."[13] Certainly Isabella Knightley, in *Emma,* was thinking only of the health of her children and husband when she made her impassioned defense of the Foundling Hospital estate against the aspersions of Mr. Woodhouse:

> No indeed—*we* are not at all in a bad air. Our part of London is so very superior to most others! You must not confound us with London in general, my dear sir. The neighborhood of Brunswick Square is very different from almost all the rest. We are so very airy! I should be unwilling, I own, to live in any other part of the town; there is hardly any other that I could be satisfied to have my children in: but *we* are so remarkably airy! Mr. Wingfield thinks the vicinity of Brunswick Square decidedly the most favorable as to air.

In setting forth in 1836 a building plan for the Bedford properties north of the Euston Road, the steward of the estate emphasized the desirability of giving it "the character of an open, pleasant, airy, and (as far as attention to those points can make it so) healthy part of the town . . ." He therefore "proposed to make all the streets wide, and to give sufficient ground as gardens to the houses . . ."[14]

So far, the interests of the landlord and of the builder seem to be identical. No builder would object to the estate plan having an over-all architectural pattern. It added little to the cost of construction and made the new houses more attractive to purchasers. The initiative for making a range of houses or an entire square an imposing architectural unit often came from the builders themselves, who well understood the value of such devices in promoting a quick sale of house property. Similarly no builder would object to a plan which devoted a great deal of space to wide streets and garden squares. Large and conspicuous open spaces added to the selling value of his houses; since he was not the freeholder, he did not suffer from the sacrifice of building land. Landowners in

13. Ibid., p. 769.
14. [Christopher Haedy], "Observations on the Proposed Plan for Building upon Figs Mead, 1836."

fact consciously introduced such squares partly as a means of attracting builders and encouraging them to put up larger and more substantial houses than they might otherwise have done.[15]

The real conflict of interest usually arose not over questions of architectural design or external ornament but over the quality of materials and workmanship. The builder naturally wanted to keep his costs to a minimum. The freeholder wanted houses that would still be sound and valuable when the leases expired. By actuarial tables the reversionary value of a lease with more than forty years to run was said to be negligible, less than a single year's purchase.[16] Yet landlords did not act as if it were negligible, or as if their sole interest was to secure the immediate ground rents. The whole day-to-day business of an estate office would be unintelligible without the assumption that the first duty of the ground landlord was to pass on to succeeding generations the value of the property unimpaired and if possible enhanced.

The building plan could contribute to this end by demanding the construction of the most valuable property that builders could be persuaded to erect. Other things being equal, first-rate houses were to be preferred to second-rate ones, second-rate ones to the third-rate. In addition, the building contract would usually go beyond the minimum requirements of the building acts with respect to the quality of materials used, the thickness of walls, and the standards of workmanship.

Perhaps the fundamental aim of all the planning was to attract to the estate tenants of fashion or at least of respectability. No landlord would feel the same pride in an estate of working-class tenements as in one whose residents stood higher on the social ladder. For one thing, both the rents and the reversionary value of a piece of residential property would vary directly with the degree of respectability of its occupants. But purely economic motives cannot entirely explain the preference of landlords for upper-class residential property. There was, for instance, a feeling that, although shop property might produce higher rents, it was better to accept lower rents from a resident private gentleman than from a business concern. A street of single family houses was regarded as better in itself than a street of business property.[17]

Working-class property was rarely thought desirable in itself. When Edward Bailey described the Portland Town portion of the Howard de Walden es-

15. For the reasons behind the generous supply of squares and gardens in Bedford New Town, see below, pp. 65–70.

16. TH, p. 330; 1886 (213) xii.

17. An illustration of this attitude is to be found in the policy of the Bedford estate toward Gower Street in the 1880s, described below, pp. 174–77.

tate—the area north of Regent's Park and west of Primrose Hill—as having been "let disadvantageously and laid out injudiciously," what he meant was that "a better class of house altogether might have been erected there."[18] Ralph Clutton, agent for the estates of the Ecclesiastical Commissioners, admitted the general truth of the assertion, made by Lyulph Stanley, "that there is a great tendency on the part of people who have building estates rather to seek to develop them for dwellings for the middle class, and not to develop them in the first instance for dwellings for the laboring class."[19] John Robert Bourne, the London steward of the Bedford estate, justified such a policy of exclusion by arguing that "where you get a large working-class population you eventually get decadence, rottenness, and decay."[20]

Insofar as it was necessary to house the poor at all, it was felt that they should be placed where they would not offend the eyes of their betters. Speaking of the policies of an estate in Beckenham, John George Rhodes, a merchant in that community, reported: "I believe it is the view of the estate (if a neuter thing like an estate can have a view) that houses for the class of people that we have been speaking about [the lower orders], and houses for the class of people to which, if you will allow me to say so, I belong, should be kept very widely apart ..."[21]

The ability to segregate decently the various classes of society was one of the virtues attributed to the large estate by its defenders. Mr. Tyssen-Amherst, a member of the Select Committee on Town Holdings and himself a ground landlord in southeast London, spoke of the advantages of systematic building plans on big estates: "Different classes of houses to be built in the most suitable localities, large streets, small streets, artisans' dwellings; everything necessary for the development of a large town ..." While admitting the desirability of an estate having "artisans' dwellings as well as large and small houses," he argued that "it is better for them all that they should be arranged so as to suit each other"; his witness, Edward Ryde, a London builder, agreed that it was desirable "for the large houses to stand together, and the small houses to stand together."[22]

If the great task of the estate plan was to entice respectable tenants, the great

18. TH, p. 455; 1887 (260) xiii. "Portland Town furnishes an example: most of the houses are occupied by a poor description of inhabitants, living in courts, alleys, and places where there is stabling and mews; where cows, horses, pigs, and other animals are kept and slaughtered; it is drained by means of small drains, which pass through the backs of the gardens ..." Parliamentary Papers. State of Large Towns and Populous Districts. R. Comm. mins. of ev., p. 227; 1844 [572] xvii. See also Ibid., pp. 284–86.

19. HWC, p. 211; 1884–85 (4402-I) xxx.
20. TH, p. 579; 1887 (260) xiii.
21. Ibid., p. 33.
22. Ibid., p. 367; 1886 (213) xii.

task of management during the terms of the leases was to keep them there. In the eyes of a ground landlord, the success of a housing venture depended on how high a character it attained at the start, and how well it was able to maintain that character over the years.

The usual assumption was that the best way to maintain the reversionary value of an estate was to preserve its original form as closely as possible. Estate offices generally chose to do this by using all means in their power to prevent decay, and even change itself. From the point of view of the ground landlord the ideal house would be one that remained miraculously in repair throughout the term of its lease, without alterations or additions of any sort, inhabited by precisely the same sort of tenant at the end of ninety-nine years as had lived there in the beginning. The ideal street would consist exclusively of such houses, the ideal estate exclusively of such streets.

Ground landlords never expected to achieve such a static ideal, at least not in a century as dynamic as the nineteenth. What they did attempt was to preserve as much as they could of the original plan, by fighting a series of delaying actions. Sometimes they would not attempt to prevent the changes, but instead try to modify their direction and turn them into more desirable channels. Since for the most part their powers were limited to enforcing the provisions in the existing leases, they had to be content with a defensive strategy. Not until the leases expired could an estate play a more heroic role; only then could it become itself one of the forces of change.

The redevelopment projects which took place when leases fell in were seldom revolutionary. For the most part they were an attempt to express more strongly the values inherent in the original plan. Thus narrow streets might be widened, small houses replaced by larger ones, new garden enclosures made, greater architectural regularity enforced. The representatives of the ground landlords who appeared before the Town Holdings Committee in the 1880s stressed the flexibility which the London leasehold system made possible, but their own ideas of what constituted a good town plan differed little from those which had governed estate policies since the seventeenth century. The methods which they used to put their ideals into practice had grown steadily more efficient, and the external form of their planned towns varied with changing fashions. But the basic principles of spaciousness, uniformity, and respectability persisted throughout.

Henry Trelawny Boodle, agent for the Grosvenor and Northampton estates, thus defined the aims of great landlords in rebuilding their properties:

A well-disposed landlord of house property naturally takes an interest

in his estate as a whole. His aim, for instance, is to have wide thoroughfares instead of narrow, to set back the houses in rebuilding so as to obtain broad areas and a good basement for the servants. . . . He also
wishes to have effective architecture, to insist upon good sanitary arrangements in houses, to promote churches, chapels, and schools, and
open spaces for recreation, and so forth. That is what the Duke of
Westminster, and other owners of large estates, have done and are
doing.

The ultimate motives that impelled a landlord to engage in rebuilding programs he thought "simply the improvement of the town in which their estate is
situated," along with their pride in an improved estate, and a desire to further
the economic interests of their descendants. The Duke of Westminster, he said,
carried out such improvements "chiefly . . . on public grounds. . . . because he
desires better houses, and he is a great lover of architecture and likes a handsome town, and he would sacrifice enormously to carry that out on his estate. By
far the most important element, in his mind," Mr. Boodle believed, was "the
present improvement of London quite irrespective of what his children or
grandchildren may succeed to."[23]

On the other hand, he later admitted that "with modern improvements constantly being introduced, if you do not rebuild the estate, you will find that the
people will go off to a remote part of London, where they can get modern improvements."[24] Edward Bailey, of the Portland Marylebone estate, similarly
thought that "a liberal policy in the long run is a wise policy." On the Portland
estate, "some 30 or 40 years ago it seemed as though that class of residential
property would fall almost into desuetude owing to people residing at a distance
from town; but by granting favorable terms, and requiring premises to be mod-
ernised and sanitary requirements attended to, the estate got into good repute,
and now . . . we have the greatest . . . pressure to get the houses." Rebuilding
would result in an immediate loss in rents; but in the long run the estate would
benefit.[25]

Lewis Mumford frequently urges that town planning be regarded not as an
isolated set of mechanical techniques but as a way of making men happier and
better:

Our job is to repair the mistakes of a one-sided specialization that
has distintegrated the human personality, and of a pursuit of power

23. Ibid., pp. 324–25; 1887 (260) xiii.   25. Ibid., p. 444.
24. Ibid., p. 351.

and material wealth that has crippled Western man's capacity for life-fulfilment. We must provide an environment and a routine in which the inner life can flourish, no less than the outer life . . .

The ideal personality for the opening age is a balanced personality, one that is in dynamic interaction with every part of his environment, one that is capable of treating economic experiences and aesthetic experiences, parental experiences and vocational experiences as the related parts of a single whole: namely, life itself.[26]

The main job of the town planner, then, is to help create an integrated personality, and encourage an "even deeper exploration of man's feeling and emotions . . . the whole obscure inner world of the personality, with its desires, its dreams, its projections, its insurgences, its arts." Planning must therefore provide for solitude as much as for communal activity:

There is not a village or a housing estate that is well planned unless it has made provision for places of withdrawal—solitary walks, devious woodland paths, unfrequented towers, hard to climb—no less than places where people can gather together in groups for social communion or common recreation. . . .

In short, the balanced personality needs a balanced environment to support it, to encourage it, to give it the variety of stimuli and interests it needs in order to grow steadily and to maintain its equilibrium during this process.[27]

Mumford differs from earlier planners not so much in wanting to create an urban environment to promote human values as in the kind of values he wants to promote. Every town planner has, consciously or unconsciously, the vision of an ideal townsman, either one whose needs and desires will be particularly well fulfilled by the town plan, or whose way of life will be altered in a particularly beneficial way by the new environment created for him. The twentieth-century town planner is more of a moral reformer than the promoters of the West End estates in London, who were more interested in giving the customer what he wanted than in remaking the customer into something better than he had been. But they were interested in attracting only those customers who already lived up to their image of a proper, respectable tenant.

Ebenezer Howard and his followers in the garden-city movement hoped to create a kind of individual who would combine the gregarious pleasures of the

---

26. *City Development,* pp. 150–51.   27. Ibid., pp. 153–54.

town with a mystic communion with nature: a man who would walk from a well-designed factory through leafy streets to his country cottage, and settle down to a satisfying evening cultivating swedes and vegetable marrow in the company of his wife and numerous offspring. After a supper consisting mostly of the products of his own garden, he would accompany his family to a rehearsal of the local choral society, or a Fabian discussion group. Week ends would be devoted to nature walks and field sports. He would neither drink nor smoke, and would shun the false pleasures of the cinema and television. He would be a well-rounded participant in all of the healthier human activities, not a passive spectator. He would take cold baths and scoff at central heating. He might well be a vegetarian. He might own a bicycle, but would not desire a motor car. He would encourage his wife to engage in peasant handicrafts, when she was not engaged in bottling fruit and vegetables from the garden or nursing her latest infant.

What sort of person, in comparison, would the ideal tenant of the Bedford or Foundling estate have been? Like the resident of Letchworth or Welwyn, he would be the father of a large and growing family; but nurses and nannies would relieve his wife of the more irksome duties of motherhood. His exercise would consist for the most part of reflective walks within the barriers of a private square. He would be a member of one of the more respectable professions, and travel to and from the Inns of Court or the City in a carriage which he kept in a nearby mews. He would frequently entertain friends as respectable as himself at sober and dignified dinner parties. He would retire regularly at ten every night and sleep soundly, with an untroubled conscience.

He would keep his house in good, substantial repair, but never wish to make any substantial alterations in the structure or façade. If he were the leaseholder, he would be providently putting down a sinking fund to meet the expenses of renewal when the existing term expired. He would be completely content only if he knew that everyone else in his street or square was leading the same sober, unexceptionable life behind the same sober, unexceptionable walls.

The abstract values and theoretical aims of the London estate offices were inevitably deflected and modified by external circumstances. The following chapters will try to decide how well the big landed estates—in particular those of the Foundling Hospital and the Duke of Bedford—succeeded in putting into practice their principles of urban planning.

II *BUILDING THE NEW TOWNS*

3 Landlord and Builder

It has ever been the practice of the London builders to erect houses at the least possible expense, because their tenures are almost exclusively leasehold. Hence it is that the editors of the newspapers of the last century were compelled from time to time to notice the horrid effects produced by the fall of those frail buildings. I am fully convinced that not less than one hundred lives have been lost in this way between 1700 and 1807; and that at least three times as many persons were maimed.—Malcolm, Anecdotes of the Manners and Customs of London during the Eighteenth Century (1810)

The history of town planning has seen ideal cities in all possible shapes. With ruler and compass, countless well-wishers of humanity have provided it with plans for towns in which the good life could be lived to the fullest. But town planning is, like politics, the art of the possible. The execution of a plan is far more difficult and far more important than its formulation. The only valid test of a plan is how it works in practice.

On the ordinary London estate the two phases of formulation and execution usually overlapped. Building ordinarily began before the estate had decided on all the features of the general plan, and modifications were usually introduced into the original scheme while building was going on. The more important contractors often had some part in the drafting of the building plan, and were sometimes wholly responsible for it. In any event the estate surveyor had to prepare his plan with the builders in mind: the best of plans would be worthless if they refused to cooperate.

In order to put his plan into effect, the landowner had to enter negotiations with one or more large-scale builders. The resulting building contracts, or "articles of agreement," were in fact miniature town plans, designed to ensure that the scheme was carried out in detail. Edward Ryde, a London builder, thus defined a building contract for the Town Holdings Committee:

> It is an agreement by which the ground landlord, on the one hand, agrees to let, and the builder agrees to take, a block of land, as a rule, upon which the builder agrees to build one or more houses, usually a number of houses. Those houses are to be of a certain character and

quality and to be built with good materials, and in an approved manner, and upon plans of which the freeholder is to approve. . . . Therefore the whole operation of the builder is controlled by the terms of
his agreement, which, of course, are varied with different men in
different places.

He reminded the committee that although the covenants were "extremely
stringent," the contractor was by no means at the mercy of the landlord: "I need
hardly say that a man who is a substantial builder, who comes to take a block
of land like that, has and does exercise a good deal of control over the nature
of the agreement, in fact, quite as much as the freeholder."[1] The agreement
often specified a definite outlay for each house.[2] In addition there would ordinarily be "provisions for laying out all the new roads, where new roads are required," and for the necessary sewers. The ground landlord would agree that as
each house was duly completed to the satisfaction of his surveyor, he would grant
to the contractor, or to any individual whom the contractor might nominate, a
building lease, a copy of which would be attached to the agreement.[3]

The contractor would agree to pay a certain annual rent for the whole plot of
land; within limitations, he could usually apportion the ground rents among the
separate houses as he saw fit. For this reason, "it does often happen," Edward
Ryde told the Town Holdings Committee, "that you will find houses of exactly
the same quality standing side by side, and owned in exactly the same way where
there is a ground rent to the freeholder of £25 on one house, £15 on the second
house, and of £5 on the third house."[4] The ground rent was not ordinarily paid
until the houses were completed; for the first year or two the rent might be a
peppercorn, after which the rent would rise gradually to its full figure.[5] If the
builder could dispose of his houses quickly enough, he need spend none of his
capital on rent.

The customary length of building leases increased from the seventeenth to the
eighteenth century but contracted somewhat toward the close of the nineteenth.
At the time of the original development of the Bedford estate in Covent Garden
in the 1630s, thirty-one-year leases were the rule.[6] Sixty-one-year leases were
common on the Bloomsbury estate in the early eighteenth century; later, eighty-

1. TH, p. 317; 1886 (213) xii.
2. "The character of the house and the quality of the house is often measured by the cost of
the house; but in all cases the plans have to be
submitted to the freeholder . . ." Edward Ryde,
ibid., p. 306.
3. Ibid., pp. 306–07. For a description of a

typical building agreement from an estate in
Kensington, dated 1844, see ibid., pp. 172–73;
1887 (260) xiii.
4. Ibid., p. 305; 1886 (213) xii.
5. Ibid., p. 306.
6. Ibid., p. 573; 1887 (260) xiii.

year terms were granted. From the latter part of the eighteenth century to the middle of the nineteenth, the ninety-nine-year lease was standard in London.[7] But by the 1880s, although ninety-nine-year leases were still being granted on many estates on the outskirts of London, the tendency was to offer shorter terms, of eighty years or even less.[8]

Although the contractor was legally responsible for building all the houses in the agreement, he usually disposed of some of the plots to smaller builders, who worked under his supervision. Sometimes he would build only the carcass of a house, which he would then sell to a smaller man to finish. Edward Ryde argued that one of the advantages of the system of land tenure in London was that it encouraged rational large-scale development while allowing men of small capital to participate:

> The owner of the land in the first instance lets it to one substantial builder . . . It very often happens that that piece of land . . . is not capable in itself of being developed in the most beneficial manner without the assistance of the adjoining lands. The builder then makes arrangements with the adjoining landowners, one, two, or three, as the case may require. Cromwell Road, for instance . . . goes through the freeholds of several freeholders. . . .
>
> The one builder takes the three properties, say, and lays out his main roads. He cuts the land up. Although the land is ripening for building, if he were to build upon it all at once he would create such a supply that it would be beyond the demand, therefore he, having eventually got the profit rent to look to, waits and gets a smaller builder, a man of his own class, but a smaller man, to take a portion of this land of which he has got the whole. Then that man has a profit rent there, because the second man pays a higher rent per acre or per yard than the first man. Then that man in his turn lets to some one else, or, perhaps, to a number of small builders, who are able to build two, three, or four houses, and who could not . . . be trusted with the land to build more. They would come to grief before they had finished, and so in that way some four or five interests are carved out before you get to the actual occupier.[9]

7. From the 1770s to the end of the original building in Bloomsbury the ninety-nine-year lease was universal on both the Bedford and Foundling estates. The original Portman estate leases were for the same period, as were those on the adjoining Portland estate. Ibid., p. 450. The original development in Paddington and South Kensington was likewise mostly on ninety-nine-year terms. Ibid., p. 330; 1886 (213) xii.

8. Ibid., pp. 329–30, 307; 1886 (213) xii; pp. 375–76, 574; 1887 (260) xiii.

9. Ibid., p. 304; 1886 (213) xii.

The financial arrangements the contractor might make were often of the greatest complexity:

> The builder . . . taking a large block of land, must be himself a man of some capital; then he is connected with men who advance him money, and, of course, they are not always of the same class; they are as various as possible . . . they generally spend the first money on the drains, the sewers, and the roads. . . . [Money can be raised on the building agreement, and] when the builder is associated with a man whom we will call the capitalist, he has to deposit his agreement with the lender . . . the ground landlord himself . . . sometimes makes advances as the houses go up; up to the first floor so much money is advanced; up to the next floor so much, and so on; and the builders cannot get a mortgage upon the leasehold house until they have finished it in carcass, and have got their lease.

The builder, he admitted, very often broke down, "and what generally happens in my experience," Ryde concluded, "is that the builder has got into debt with the brick merchant and the timber merchant, and sometimes those men come in" to take over the contract.[10]

A recurring criticism of the leasehold system was that it encouraged builders to put up less substantial houses than they would if they owned the freehold. Some even suggested that houses were nicely calculated to last exactly the term of the lease and no longer. Sir John Soane contended that the leasehold system was necessarily "opposed to sound construction, whereby not a year passes without lives being lost through this wretched practice."[11]

Others argued that the stringent provisions of the building agreements made leasehold houses more substantial than those on freehold land. "My experience," reported Robert Vigers, surveyor to the Peabody Trustees, "leads me to the conclusion that houses built upon leaseholds, with the supervision of the freeholder and his agents, are better built, as a rule, than those built upon freeholds, with the exception of large mansions, where a man builds a house for his own occupation."[12] Edward Ryde agreed, pointing out how much it was to the interest of the ground landlord to make the builders live up to their agreements:

10. Ibid., pp. 317–18. For a description of the financial arrangements of builders in the eighteenth century, see Summerson, *Georgian London*, pp. 69–79.

11. *Lectures on Architecture*, p. 156. For a similar view see Friedrich Engels, *The Condition of the Working Class in England*, trans. W. O. Henderson and W. H. Chaloner (Oxford, Basil Blackwell, 1958), pp. 69–70.

12. TH, p. 46; 1887 (260) xiii.

Of course there are certain general Acts of Parliament which apply to
all parties building, whether freeholders or lessees; they must be controlled by the provisions of those Acts of Parliament, but in addition to
that the man that builds on leasehold land has the freeholder to look
after him. The freeholder is interested in the reversion of the houses
at the expiration of the lease, and also in the security of his ground-
rent, and therefore he exercises a control over the lessee, while the
freeholder who builds a similar class of house is not controlled in any
way. The freeholder pleases himself, whereas the lessee is bound to
please his ground landlord as well as himself.[13]

While admitting that improper building did in fact take place on leasehold
property, he argued that this usually happened where the freeholder had acquired the land for speculative purposes, and not on the great hereditary estates:

Jerry building takes place really, in fact, by the connivance of all parties. It is very disrespectful, I daresay, to say that there is a jerry landowner, but there is, you know, because there is the man who permits
it. Where you see jerry builders carry on, and bad houses built up, it
is generally where some small man has bought a field and has let it out
at the highest rent he can get. His object, and his only object, is to
create the ground rents and sell them as soon as they are created. The
object of the builder is to build the houses, and he does not care
whether they stand or whether they do not. Whether built on leasehold
or freehold that would equally arise. . . . Where the jerry builder has
been born and brought up is off the large estates . . .[14]

Edward Tewson, an estate agent, believed that the specifications in building
agreements were "usually enforced . . . The larger the estate," he thought, "the
more certain it would be that those covenants would be enforced, because a
surveyor is specially appointed to attend to them." Bad building was most
likely on "freehold land which has been bought by speculators, whose object
is to create ground rents, and they do not understand their business so well as
the large proprietor does. They let it to speculative builders, and so long as they
see certain houses put up, they do not know any more." It did not ordinarily pay
the builder to make use of the best materials and most careful workmanship.
"Houses are . . . generally taken," said Tewson, "by those who have not got more

13. Ibid., p. 299; 1886 (213) xii.   14. Ibid., pp. 319, 324.

than a superficial knowledge of the building; and so if a man spends £1,000 upon a house in a street, it does not follow that he will get 5s. a year more rent for his house than the man who spends £800 will get." In time, of course, the difference between the two houses would become evident, but the builder interested only in a quick sale would not be influenced by such a consideration. The ground landlord, on the other hand, had every motive for seeing that the houses were built as substantially as possible.[15]

Several witnesses told the Town Holdings Committee that ground landlords did not in fact exercise much supervision over the building on their estates. Edward Yates, a builder in south London, thought that in the suburbs at least, "where a man wants his land covered, he wants to see the roof on a building whereby his ground rents are secured; he will worry the builder as little as possible as long [as] he can get his ground rents secured." He had himself recently bought an estate of nearly fifty acres for speculative purposes, and in insisting that he himself was, "from a business point of view," chiefly interested in getting the ground covered and securing his ground rent, inadvertently lived up to Edward Ryde's description of the "jerry landowner." It would be foolish, Yates thought, to enforce building covenants too strictly:

> One of the great points is this . . . a man has got his land to let for building purposes, he is most anxious to get sufficient buildings to put upon his land to secure his ground rent; he knows very well that building is cut very fine; in fact you may say the art of building is building to pay. Of course if you cannot get the money you cannot bring your money home on Friday to pay the workmen's wages and materials . . . People who are owners of land are of course most anxious to get their rent secured by sufficient buildings or capital put upon it, and they know very well under the circumstances that if they were to exercise too strict a supervision the consequence would be that the builder most likely would fail in carrying out his arrangement, and they would not get their land covered.

He admitted that "in the case of some large estates the ground landlord's surveyor comes round and sees that the proper materials are used, and that proper work is done," but in general he thought that leasehold houses were no better built than freehold ones.[16]

15. Ibid., pp. 142–43; 1887 (260) xiii.

16. Ibid., pp. 377–78. For Yates see Dyos, *Victorian Suburb*, pp. 82, 91, 127–35. Dyos finds him a model builder and landlord, whose houses were "modern, solid, and respectable," and whose leasehold development "was conducted irreproachably."

An exchange of letters which took place in 1807 between the Duke of Bedford's solicitor and a builder on his estate gives some idea why the Town Holdings Committee was to find it so difficult to get any simple answers to their questions about the effect of the leasehold system on the structural soundness of houses. The builder, Thomas Lewis, had contracted to put up some houses in Keppel Street, Bloomsbury. The significance of the correspondence is not so much the information it gives about the origins of Keppel Street as what it tells of the conflict that was continually going on between landlords and builders: the one wanted large, well-constructed houses which would still be sound and valuable at the end of ninety-nine years; the other wanted small, cheap houses which could easily be sold for an immediate profit. It was not that the builder was thinking of profits while the landlord was not: it was rather that the landlord's real profits lay ninety-nine years in the future (see Appendix II).

The outcome of the struggle is not wholly clear. Since photographs of Keppel Street in the 1890s show its houses to have been unusually small for the Bedford estate, it is likely that the Bedford Office had ultimately to come to some sort of compromise with Lewis and the builders under him. By the time the original leases of Keppel Street fell in, the houses were in such bad condition as to impel the estate to take them down and clear the entire site.[17]

Similar conflicts enlivened the building history of the other estates.[18] Ordinarily it was to the interest of the landlord to enforce building agreements and to the interest of the builder to evade them. Where the interests of the landlord conflicted with those of the builder, they tended to coincide with those of the future tenants. But in practice, as the experience of Thomas Pearce Brown with Thomas Lewis shows, it was often impossible to enforce a strict observance, which could drive the builders into bankruptcy, leaving the freeholder with a row of useless carcasses. The Napoleonic Wars, which saw a great rise in the cost of building materials, made it particularly hard to enforce the specifications, even if the landlord was willing to compensate the builder for his extra expenses by lowering the ground rent. In the end the houses were usually neither as cheap as the builders would have liked nor as substantial as the landlord might have wished.

17. The University of London purchased the cleared building site in 1927. It might be argued that the present location of the Senate House is an indirect result of the stubbornness of Thomas Lewis in 1807.

18. For a discussion of the responsibility for some badly built working-class houses on the estate of the Ecclesiastical Commissioners at Harrow, see TH, pp. 342–43; 1886 (213) xii. For the practices of the Evelyn estate in Deptford in enforcing the provisions of building agreements, see ibid., p. 470; 1887 (260) xiii. For the Portland Marylebone estate see ibid., p. 446. For the Foundling estate, see below, pp. 81–82, 86–88, 91–92.

The landlord was as eager as the builders that the houses should be speedily erected and disposed of. "I have known hundreds of times," Edward Ryde told the Town Holdings Committee, "of cases where ground landlords have given extension of time to builders and allowed them every facility in fact for going on with their work, although they had long since broken the provisions of their building agreement."[19] Even when such emergency measures were unnecessary, the landlord often gave financial assistance to the builders, usually by purchasing improved ground rents from them. The improved ground rent of a plot of building land was the difference between the rent stipulated in the building agreement and the rent the contractor could get for the site. Howard Martin explained the practice to the Town Holdings Committee:

> A builder can apportion his ground rent at a higher rate on each house than the proportionate rate which he pays the ground landlord. The difference between the two rents is the improved rent. In many cases the ground landlord agrees to take these improved ground rents of the builder at 18 or 20 years' purchase. . . . Sometimes the ground landlord agrees either to convey the freehold or grant a lease at a peppercorn of whatever land is left over after the improved ground rents have secured the original ground rent, and gives the builder the value of his improvement in that way.[20]

Ryde gave a similar description:

> The general mode of dealing with building land which is ripening up for building is for the freeholder to let it in a large block to a well-to-do builder. . . . and to let it at such a rent as will give the builder about one-third of the ground rents as profit to himself. . . . supposing, for instance, that the ultimate ground rent to be realized would amount to £3,000, the builder only agrees to pay the ground landlord £2,000, and secures the £1,000 as a profit ground rent to himself. That may be done, and is done in various ways. For instance, a builder himself may take up a lease at £60 a year ground rent for a large house, or any number of houses you like, and may grant an under lease to someone else at £90 ground rent. The £30 is his apparent profit; it is not to be assumed that that is an absolute profit, because the first thing a builder with capital, or associated with men of capital (as is generally the case), has to do is to lay out his roads. All the new streets have to be

19. TH, p. 367; 1886 (213) xii.   20. Ibid., p. 83; 1887 (260) xiii.

marked out, and not only marked out but made, sewered, and paved
. . . and that involves a very large outlay.[21]

By purchasing the improved ground rents, the landlord was in fact giving a loan
whose principal would never be repaid; instead, a certain percentage was added
to the ground rent which he would receive. Sometimes the improved ground
rent would be purchased by a private investor, or by the purchaser of the house
itself.[22] The whole system compensated, in part at least, for the impossibility
of getting a mortgage on a building agreement, and for the higher rate of interest which was usually demanded for a loan on leasehold property than for
one on freehold.[23]

Ryde was convinced that the leasehold system ultimately kept rents down by
promoting building and thus increasing the supply of houses on the market. "In
building new property, and starting to develop building land," he thought that
the leasehold system "enables a builder . . . to embark in a building operation,
with less capital than otherwise would be necessary if he had to buy the land."[24]
The freeholder by himself would ordinarily be reluctant to risk his capital in
building:

> No freeholder would undertake a building operation which, after all,
> is the most risky operation you can undertake. It is a most capricious
> thing. You think building land is as ripe as possible, and to all appear-
> ance it is, and presently you build upon it, but no tenant comes, and
> there it remains a howling wilderness for years sometimes. . . . [The
> leasehold system] brings into operation first a very substantial builder,
> then the smaller man, who is the little builder, and at last you see
> the houses built.[25]

The building histories of the Bedford and Foundling Hospital estates illustrate
how difficult it was to impose a coherent plan on the expanding metropolis. The
transformation of the Bedford lands from a collection of fields and market
gardens to a residential suburb lasted from the 1630s to the 1850s. The building
of the smaller Foundling estate came between 1790 and 1826. On neither estate
was building steady or gradual, but took place in a number of separate developments. Although the later developments are better documented than the early
ones, and although each presented its own problems, which had to be dealt with

21. Ibid., pp. 303–04; 1886 (213) xii. Ryde
went on to explain that landlords occasionally
built the roads themselves, but that this rarely
happened in London.

22. Ibid., p. 367.
23. Ibid., p. 376; 1887 (260) xiii.
24. Ibid., p. 355; 1886 (213) xii.
25. Ibid., p. 305.

pragmatically, a recurring pattern can be discerned. The evidence in the minutes of the Royal Commission on the Housing of the Working Classes and the Select Committee on Town Holdings indicates that the practices of the Bedford Office and the Foundling Hospital in planning and supervising the original building on their estates did not differ in essentials from those of other great landlords.

4 The Bedford Estate

*Pure air, so essential to the preservation of life, now circulates freely
through the new streets; squares, calculated for ornament, health, and
the higher ranks of the community, are judiciously dispersed, and their
centres converted into beautiful gardens; the tall houses have a sufficient
number of large windows; the areas in front are wide, and handsomely
railed with cast iron; lamps on scrollwork are suspended at due distances
from each other; and admirable level smooth footways of great breadth
protect the passenger from the carts and carriages* . . . —Malcolm, Anecdotes of the Manners and Customs of London during the Eighteenth
Century (1810)

The Duke of Bedford owned three estates in London: Covent Garden, Bloomsbury, and Figs Mead. The Covent Garden estate was roughly limited by the
present lines of St. Martin's Lane on the west, Long Acre on the north, Drury
Lane on the east, and the Strand on the south (see Fig. 7 for its exact boundaries
in 1795). The Bloomsbury estate lay within the rectangle formed by Tottenham
Court Road, Euston Road, Woburn Place and Southampton Row, and New
Oxford Street (Figs. 7, 8). Figs Mead lay north of Euston station, bounded on
the west by Hampstead Road and on the north by Crowndale Road (Figs. 51,
52).

The first of the estates to be acquired by the Russell family was Covent Garden, which Edward VI granted to John, first Earl of Bedford, in 1553. The
annual rental of the estate, which had belonged to the Abbey of Westminster before 1536, was £5 6s. 8d. The Earl continued to let the greater part of the property for grazing purposes. In 1559 he granted a twenty-one-year lease of twenty-
eight acres at £1 16s. per acre of annual rent.[1] Facing the Strand, the Earl built
himself a large wooden house on his new property, but the rest of the estate
changed little during the sixteenth century. Unplanned groups of houses began to appear around 1603, but orderly development did not begin until 1630,
when the fourth Earl obtained a royal license to demolish the old buildings and
replace them with new, handsome, and substantial structures.

In order to fulfill the conditions of the license, which called for buildings
that would serve to ornament the town, the Earl called upon Inigo Jones, Sur-

1. TH, p. 577; 1887 (260) xiii.

veyor of the King's Works, to design the church of St. Paul, Covent Garden and, together with Isaac de Caus, the adjacent Piazza to the north of Bedford House in the Strand (Fig. 7).[2] The church formed the west side of an open square; the north and east sides consisted of a uniform, arcaded terrace of town houses, reminiscent of the Place des Vosges. The regular, classical layout of the Piazza in Covent Garden set standards in town planning that were to dominate upper- and middle-class urban architecture in the British Isles for more than two centuries. The Earl of Bedford and Inigo Jones had done more than provide a noble ornament for the expanding capital; they had created the prototype of the London square (see Fig. 9).

However admirable the architectural treatment of the Piazza, the planning of the Covent Garden estate was, by later standards, only partly successful. The fruit and vegetable market that grew up north of the garden wall of Bedford House gradually expanded to cover the whole of the open space in the square; by the close of the century the fashionable residents of the Piazza understandably had begun to move to more agreeable locations. The rest of the estate —although it abounded with large and expensive houses and remained fashionable until the early eighteenth century—was laid out in a fashion that was neither regular nor generous. Many of the streets were fairly wide, but behind them were narrow, mean, and unsanitary courts. There were no squares apart from the main Piazza (see Figs. 10–14).

More serious than the deficiencies of the street plan was the inconsistency of the Earl of Bedford in disposing of building sites. Most of the plots he let on leases for years, but others he granted in perpetuity, subject to fee-farm rents. The owners of such property became for all practical purposes freeholders; so long as they continued to pay the fixed annual rents, the Earl and his heirs had no control over their buildings. The map of the Covent Garden estate in 1795 (Fig. 7) shows the location of some of the resulting foreign enclaves within the estate. One street, Bedfordbury, was granted out almost wholly in fee-farm rents. John Robert Bourne, steward of the Bedford estate in 1887, thus described the results to the Town Holdings Committee:

> Those fee-farm rents were created by means of grants containing no restrictions, but the people who took the grants became the absolute owners of the property without any obligations as to building, without any restraint as to the mode of occupation. Every grantee became

2. See Summerson, *Georgian London,* pp. 29–31; also his *Architecture in Britain, 1530–1830* (Baltimore, Penguin Books, 1954), pp. 83–4.

7. Duke of Bedford's Covent Garden estate and southern portion of Bloomsbury estate, with surrounding areas, c. 1795

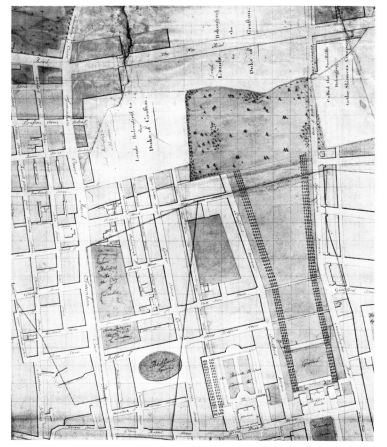

8. Northern portion of Bedford estate in Bloomsbury, with surrounding areas, c. 1795

9. Piazza in Covent Garden, showing St. Paul's, Covent Garden. Pieter Angillis (1685–1735)

10. Piazza in Covent Garden and Market, 1751

11. Perspective view of Covent Garden, 1741

12. St. Paul's, Covent Garden, 1796

13. Piazza in Covent Garden,
1796

14. View beneath Piazza,
Covent Garden, 1796

his own freeholder, and his plot of land was under his own absolute control, with this result: that Bedfordbury commenced its career by every man doing what was right in his own eyes in the way of building. A number of alleys came into existence, and instead of a single house being put upon a single plot . . . [such as was then stipulated in the regular building leases on the estate], a man would put two or three or four or it may be half-a-dozen houses, or cottages, or anything he pleased upon it, and that went on in perpetuity . . . It was a perfect by-word and a proverb for everything that was disorderly and disgraceful; the reason being that there were so many independent freeholders, every man being his own master and under nobody's control, except that control which a man chooses to exercise over himself, and with the result that the Metropolitan Board had to step in, condemn the area under Sir Richard Cross's Act, buy up all the people who were living there, make a clean sweep of the whole lot, and begin afresh by making a grant of it to the Peabody Trustees.[3]

The passage is perhaps as significant as an indication of the horror with which Mr. Bourne regarded "every man doing what was right in his own eyes . . . being his own master and under nobody's control," as a piece of the early history of the Covent Garden estate. But his seventeenth-century predecessors must have come to similar conclusions, for they granted no more fee-farm rents after 1660. During the eighteenth and nineteenth centuries the estate bought up premises paying fee-farm rents from time to time so that they might be restored to centralized control. Often this was a necessary prerequisite for a general rebuilding scheme.

Why the fee-farm rents were granted at all is far from clear. Mr. Bourne pointed out that in Maiden Lane the estate tried the leasehold and fee-farm systems side by side: "in one case they granted a lease for building, and in the next they granted a fee-farm rent, and so on, with this curious result, that you may walk down Maiden Lane at the present time, and . . . a blind man could almost put his hand upon the houses that were let out on fee-farm and those let out on lease, the difference is so great between them."[4]

The Russell family acquired Bloomsbury and Figs Mead through the marriage in 1669 of William Russell, second son of the fifth Earl (later first Duke) of Bedford, to Rachel, Lady Vaughan, daughter and co-heir of the fourth Earl

3. TH, pp. 575–76; 1887 (260) xiii.   4. Ibid., p. 576.

of Southampton, who had died two years before. Thomas, Lord Wriothesley, later the first Earl of Southampton, had purchased the manor of Bloomsbury in 1545 from the Crown. In 1616 the Earl of Southampton had acquired a portion of the adjoining manor of St. Giles, which became thereafter an integral part of the Bloomsbury estate.[5]

Irregular clusters of houses began to appear in Bloomsbury as early as 1623, but not until 1661 did the Earl of Southampton impose a formal building plan on the estate. In that year Charles II granted the Earl a building license, authorizing him to tear down the old wooden houses and replace them with buildings of brick and stone.[6] Although the construction of Bloomsbury Square and a number of streets to the west and south followed shortly thereafter, the whole of the estate was not covered with buildings until 1860, with the completion of Gordon Square.

The building history of Bloomsbury can be divided chronologically by the year 1776, and geographically by Great Russell Street (Figs. 7, 8). The development prior to 1776 lay, with minor exceptions, to the south of Great Russell Street, and represented only a minor advance over the planning of the Covent Garden estate. The building north of Great Russell Street, beginning with the granting of articles of agreement for Bedford Square in 1776, involved town planning of a most sophisticated variety, surpassed nowhere else in London.

The central feature of the seventeenth-century Bloomsbury plan was Southampton—later Bedford—House, which formed the north side of what came to be called Bloomsbury Square, an arrangement comparable to that at Covent Garden. The houses forming the other three sides of the square were big and costly for the most part, like those in the Piazza. Unlike the Piazza, the houses in Bloomsbury Square made no attempt at uniformity, much less at an over-all monumental design (see Figs. 15–19).

Next in importance on the estate was Great Russell Street, the westward extension of the north side of the square. Two mansions, comparable in importance with Bedford House itself, Montague House (later the British Museum) and Thanet House, together with many lesser residences, lined the north side of the street, enjoying an uninterrupted view of the green hills of Highgate and Hampstead. The only other streets of reasonable width were Hart Street (now Bloomsbury Way), paralleling Great Russell Street to the south; Southampton Street (now Southampton Place; see Fig. 20), providing a dramatic ap-

5. Gladys Scott Thomson, *The Russells in Bloomsbury* (London, Cape, 1940), pp. 1, 19–20, 24.

6. Ibid., pp. 38–39.

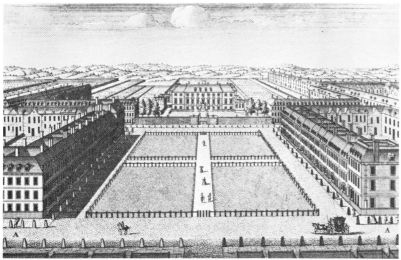

15. Bird's-eye view of Bloomsbury
Square, looking north, 1727

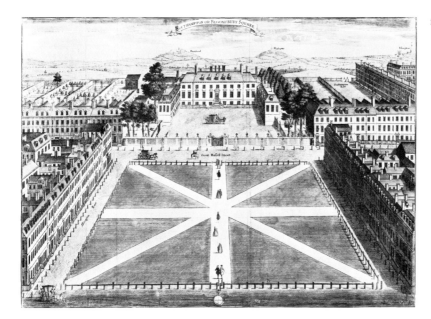

16. Bloomsbury Square, 1746

17. Bloomsbury Square, 1787

18. Bedford House, north side of Bloomsbury Square

19. Bedford House, north front, before demolition in 1800

proach to the square and Bedford House from the south; and King Street (now Southampton Row), paralleling the eastern boundary of the estate.

After Bedford House and Montague House, the principal building on the estate was the parish church of St. George, Bloomsbury, in Hart Street, erected between 1720 and 1731 (see Frontispiece). Slightly to the southeast of the church was Bloomsbury Market; it proved to be far less profitable than Covent Garden Market and was abandoned in the 1780s. Bloomsbury never became an important commercial or shopping center.

Aside from such features, Bloomsbury south of Great Russell Street left something to be desired. Behind its wide and respectable streets lurked mean alleys, courts, and passages wherein dwelt the lower classes. In contrast with the notorious rookery of St. Giles to the west and southwest, the streets on the estate were models of decency and propriety, but they represented no more than tentative gropings toward the sort of town planning involved in the neighborhoods laid out after 1776. Not only was there no attempt to impose uniform façades even in the principal streets, but in a single row there might be houses of widely varying size and importance. Even in Bloomsbury Square the frontages and ground rents varied greatly from house to house.[7] The early leases did not forbid the conversion of houses into shops; no system of zoning was therefore possible. By the 1720s inns had established themselves in aristocratic Great Russell Street itself, and shops appeared there shortly thereafter.[8] Yet by the standards of the early eighteenth century southern Bloomsbury—with its square, its church, its market, and its conspicuous great houses—was an admirable residential quarter.

The Earl of Southampton provided for future redevelopment with more foresight than the Earl of Bedford had done in Covent Garden. He granted no property on fee-farm rents, but disposed of the whole of the building land on forty-two-year leases. When the leases fell in, the estate would be able to pull down, replan, and rebuild.

The granting of building agreements for Bedford Square in 1776 marked the beginning of the second phase in the history of Bloomsbury, a phase that was not to end until the completion of Gordon Square in 1860. For the previous generation there had been virtually no expansion of the estate. What building there was consisted chiefly of repairing or reconstructing old houses, or of replacing them with new buildings. The estate concentrated on the consolidation and maintenance of older developments, ignoring more adventurous possibilities. Great Russell Street marked for all practical purposes the northern boun-

7. Ibid., pp. 37–54.   8. Ibid., pp. 178–79.

dary of urban Bloomsbury in 1775 as it had in 1720, and indeed in 1680.

The building of Bedford Square and the adjacent streets inaugurated the systematic transformation of the pastures of northern Bloomsbury into a restricted upper-middle-class suburb. While the older parts of the estate had provided for all but the very lowest classes, the whole area north of Great Russell Street and west of Southampton Row was laid out as a neighborhood of big town houses. There were of course mews for the carriages and horses of the residents in the streets and squares, but there were no mean streets or courts, except to the east of Southampton Row and Woburn Place. Neither, with one or two negligible exceptions, were there any shopping or business districts. The uniformity of occupation was matched by a general uniformity of façade within each of the various streets and squares as they came into existence. Nearly eighty-five years were required to complete northern Bloomsbury, but when finished it possessed an essential unity. If Bloomsbury is today more than a geographical expression, the continuous efforts of the Bedford Office since the 1770s are in large part responsible.

There had been indications of the approaching building scheme for some years prior to 1776. The 1760s had seen a great deal of new construction in Great Russell Street. In 1766 a builder named Leadbetter had agreed to put up a row of seventeen houses to form the east side of a new street running north from Great Russell Street, to be called Charlotte Street (now Bloomsbury Street).[9] By that year the fourth Duke had already determined to build a new square to the east of Tottenham Court Road, to be called Bedford Square, modeled on the King's Circus at Bath.[10]

In 1771 the fourth Duke died, succeeded by his five-year-old grandson. The estates were held in trust for him by his grandmother, the dowager Duchess of Bedford; his aunt, the Duchess of Marlborough; and Robert Palmer, the chief agent of the late Duke. Of the three, the dowager Duchess occupied the dominant position, and it was she, according to Miss Scott Thomson, who was principally responsible for the vigorous execution of the Bedford Square scheme.[11] As a preliminary step, the trustees purchased from the Duke of Newcastle in 1772 Cantelowe Close, a field of nine acres, north of the site of the square, for £2,500. On Cantelowe Close parts of Gower Street, Store Street, and Chenies Street were subsequently built.[12]

9. Robert Palmer to the Duke of Bedford, 14 June 1766, in Palmer's Letter Book, *I*, 99.

10. Gladys Scott Thomson, quoted by Eliza Jeffries Davis, "The University Site, Bloomsbury," *London Topographical Record, 17* (1936), 76.

11. Ibid., p. 77.

12. Abstract of the Duke of Bedford's title to ground rents in Gower Street, etc. Copy in Bedford Office dated 22 March 1797.

Bedford Square is important today as the only intact eighteenth-century square remaining in London. It was important, when it was built, as the first square in London since the Piazza in Covent Garden to be planned and built as a unit (Figs. 21–23). The evidence as to who actually designed the façades is confused and contradictory. On the one hand, Robert Grews in 1784 gives the impression that he and the other contractor, William Scott, were responsible:

> Permit me to remind you, that in the year 1776 I, in conjunction [with] Mr. William Scott, engaged to build the west and north sides of Bedford Square, and formed and prepared plans and elevations of the whole square at a very considerable expense, which being submitted for the perusal of Her Grace the Duchess of Bedford and yourself met with approbation.
>
> As the business might have been impeded, or the plan deviated from had more persons been concerned, we were induced to engage for the completion of the whole square and the several streets leading into the same.[13]

On the other hand, Thomas Malton, writing in the late 1790s, implies that Scott and Grews employed a third person to design the actual façades, which they altered somewhat in execution:

> In Bedford Square . . . we have an example of the beauty resulting from an uniform design, carried into execution under individual direction; and an instance of the deformities, which are too frequently occasioned by the shackles of interested speculation. Each of the four sides of this square has a pediment in the center, supported by pilasters; but on two of the sides [the east and the south] the pediments extend over two houses, and have a pilaster in the middle; destroying that appearance of unity which is the characteristic of a pediment. It is scarcely to be imagined that such a fault could be committed, at a time when architecture has been so much studied and improved; yet justice requires it to be told, that the gentleman who made the design, felt this impropriety, and would have removed it; but the builder, who held the ground under the Duke of Bedford, having limited the number of houses, and determined to have a pediment on every side, could not be prevailed upon to alter his arrangement.[14]

13. Robert Grews to Robert Palmer, 4 February 1784.

14. Thomas Malton, *A Picturesque Tour* *through the Cities of London and Westminster* (London, 1792–1800), 98–99.

Possibly the third person was Thomas Leverton (1743–1824), whom Sir John Summerson thinks at least partly responsible for the design.[15]

Whoever was ultimately responsible, the Bedford estate put into the building contracts a requirement that the façades follow the original design. On each side of the square Scott and Grews agreed to build, within five years from Michaelmas 1775, "one uniform row of houses to front . . . on the . . . intended new square, agreeable to an elevation for the same signed by the said Robert Palmer, William Scott, and Robert Grews, and deposited in the steward's office at Bedford House." The agreement went on to enumerate the dimensions of each story, and the quality of materials for the different parts of the houses. For example, only the "best Memel or Riga timber" might be used, the floors were to be laid with "good yellow seasoned deals free from sap," and the houses as a whole were to be built "with hard place brick, faced with good grey stocks of uniform color, the walls . . . to be flushed solid with good mortar."

Scott and Grews agreed to make a footway in front of the houses, 9 ft. 6 in. wide in Bedford Square, and 6 ft. wide in the streets leading off the square.[16] They also contracted to pave the streets, and to make the carriage way in Bedford Square as far as sixty feet from the fronts of the houses, and to lay the necessary sewers throughout. Behind the houses they agreed to build coach houses and stables, and to pave the mews. The Duke's trustees promised on their part to undertake the expense of paving the roadway in Bedford Square beginning at sixty feet from the house fronts, and also to make the garden in the center. Scott and Grews were to do the actual work of forming and enclosing the garden, under the direction of Palmer, who would settle the bills.

Covenants prohibiting nuisances and all forms of business and trade were included. The Duke's agents were to supervise the whole of the works, and might enter and inspect any of the premises at any time, to see that the covenants were being observed. When the houses were completed, the trustees promised to grant ninety-nine-year building leases to Scott and Grews, or to "such person or persons as they shall name."[17] The leases would contain covenants by which the lessees were to pay "a reasonable share and proportion for and towards the maintaining, supporting, repairing, lighting, cleansing, paving,

15. *Georgian London*, pp. 165–66. See also H. M. Colvin, *A Biographical Dictionary of English Architects* (London, John Murray, 1954), p. 364.

16. The agreements covered, in addition to the whole of Bedford Square, houses to be built in Bedford (now Bayley) Street, Tavistock Street (now part of Bedford Avenue), Charlotte (now Bloomsbury) Street, Caroline (now Adeline) Street, Gower Street, and Store Street.

17. The Bedford Square leases were the first ninety-nine-year leases on the estate. Earlier building leases had been for terms of sixty-two or eighty years.

20. Southampton Street (now Southampton Place), east side, in 1982. Henry Flitcroft(?), c. 1740–50

21. Bedford Square, west side, in 1982. Robert Grews and William Scott, c. 1776

23. Bedford Square, east side, in 1982

22 (facing page). Bedford Square, south side, in 1982

24. Gower Street, west side, at Store Street, in 1982. Various builders, c. 1781

25. Gower Street, nos. 87–97, in 1982

26. Gower Street, nos. 123–31, in 1982

and keeping in good order and condition the said square intended to be called Bedford Square, and the iron rails thereof, and the inside thereof."[18]

Later building agreements do not differ in essentials from the Bedford Square contracts. Lists of dimensions, specifications of materials and quality, stipulations for uniformity of line, and covenants against nuisances and trade are to be found in building agreements generally. While the pattern remained the same, building agreements tended to grow longer and more detailed over the years. The culmination was reached with the printed form of agreement for houses on the Figs Mead estate, developed in the 1840s and 1850s, in which page after page is devoted to specifications of the most minute sort. As might be expected, agreements for big houses in important streets were longer and more exacting than were agreements for small houses in secondary streets. In particular the latter did not ordinarily require the builder to conform to a predetermined elevation; instead he had to submit his own elevations to the estate surveyor for approval. In addition, such agreements required that all houses in a street form a uniform row and that the levels of the windows be the same in each house.

From a study of building agreements it is easy to gain the impression that the estate office played a passive and certainly unheroic role in a building development, merely setting forth specifications and seeing that the contractors lived up to them. What the agreements and leases do not make clear is the active financial participation that the Bedford estate took in its building schemes. Such participation ordinarily took the form of loans to the contractors and to the lesser builders. At the time of the building of Bedford Square and Gower Street the trustees lent money to the builders without interest for the first year, and afterward at four per cent. At the close of 1782 the estate had lent, mostly on mortgages of houses in Bedford Square, a total of £22,500. It had also lent considerable sums to the paving commissioners for the parish of St. George, Bloomsbury, in order to speed the paving of the new streets.[19]

18. All the preceding quotations and information are taken from three counterpart building agreements between "the devisees of the late Duke of Bedford and Mr. William Scott and Mr. Robert Grews," dated 18 January and 6 July 1776.

19. Foundling Hospital General Court Minutes, 4, 225–26 (hereafter cited as General Court). "Account of Interest due on Mortgages of Houses in Bedford Square etc., December 31st 1782 or at times near thereto," in Bedford Office. Although building agreements usually included the obligation of the contractor to pave to the center of the roadway in front of his house, the actual paving was ordinarily carried out by the local paving commissioners, who reimbursed themselves by levying rates on the householders who were benefited. Summerson, *Georgian London*, p. 165, states that Robert Palmer, one of the trustees, lent money from his personal fortune to the builders in Bedford Square. A pamphlet in the British Museum by John Holliday, *A Further Appeal to the Governors of the Foundling Hospital* (London, 1788), implies that the money Palmer lent came instead from the estate: "Were not the lessees of the Portland and Bedford estates enabled to build upon, and give large prices for the ground . . . from the builders

Although Scott and Grews took on the responsibility for building the whole of Bedford Square, they sold to smaller builders the rights to build on many of the sites. The estate granted a lease of each house to the actual builder. Scott and Grews themselves built the whole of the south side of the square, as well as many of the houses on the other sides.[20] John Utterton and Thomas Leverton were important subcontractors.[21]

Bedford Square served as the focal point for a whole new network of streets and mews. Charlotte and Caroline streets to the south, Bedford and Tavistock streets to the west, and Gower, Store, and Chenies streets to the north took shape in the years following 1776 (Figs. 24–26). Scott and Grews were the principal leaseholders in the subsidiary streets, but others, such as Utterton, Leverton, and Alexander Hendy, also built on a large scale. By 1786 the northwestern section of the Bloomsbury estate, bounded on the east by Gower Street, was covered with houses.[22]

The desire of the Duke that Bedford House retain its uninterrupted prospect to the north forbade any building north of Great Russell Street and east of Gower Street. In a draft of a letter to the Secretary of the Foundling Hospital in June 1787, Henry Holland, who was then acting as the Duke's surveyor, wrote:

> His Grace the Duke of Bedford would be very glad to aid and assist the interest of the Charity but is advised he cannot permit any openings into his private Road or give encouragement to any plan of

being supplied with large savings during long minorities? Witness the many hundreds of leases granted by the Dowager Duchess of Portland, the Honourable Mr. Harley, and other Trustees, before the present Duke of Portland came of age—witness the immense sums lent by the late Mr. Palmer to those who built Bedford Square, and Gower Street—without which (as he frequently owned) the buildings would never have been finished."

20. In the end they built more of the square than they had at first intended. As Grews wrote to Palmer on 4 February 1784, "The great scarcity of money, occasioned by the unhappy American War, so severely affected many of the persons concerned under us, that some were compelled to stop, and we found ourselves under the unfortunate necessity of taking back the ground, and completing the houses thereon, which their inability had rendered them incapable of doing . . ."

21. Information as to who the principal builders were comes mainly from the appropri-

ate volumes of rentals. Leverton, in connection with an unsuccessful application for the post of surveyor to the London estate, wrote in 1797 that he had "actually laid out for my friends and myself above forty thousand pounds in new buildings and improvements on it," and that he "had a principal concern in promoting the finishing of Bedford Square, and built among other houses in it that of the Lord Chancellor [Mansfield, nos. 6 and 6a], besides several on my own account, in one of which I now reside [no. 13]." Thomas Leverton to the Duke of Bedford, 17 July 1797. See also his letter to Robert Palmer, 29 September 1785.

22. In his Annual Report for 1851, p. 10, Christopher Haedy, then the Duke's chief agent, wrote that the development of the streets around Bedford Square was "proceeded with, with occasional interruptions, till 1786, about which time they were finished; and that completed the building plan as to all the ground on your Grace's estate which was then considered to be applicable to building purposes.

building as referring to the estate west [meaning east?] of Bedford House without considerable prejudice to his property and without a decision respecting Bedford House for which his Grace is not prepared.[23]

The implication is that the Duke felt that any building to the north of Bedford House would so diminish its desirability as to make him decide to give up the house altogether. This he was not prepared to do, at least not in 1787.

By 1795 circumstances had changed. Despite the Duke's reluctance to cooperate, building was rapidly progressing on the Foundling estate, and an agreement had been made to permit the Hospital to make street openings from its estate onto the Duke's private road. Accordingly, the Duke had determined to develop the rest of the Bloomsbury estate, except for the portion of the Long Fields directly north of Bedford House, which were to remain permanently free of buildings. The 1795 map of the Bedford estates in London (Fig. 8) shows the newly projected scheme. The author of the plan is unknown, but it is reasonable to assume that Henry Holland had some part in its formulation.[24]

The plan showed considerable ingenuity. It made Bedford House and its grounds the central feature of the new northern Bloomsbury development, as they already were of southern Bloomsbury. The Long Fields north of the ducal mansion were to be landscaped and made an ornamental pleasure ground, fronted on either side by a row of houses. The essential idea was the same as that which had placed Bloomsbury Square to the south of Southampton House in 1661. In both instances the great mansion added lustre to the smaller houses surrounding it by forming one side of a large enclosed open space. The plan isolated Bedford House and made it conspicuous. The conception of a great parklike area surrounded by terraces of imposing town houses calls to mind the later, more elaborate plans of John Nash for his Regent's Park development.

A covenant inserted in the building agreements for Southampton Terrace, which was to face the Long Fields from the east, proves that the Duke at that time intended the open space to be a permanent feature of the estate. The Duke promised that "the area or lawn extending northwards from the garden belonging to Bedford House to the estate of Lord Southampton, and also extending

---

23. "Draft of Letter proposed by Mr. Holland to be sent to Thomas Collingwood Esq. Secretary to the Foundling Hospital but on laying it before Mr. Macnamara he was of opinion it will be better not to give an answer in writing. (Call on Dr. White)."

24. See Dorothy Stroud, *Henry Holland* (London, 1950), for a general account of the architect.

from the said intended [Southampton] terrace westward to another intended terrace to be called Bedford Terrace shall not be let or granted for building, nor shall the said Duke of Bedford . . . permit any buildings to be erected thereon, except ornamental or other buildings for the use of the ground, during the said term of ninety-nine years."[25]

West of Bedford Terrace two new streets, New Bedford Street and New Store Street, were to form continuations of the north side of Bedford Square and Store Street respectively, as Montague Place and Keppel Street now do. Slightly to the east of Southampton Terrace lay the western boundary of the Foundling Hospital estate. The Duke's streets east of Southampton Terrace were therefore the western continuation of the Foundling estate plan, and were for the most part built on ground which the Hospital estate granted to the Bedford estate in exchange for the openings onto the Terrace.

Not only was the portion of the estate east of Southampton Terrace linked geographically with the Foundling estate, but it resembled it socially as well. Much of the building development on the latter estate, which had begun in 1790, was intended for a less substantial class of tenants than was the Bedford estate. Therefore, unlike the rest of his Bloomsbury development, the Duke's property east of Southampton Terrace was let for the construction of narrow streets and small houses, similar to those going up on the neighboring property. The circumstance was later to cause the Bedford estate great embarrassment: it was in these streets that the only slums on the Bloomsbury estate developed.

The line of Southampton Terrace ran, roughly speaking, along the line of the Duke's private road, which had been in existence since the 1750s. Bedford Terrace was, on the other hand, to cut across open fields, and its development was therefore delayed. Before any building took place along it, the Duke had abandoned the 1795 plan and substituted for it a new building scheme that contained the essential features of the Bloomsbury of today.[26]

The new plan, which the estate put into effect in 1800 (Fig. 27), provided for the demolition of Bedford House and the covering of its site and the Long Fields

25. Building contract to James Burton and Henry Scrimshaw for Southampton Terrace, 6 July 1795. The contractors released the Duke from this covenant when the 1800 building plan was decided upon.

26. Christopher Haedy, in the 1851 Annual Report, p. 10, described the events in the following manner: "A scheme was proposed for building on part of the Long Fields by carrying out two lines of houses running from south to north in such manner as to leave open the view over those fields from the north side of Bedford House, the taking down of which was not then contemplated. After one of those lines of houses (the one to the eastward) was commenced by the erection of the houses which now form the part of the east side of Russell Square which lies between Guilford Street and Bernard Street, your Grace's uncle determined upon taking down Bedford House, and letting the site of it and the Long Fields for building."

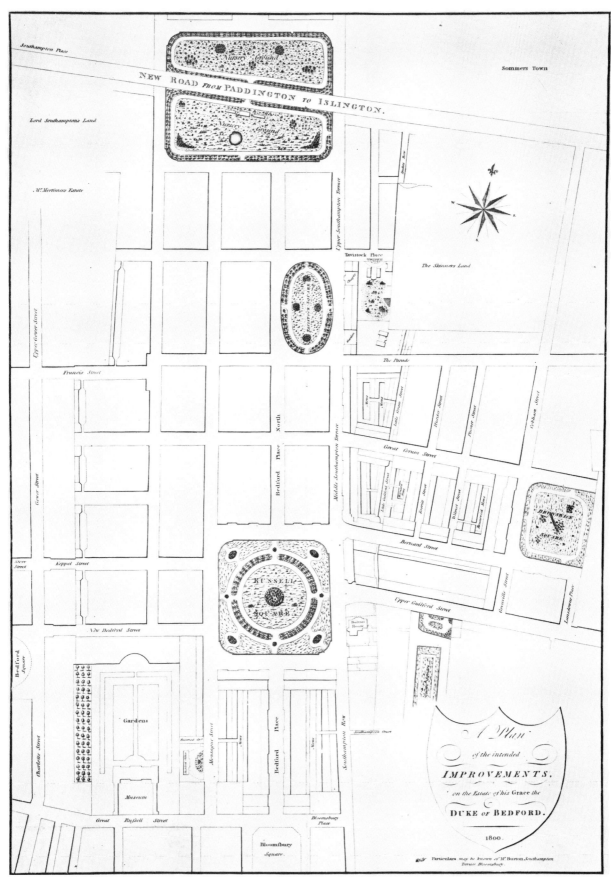

27. Bloomsbury estate plan, 1800

28. Bloomsbury Square gardens, looking north, in 1982

29. Bloomsbury Square, north side, and Bedford Place, looking toward Russell Square, in 1982. James Burton, c. 1800

to the north with a dramatic succession of streets and squares. The reason for the abrupt change of program is not clear, although the new plan was clearly more sensible than the discarded scheme of 1795.

By 1800 the detached mansion had become an anachronism in London. Most of the big seventeenth-century houses in Piccadilly, like the sixteenth-century palaces in the Strand, had long since been pulled down, and their sites taken by speculative builders. Yet even they had not been set in grounds as extensive as the portion of the Long Fields which the 1795 plan had marked for preservation. The potential value as building land of so large an area was obviously too great for the Duke to ignore.

The original building scheme itself was open to practical objections. The Long Fields would inevitably have tended to isolate the houses in Southampton Terrace, which would have had easy communication only with the less fashionable streets of the Foundling estate to the east. Remote and inaccessible, they would almost certainly have proved difficult to let.

Quite apart from considerations of estate management, Bloomsbury had ceased to be a fashionable address for a duke, and even the view of Hampstead and Highgate could not wholly compensate for such a situation. In 1800 the Duke moved not only out of Bedford House but off his own estate, and transferred his town residence to Arlington Street, St. James's.[27]

The new plan retained the general pattern of the streets projected in the 1795 map, but continued them across the Long Fields. The principal new features of the development were to be two garden squares, which would compensate in part for the loss of the amenities of the open fields. One of the squares would be, after Lincoln's Inn Fields, the biggest in London. The proposed streets were without exception wide and regular. The building agreements ensured that they would be lined with imposing houses, set in uniform terraces. The squares and the more important streets would be formal architectural compositions, in the manner of the Piazza in Covent Garden and Bedford Square.

For the part of the development included in the parish of St. Pancras the Bedford Office obtained a paving act (40 Geo. III, cap. 49), providing for a commission elected by the ratepayers involved. The twenty-one commissioners were

27. Shortly before he did so, Thomas Malton wrote of Bedford House: "No mansion in town has the advantage of such a beautiful situation; the garden front in particular commands a delightful view of Hampstead and Highgate; and although the house wants elevation and dignity to render it worthy of the owner; yet we are surprised to hear that a situation so peculiarly favourable for a town residence is shortly to be sacrificed to the more profitable purpose of letting the ground on building leases." *A Picturesque Tour through the Cities of London and Westminster*, p. 96.

to levy rates on the inhabitants and make provision for "forming, paving, repairing, and keeping in repair . . . [the] intended streets, squares, passages, and
places; and also for cleansing, lighting, watching, and watering the same; and
for removing and preventing nuisances, annoyances, and encroachments therein . . ." Russell Square, being in the parish of St. George, Bloomsbury, required a
separate Act, which provided for the maintenance of the garden enclosure by a
committee of ratepayers. A similar Act in 1806 dealt with Bloomsbury Square.

By far the most important of the contractors who came forward to execute the
plan was James Burton (1761–1837).[28] Burton, together with Henry Scrimshaw,
had already built part of Southampton Terrace and the less imposing streets
behind it for the Duke of Bedford. He had been the leading figure in the development of the western portion of the Foundling estate in the 1790s.

Burton agreed in December 1799 to pull down Bedford House, offering 5,000
guineas for the materials and furniture. He proposed to engage for the whole of
the north side of Bloomsbury Square, the south side of Russell Square, and the
whole of the central street (Bedford Place) connecting the two, building in addition a mews behind the houses. For the 1,328 feet of frontage, he agreed to
pay ground rent at the rate of 12s. per foot, or £996 a year for the whole, the
first five years to be at a peppercorn rent. He would enclose and plant the areas
of the two squares, either according to his own plan or according to the more
elaborate plan of James Gubbins, the Duke's surveyor.[29] Finally, he proposed to
build the necessary sewers at 12s. a foot.

The estate, according to Burton's proposals, would pay him for the cost of the
square enclosures and the sewers. The commissioners of the intended Russell
Square Act and the St. Pancras Paving Act would reimburse the estate for the
cost of enclosing the squares, while the residents would eventually pay for the
sewers.[30]

The actual building contract for the site of Bedford House, dated 24 June
1800, differs only in minor ways from Burton's original proposals of the previous
December. The total ground rent was raised to £1,572 per annum, and the
frontage let was proportionally increased. The contract included the whole of the
north side of Bloomsbury Square, both sides of Bedford Place, and the south
side of Russell Square. In addition Burton contracted to build along the west
side of Southampton Row for a distance of 559 feet southward from Russell
Square, and along the east side of Montague Street for 519 feet southward from

28. See Summerson, *Georgian London*, pp.
169–73, and Colvin, pp. 113–14.

29. For Russell Square, Burton's plan would
cost £2,570; the Gubbins plan would cost £3,000.

The alternative prices for Tavistock Square were
£1,650 and £1,850.

30. Memoranda from Burton in the Bedford
Office, with comments by Gubbins.

Russell Square. Finally, he contracted for the west side of Russell Square and Montague Street southward from New Bedford Street (now Montague Place) for 465 feet (Figs. 28–30).

Burton's houses in Montague Street and Southampton Row could be either of the first or second rate. The rest were all to be "capital first-rate houses." He agreed to build the houses in Bedford Place and along the south side of Russell Square to conform with detailed elevations drawn on the backs of the contract. The elevations are signed by James Gubbins, although it is almost certain that the designs were by Burton himself.[31]

Although Burton designed the façades, the responsibility for the over-all appearance of Russell Square lay with Gubbins and the estate office. They alone were able to impose on the contractors for the north side of the square—Henry Scrimshaw, Thomas Lewis, and David Alston, Jr.—elevations practically identical with Burton's on the south. Some idea of the simple but pleasing design of the square can be seen in Figure 31, showing a portion of the range of houses built by Lewis and Alston, west of Upper Bedford Place (now Bedford Way). The photograph does not show the symmetrical arrangement of the blocks, which in their original state was emphasized by the placing of the ornamental breaks and balustrades.[32]

Since part of the east side of the square had already been built before 1800, as part of Southampton Terrace, that part could not be given a unified façade. The central block of the western side, between Montague Place and Keppel Street, had a different design from that imposed on the northern and southern blocks. The "elevations . . . deposited in Bedford Office," to which Thomas Lewis and David Alston, Jr., agreed in their contracts to conform, called for a central pediment and Ionic pilasters. The other houses on the west side—the only ones in the square that still retain their original appearance—had merely "to conform as nearly as possible" with the other houses in the square, which Britton's *Picture of London* later described as "one of the largest and most handsome in London."[33]

31. The fact that Burton exhibited at the Royal Academy in 1800 a "West view of the houses erecting at the back of Bedford House, the south side of Russell Square," indicates that the design was his own. See Summerson, *Georgian London*, p. 170.

32. The symmetrical arrangement of the ornamentation on the north and south sides survived the improvements of 1900 and can still be seen. See Fig. 32.

33. "Broad streets intersect it at the centers and angles, which not only add to its beauty, but remove an objection made by some to squares in general, by securing a thorough ventilation. Pilasters adorn the central houses, and balconies are appended to the first stories, nearly throughout; the basements in general are stuccoed. The extensive enclosure in the center is a miniature landscape-garden, combining beauty and variety." John Britton, ed., *The Original Picture of London, Enlarged and Improved* (24th ed. London, 1826), p. 187.

Burton himself took leases of all the houses in Bedford Place and the north side of Bloomsbury Square, along with nine in Russell Square and some in Southampton Row; smaller builders working under his supervision took the rest. Among other streets in which Burton contracted to build are Tavistock Place, Tavistock Mews, Abbey Place, Little Coram Street, the east side of Woburn Place north of Great Coram Street, and the east side of Tavistock Square.[34]

Burton's contract for the east side of Tavistock Square, dated 21 November 1800, did not mention any specific elevation. The Bedford Office obviously considered it less important than Russell Square. Beyond the usual lists of dimensions and materials, the agreement merely stipulated that "the west fronts of the said houses with the windows therein [were] to range in a line, and be regular, and correspond in height of stories, and in all other respects with the houses last built in the said [Woburn] place by Henry Scrimshaw, or as near thereto as the different levels of the pavements on the said place and square will allow, and all external walls [were] to be built and finished with materials of equal goodness as the fronts of the said several houses . . ." That Burton did in fact attempt to give his block of houses in Tavistock Square a certain architectural distinction is indicated by Figure 39. When Thomas Cubitt built the rest of the square twenty years later, he adapted Burton's Ionic pilasters on his houses in order to give the whole square a unified appearance (Figs. 40, 41).

Montague Place, like Russell Square and Bedford Place, was sufficiently important to warrant a special elevation in the Bedford Office, to which the builders—among whom Thomas Lewis and Alexander Hendy were prominent—had to conform. Lewis' building agreement for houses in Montague Place is dated 1802, but the street was a long time in the making; eleven of the building leases date from 1810, and two more from 1811.[35]

Keppel Street, paralleling Montague Place to the north, was the scene of Lewis' difficulties.[36] As a result, its houses, built toward the end of the decade, were much smaller than those Lewis and others had put up in Montague Place. With its completion, new building practically ceased in Bloomsbury.

The remarkable thing was not so much that the building boom came to an end but that it could have existed at all in the middle of the Revolutionary and Napoleonic wars. The less serious wars of the eighteenth century had each in

34. All these streets were at the eastern boundary of the estate, bordering on the property of the Foundling Hospital, where Burton was carrying on an even more ambitious building scheme.

35. A building lease ordinarily dates from the time that the articles of agreement for the house were granted, not from the time that the lease itself was granted.

36. See above, p. 35, and Appendix II.

30. Montague Street, east side, in 1982. James Burton, c. 1800

31. Russell Square, north side, before the alteration of the facades in 1899

32. Russell Square, south side, in 1982

33. Upper Bedford Place (now Bedford Way), east side. Mostly by John McGill, c. 1810–21.

its turn slowed or halted building developments, as laborers joined the army or navy and the cost of materials rose. The American War had brought many speculative builders to ruin.[37]

"The present war," wrote Malcolm in the first volume of his *Londinium Redivivum* in 1802, "has been a great check to the enterprising spirit of builders; consequently the improvements have been nearly confined to the northern side of the metropolis, and have chiefly been in the hands of one eminent builder, Mr. Burton."[38] While lamenting that with the demolition of Bedford House and the covering of its site with buildings the residents of Southampton Row were being "deprived of the cheering prospect of Bedford gardens and the fields, with the beautiful Hampstead Hills," he found much to admire in the development. "Perhaps, in these times of difficulty and distress," he thought, "no plan has a more beneficial effect than thus employing so many hands, which would have otherwise been idle. When the excessive price of every article of necessity is considered, what heart is there but must rejoice at the busy scene this neighborhood presents, and bless the proprietors?"[39]

While writing the second volume in 1805, Malcolm remarked on the "wonderfully rapid" increase in the population of the parish of St. George, Bloomsbury: "Squares, and spacious streets of the first respectability, are rising in every direction; and the north side of the parish will, in a few years, contain an immense accumulation of riches, attracted by the grand structures in Russell Square, now almost completed, Tavistock Square, Woburn Place, Upper Bedford Place, etc. etc. which has entirely obliterated every vestige, except two poplar trees, of the house and gardens of the Duke of Bedford, and great part of the verdant fields between them and the New Road."[40]

"The immense accumulations of building that have lately taken place on this side of the metropolis, are apparently beyond credibility," wrote another London historian with respect to the Bedford and Foundling estates in 1807. "In 1803, all the new houses between Russell and Bloomsbury squares, were erected; and most of the large tract, formerly known by the name of the Long Fields, have [sic] been covered with magnificent houses since 1801."[41]

In fact the boom had ended long before 1807. Of the streets projected in the original plan, Upper Bedford Place, together with three sides of Tavistock

37. M. Dorothy George, *London Life in the XVIIIth Century* (London, Kegan Paul, 1925), p. 79.

38. James Peller Malcolm, *Londinium Redivivum* (4 vols. London, 1802–07), *1*, 5.

39. Ibid., p. 7.

40. Ibid., *2*, 480.

41. Edward Pugh (David Hughson, pseud.), *London* (London, 1805–09), *4*, 384.

Square, were not to be completed until the 1820s. The closing decade of the European war brought with it both a rise in the cost of building materials and an acute scarcity of credit, while the rigid specifications of a Bedford contract prevented the builder from cutting corners. To make matters worse, the first-rate houses which the agreements usually called for were not selling as readily in the relatively remote and unfashionable Bloomsbury as the writers of contemporary guidebooks seemed to think.[42] One of them, in the following decade, admitted that "at the time of writing (1814) the town is overbuilt, many thousands of houses in private situations being unlet, and very numerous families engaged in building speculations have been ruined, besides above 20,000 workmen being out of employment."[43]

To help the builders overcome such difficulties, and thereby speed the development, the Duke made them liberal loans, as the estate had earlier done to encourage the builders of Bedford Square and Gower Street. The total sum of money that the Duke loaned on mortgages cannot be ascertained, but it must have been considerable.[44] In certain instances the Duke redeemed the land tax on the houses being built in return for an increased ground rent.[45] In addition the estate frequently extended the period of peppercorn rent when the builder

42. A letter from Thomas Lewis to T. P. Brown, 5 October 1821, recalls the difficulties of letting the houses in Russell Square during the war.

43. John Feltham, *The Picture of London, for 1815*, p. 358. In their study of the cycles in building in Britain between 1785 and 1849, A. K. Cairncross and B. Weber write as follows: "A rise beginning early in the 1780's seems to have been checked in 1788 or 1789 and, when resumed, continued until 1793 or 1794. From then until the next trough in 1799 there was a gradual fall, temporarily checked in 1796. This cycle of about eighteen years was followed by a second of the same length with a fresh trough in 1816 or (less probably) in 1817. There was no clear intervening peak but instead a high plateau stretching from about 1803 to 1813." "Fluctuations in Building in Great Britain, 1785–1849," *Economic History Review*, 2nd ser. 9 (1956–57), 285. The building history of the Bedford estate clearly did not conform to this pattern.

44. There are references to building loans in the 1790s. See, for example, John Hobcroft to Daniel Beaumont, 14 March 1793; also the Foundling Hospital General Court Minutes, *4*,

226 (26 November 1798). On 13 June 1800 the Duke advanced £7,000 to Burton on mortgage (building agreement for the east side of Tavistock Square and Woburn Place, 21 November 1800). According to Malcolm, the Bedford estate was in 1802 lending "sums of £150 to £600 for three years, to such persons as choose to accept them . . ." (*Londinium Redivivum, 1,* 7). In January of that year it advanced £5,000 to Burton on the security of seven houses on the south side of Russell Square (James Gubbins to John Gotobed, 20 January 1802). In September 1803 Scrimshaw requested a loan of £1,400 on the security of one of his houses in Russell Square (Henry Scrimshaw to John Gotobed, 5 September 1803). In December 1805 Burton and certain unnamed associates paid off a mortgage of an unspecified amount on a house in Keppel Street (James Burton to Messrs. Brown, 30 November 1805). There is a reference in 1810 to a loan of £1,000 to Thomas Lewis (Duke of Bedford to Thomas Pearce Brown, 29 October 1810).

45. See endorsement dated 25 January 1802 on the back of the building agreement with Henry Scrimshaw for the north side of Russell Square, 10 November 1800.

was unable to finish his house in the allotted time, or could not immediately find a purchaser or tenant.

While loans and a liberal policy of extending peppercorn rents no doubt did much to encourage construction, not even the Duke of Bedford could escape the effects of a general stagnation in speculative building. The extension of the estate northward from Russell Square proceeded slowly and deliberately. Although Henry Scrimshaw built two houses at the south end of Upper Bedford Place as early as 1802, the street was not extended beyond his houses until 1810; the final lease for its northernmost portion dates from Midsummer 1824. John McGill, who was also responsible for much of the west side of Woburn Place, built most of Upper Bedford Place (Fig. 33).[46]

The remaining undeveloped portion of the Long Fields in no sense constituted one of the amenities of Bloomsbury. The Duke in a letter to his solicitor in 1817 wrote of "the general nuisance which has caused so many representations to be made to me from that neighborhood, and if there are any means of getting rid of these ponds without difficulty, it certainly must be a desirable object to the more respectable inhabitants of the vicinity."[47] Brown replied that the ponds formed part of "the general nuisance which we are in daily hopes of getting rid of by letting the whole ground to one person. What has impeded the matter," he explained, "is the large sum which each proposer for the ground requires your Grace to expend in fencing, and in one plan these ponds are intended to be kept as objects of beauty."[48]

The period of stagnation came to an end in the 1820s, when two new builders came forward to transform the swampy lowlands of northern Bloomsbury into something more pleasing to the respectable householders of Tavistock Square. The first of these was James Sim, who, in partnership with his sons, James Sim, Jr., and Robert Sim, built Torrington and Woburn squares.[49] The second was the celebrated Thomas Cubitt, who built nearly the whole of the remainder

---

46. In a letter to the Foundling estate proposing to build along the north side of Mecklenburgh Square, McGill wrote: "For the character of my building, I beg to refer the governors to the houses which I have lately built in Upper Bedford Place, most of which have been sold and occupied as soon as finished." Building Committee, 5, 1 (27 October 1821).

47. Duke of Bedford to T. P. Brown, 24 August 1817. "Ponds" was a euphemism; much of the area was a swamp. See the print reproduced

in Davis, "University Site," p. 94. See also the 1851 Auditor's Report, p. 11.

48. T. P. Brown to the Duke of Bedford, draft copy, 25 August 1817. By 1817 romanticism had 'apparently penetrated the world of the speculative builder.

49. Summerson, *Georgian London,* p. 193. Cairncross and Weber, p. 291, speak of an upswing in building in London from 1817, reaching a peak in 1819.

of the estate south of the New Road.[50] The Sim family and Cubitt differed from their predecessors in that they ordinarily did not grant subcontracts to smaller builders but carried out the whole of their agreements with the Bedford Office.

The new construction in the 1820s and '30s involved a considerable modification of the 1800 plan. It had already suffered a number of alterations. The westward extension of Great Coram Street shown in Figure 8 had never been made, nor had the street running north from the center of Montague Place materialized. The changes of the 1820s were far more extensive; in that decade three new garden squares were superimposed on the old street plan (Fig. 34). Torrington and Woburn squares were little more than widened streets with garden strips down the center—much on the order of Montague and Bryanston squares on the Portman estate. Gordon Square, to the north, was a far grander conception, if one that proved difficult to realize. To complete the scheme gates had been, by 1830, placed across each of the four streets which crossed the northern boundary, together with one across Torrington Place—which ran to the west. These were intended to reduce the traffic on the estate to a minimum and to impede communications with adjacent and unfashionable neighborhoods.

The Sim family first appears in the Bedford records in a building agreement for two second-rate houses on the west side of Torrington Street, dated 18 March 1820.[51] There followed three more important contracts—dated 26 May 1821, 21 June 1824, and 3 June 1825, respectively—for the southern, central, and northern portions of Torrington Square (Fig. 35).

The first of the contracts called for the construction of twenty-seven second-rate houses. In addition, the Sim family was to enclose and plant the narrow garden in the center of the square. The agreement, which emerged from extended negotiations between the builders and the Bedford Office, included not only an elevation for the houses but also a detailed map of the garden, showing

50. Thomas Cubitt (1788–1855) "devoted himself to building, from his own designs and on his own ground. His plan was to take a large tract of unoccupied land, sometimes from several distinct land-owners, and to lay it out on one great plan of squares, streets, roads, etc., as a whole, sparing no expense in the outset, in drainage, forming gardens, planting, laying out wide streets, and using every endeavour to keep up the character of the whole." *Minutes of the Proceedings of the Institution of Civil Engineers, 16* (Session 1856–57), p. 159. Before embarking on his undertaking on the Bedford estate in 1821, he had engaged in building speculations on the Calthorpe estate. In 1819 Cubitt proposed to

the Foundling Hospital to build the whole of the north side of Mecklenburgh Square and the south side of Heathcote Street to the rear, but his offer was declined. Building Committee, *4*, 223–25 (4 December 1819). Ibid., *5*, 19 (15 December 1821). His best known scheme was the development of Belgravia and Pimlico on the Grosvenor and Lowndes estates. See Summerson, *Georgian London*, pp. 191–96; E. W. Cooney, "The Origins of the Victorian Master Builder," *Economic History Review*, 2nd ser. 8 (1955–56), 171–72; Colvin, pp. 160–61.

51. Torrington Street ran through what is now the Institute of Education, and connected Torrington Square with Keppel Street.

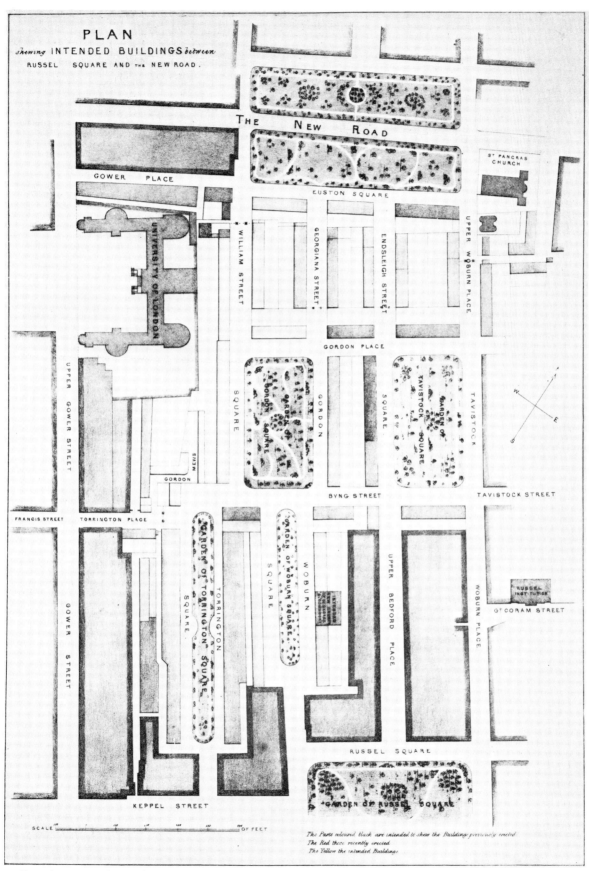

34. Bloomsbury estate plan, c. 1830

35. Torrington Square, east side, in 1939. James Sim, James Sim, Jr., and Robert Sim, c. 1821–25

36. Woburn Square, looking north toward Gordon Square, in 1964. James Sim, James Sim, Jr., and Robert Sim, c. 1829

the precise location of the intended gravel walks, grass plots, shrubbery, trees, and even the benches. There was also an elevation of the dwarf wall and railing which were to surround the garden, and a full-sized cross section of a rail head for the garden fence. The two later contracts had similar drawings, signed by T. Stead, Gubbins' successor as estate surveyor. In general, the two later ones resembled the first, except that the contract for the central portion of the square called for first-rate rather than second-rate houses. Most of the houses were of moderate size, and the square became "filled with occupants as fast as it progressed in building."[52]

Having successfully completed its speculation in Torrington Square, the Sim family proceeded to develop the vacant land immediately to the east. On 20 April 1829 it contracted to build the whole of Woburn Square, except for the church planned for the middle of the east side. The Sims agreed to build forty-one second-rate houses according to an elevation included in the contract, at an annual ground rent of £1,148, after six years at a peppercorn rent. Thomas Cubitt had already formed and enclosed the central gardens of the new square, laid the necessary sewers, and turned the vaults for the houses.[53] The elder James Sim having died in September 1833, his sons finished the northern portion of the square (Figs. 36, 37).

Thomas Cubitt began his association with northern Bloomsbury in April 1821, when he signed a contract for building the south side of Tavistock Square. After finishing his first houses, Cubitt contracted one by one for the remaining plots of building ground on the estate. His agreement for the east side of Upper Woburn Place dates from 13 November 1821; for Woburn Buildings (now Woburn Walk), from 5 June 1822. His leases for the north side and most of the west side of Tavistock Square all date from Midsummer 1824.[54] The leases for the west side of Upper Woburn Place likewise date from Midsummer 1824, as do those for Endsleigh Street, Gordon Place (Fig. 38), the south side of Gordon Square, and many of those in Gordon Street.[55] Here they stop; it was to be many

52. Rowland Dobie, *History of the United Parishes of St. Giles-in-the-Fields and St. George Bloomsbury* (London, 1834), p. 179.

53. For this the Duke paid Cubitt £5,502 8s. 2d., by extending the peppercorn rent on ground he had taken elsewhere. [Christopher Haedy], "Terms of letting the ground in Woburn Square . . . ," 1836.

54. James Alexander Frampton built the six houses at the south end of the west side of the square, following Cubitt's design.

55. "In 1824 Mr. Cubitt took all the remainder of your Grace's unbuilt-upon land southward of the New Road. It required a large outlay, in sewers, roadmaking, and raising the surface, in order to bring it into a proper state for building. This outlay was made by Mr. Cubitt, and by means of it a site, swampy, low, and having every appearance of being unsuited for the purpose, was converted into an excellent building site." Christopher Haedy, 1851 Report, p. 11.

years before Cubitt or anyone else was able to complete the estate's building plan.

In 1826 John Britton wrote that Tavistock Square "consists at present of only three sides, but the fourth side is building. . . . Immediately west of it," he continued, "a new square, called *Gordon Square,* is planted and laid out. This is intended to consist of very handsome and spacious mansions, and the adjoining streets are to be laid out in a style of corresponding beauty and appropriation [sic]."[56] Yet Cubitt's ambitious speculation, which began so auspiciously, petered out in the end. Looking back on the development in 1851 Christopher Haedy,[57] the London steward and auditor, tried to explain why:

> These buildings proceeded rapidly at first, but very slowly afterwards, in consequence of the new buildings near Hyde Park Gardens and in the neighborhood of Belgrave Square [to a great extent built by Cubitt himself] coming into successful rivalry with them. If Mr. Cubitt, when he commenced building on this part of your Grace's estate, had foreseen that rivalry, he would no doubt have erected houses which would have been less subject to its influence. When he presented his plans for building on this part of your Grace's estate, I wished him to consider whether he might not be incurring the risk of erecting too many houses adapted to one class of tenants, and whether the demand for houses of that size in that vicinity was not satisfied by the houses already erected, and whether houses one degree smaller in size and price would not be more likely to succeed on that part of the estate. He did not then concur in that suggestion, but has often since expressed his regret that he did not act upon it. The consequence of his not having done so was that the houses he built were rather too large and too expensive for the locality, and the difficulty he found in procuring purchasers and tenants for them made him hesitate to proceed with the erection of houses of a similar kind, whilst at the same time he felt that to build houses of a smaller kind and lower price would tend to lessen the value and interfere with the sale and letting of those he had already built.[58]

56. Britton, *The Original Picture of London, Enlarged and Improved,* p. 187.

57. For an excellent account of Haedy's career in the Bedford Office, see David Spring, *The English Landed Estate in the Nineteenth Century: Its Administration* (Baltimore, Johns Hop-kins Press, 1963), esp. pp. 68–78.

58. 1851 Report, pp. 11–12. Cairncross and Weber, p. 291, comment on the "extraordinarily sharp depression" which followed the boom of 1825 in London.

37. Woburn Square, east side, in 1982

38. Gordon Place (now Endsleigh Place), in 1982. Thomas Cubitt, c. 1824

39. Tavistock Square, east side, in 1911. James Burton, c. 1800

40. Tavistock Square, west side, in 1982. Thomas Cubitt, c. 1824–29

The traditional conflict between the landlord wanting expensive houses and the builder wanting cheap ones was here reversed. In other ways, too, Cubitt's role in the building history of the estate differs in kind from that of his predecessors. He built on a bigger scale than any London builder before him, and his methods differed accordingly. Instead of using the elaborate system of cross-contracting which had until his time characterized the London building trades, Cubitt employed a corps of his own workmen on a permanent wage basis. Among other advantages, this gave him a greater degree of control over the houses he contracted to build than was possible under the older system. There is little doubt that Thomas Cubitt—or, as Summerson suggests, his brother Lewis—was personally responsible for the architecture, as he was for the size, of the houses he erected. There is good reason to believe that one of the Cubitts drew the fine colored elevations which are attached to the articles of agreement for Tavistock Square, Upper Woburn Place, and Woburn Buildings.[59]

Yet although there is little doubt that one of the Cubitt family initiated the designs for the various blocks of buildings that Cubitt erected, the Duke and his various agents felt quite free to make alterations. In December 1823 W. G. Adam, the Duke's auditor, wrote from Woburn Abbey to Thomas Pearce Brown, the estate solicitor, about the arrival from London of "the box with Cubitt's plans" for Tavistock Square, which he was about to "lay before the Duke and get his opinion in point of taste. I am not quite aware however," Adam proceeded, "what the difference is between the plainer elevation sent for the north side and the actual elevation of the south."[60] He praised both "the plainer elevation now sent" for the north side, and that for the west side. Burton's terrace on the east side he pronounced "very ugly." "But," he wondered, "ought not the E[ast] & W[est] and N[orth] & S[outh] to be uniform? If not, I would have all different."[61]

What the Duke thought of the plans when he saw them, and how far, if at all, his aesthetic judgments, along with those of his auditor, solicitor, and surveyor were reflected in the final form of Tavistock Square is not easy to determine (Figs. 40, 41). One ought not to assume any unanimity on matters of taste within the Bedford Office. An extract from a letter from the auditor to the London steward dealing with the plans for the south side of Gordon Square (Fig. 42), also built by Cubitt, is typical of many:

59. They were obviously drawn by a different hand from that which produced the elevations for the Woburn and Torrington Square agreements.

60. Cubitt had already finished the south side along lines similar to Burton's houses on the west side. See Fig. 39.

61. W. G. Adam to T. P. Brown, 30 December 1823.

If I had seen your elevations before I wrote to you today, I should have written differently. I am not surprised at my differing with [Charles] Fowler [1791–1867, the architect of the new Covent Garden Market buildings] in point of taste, for I think we have seldom agreed, but I am surprised at differing with you, and still more at agreeing with Stead [the surveyor]. I very much prefer the two windows, though I don't think the pilasters important. I will not put my opinion in competition, but I think the Duke would like to see it. We will save Fowler's feelings if the Duke decides for the two windows by avowing it. When old Duke John proposed to plant the evergreens at Woburn (now so much admired), his gardener protested they would grow, and that it would injure his reputation to be considered as the adviser of such a folly—on which the old Duke painted on a board which he fixed on the wall that "this plantation was made by the D[uke] of B[edford] against the advice of his gardener." Fowler shall have a similar disclaimer if it is decided against them, if he likes it.[62]

It is clear that the sixth Duke took a lively interest in matters of architecture.[63] Toward the end of the decade the rebuilding of Covent Garden Market resulted in a flood of correspondence between London and Woburn Abbey, as the Duke accepted, rejected, or modified Fowler's plans. The Duke also interested himself in landscape architecture. He designed the gardens in Gordon Square, and personally supervised their layout and planting.[64]

The building depression of the 1830s brought new construction to a virtual halt in Bloomsbury.[65] Cubitt built a few houses in Gordon Square in the 1840s, but as late as 1852 neither the east nor the west side had been finished. In that year Cubitt began to build the west side of Taviton Street.[66] He died in 1855, leaving his son to finish the building agreement. Since his executors held houses

62. W. G. Adam to C. Haedy, 3 January 1829.

63. "He [the Duke] is particular about architectural appearance." W. G. Adam to C. Haedy, 27 January 1833.

64. "He [the Duke] went through Gordon Square the other day, and thinks the outside shrubbery quite consistent with his plan of decorating the interior. He thinks it wants thinning. When the time comes, have the trees planted according to the Duke's plan." W. G. Adam to C. Haedy, 24 July 1829. See also ibid., 1 August 1829.

65. Henry-Russell Hitchcock, in discussing the general absence of new building in the forties, explains that "too many houses had been built—or at least planned and partially completed—in the years after Waterloo; it took some time to catch up with and absorb the expansive undertakings that had been initiated in the 20's." *Early Victorian Architecture* (2 vols. New Haven, Yale University Press, 1954), *1*, 408. Cairncross and Weber, p. 292, write that "the decline in London over the years 1825–32 amounts almost to a secular drop to a new and lower level of activity, so much so that even in 1847 brick production did not regain the level reached from 1822 to 1826."

66. 1852 Report, p. 4.

41. Gardens in Tavistock Square, looking west, in 1982

42. Gordon Square, south side, in 1937. Thomas Cubitt, c. 1824

43. No. 1, Gordon Square, former residence of Charles Fowler, in 1944. Thomas Cubitt, c. 1824

44. The Nine Muses. Detail of wall of back office of No. 1, Gordon Square. Now in Warburg Institute

45. Gordon Square, east side, in 1982. Thomas Cubitt et al., c. 1824–30

46. Gordon Square, east side, in 1982. The Victorian culmination of Georgian Bloomsbury c. 1824–57

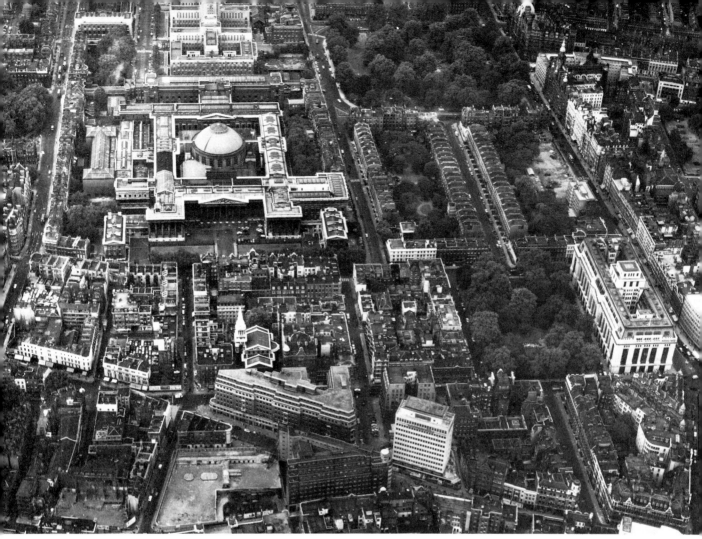

47. Aerial view of southern Bloomsbury, looking north, in 1962. Bloomsbury and Russell squares and Southampton Row to right, British Museum and portion of Bedford Square at upper left

48. Aerial view of northern Bloomsbury, looking east, in 1950. Russell Square to right, Woburn and Torrington squares center, Tavistock and Gordon squares to left

in Bloomsbury worth a total of £1,000 a year which they were unable either to let or to sell, they showed little eagerness to proceed with new building.[67] In 1857, however, they completed the east side of Gordon Square, and in 1860 the finishing of the square brought the building history of the Bedford estate to a close.[68]

When the Bloomsbury estate was finally completed, it found itself many years out of fashion. The mid-Victorians, Philistines and aesthetes alike, had nothing but contempt for the "gloomy" uniformity of Georgian street architecture, or the balance and symmetry of Georgian town planning. Gordon Square itself, spanning four decades, vividly illustrates what happened to English taste between 1824 and 1860. The contrast between the refinement of the early houses and the debased and pompous ones added later is instructive, if depressing (Figs. 42–46). Yet the unfortunate architecture of parts of Gordon Square is but a minor annoyance; the important fact is that, from an architectural point of view, the rest of northern Bloomsbury was built just in time. (Figures 47 and 48, aerial photographs of present-day Bloomsbury, show how much of the original plan has survived.)

North of, and separate from, the Bloomsbury estate lay an irregularly shaped piece of property known as Figs Mead, which Lady Rachel Vaughan had also brought into the Russell family in 1669. Not until 1834 did the Bedford Office turn its serious attention to the last substantial piece of its property in Middlesex that remained undeveloped. By that year it was obvious that Figs Mead could not remain a pasture much longer. The land immediately to the south, owned by Lord Somers, was already the thriving working-class community of Somers Town. Lord Southampton was building to the west, and to the north Camden Town was providing more suburban dwellings for the industrious artisan. Figs Mead could no more remain a pastoral enclave within the growing city than could the Long Fields behind Bedford House have so remained thirty years earlier.

No guidebook has ever suggested perambulating the streets and squares that lie immediately to the north of Euston Station. Even a specialist in Victorian domestic architecture would find little to detain him in Ampthill or Oakley squares. Since no one of note has ever lived in any part of Bedford New Town—as Figs Mead came to be called—it is wholly lacking in the historical associations so dear to another kind of writer. It was in fact a new departure in town planning for the Bedford estate, but its originality is not immediately apparent.

67. 1856 Report, p. 4.   68. 1860 Report, p. 5.

And yet it happens that the documentation for the planning and building of Bedford New Town is far more complete and detailed than that for any of the earlier developments in Bloomsbury or Covent Garden. For the first time it is possible to trace the history of one of the Duke's New Towns from a tentative idea in the mind of his steward through the gradual working out of a building plan to the actual construction of the houses. If we must conjecture as to the motives behind, say, the demolition of Bedford House, there is documentary evidence which explains even the direction in which the streets run in Figs Mead. The history of the development of Bedford New Town is therefore, significant not in itself but as a case study in how a London ground landlord went about developing one of his estates for building purposes. While it would be dangerous to conclude that because a particular set of procedures was followed in Figs Mead in the 1830s similar practices were followed in Bloomsbury in the 1770s, the later development may nevertheless shed some light on the earlier.

As early as 1826 Mr. Stead had prepared a tentative plan for the future development of the western portion of Figs Mead (Fig. 49). The plans for the eastern section, in the vicinity of what later became Goldington Crescent, were added to the map at a later date.

The 1826 plan shows no striking originality. The streets in general do no more than continue the lines of those already built on the Somers and Southampton estates.[69] The principal features that were to distinguish Figs Mead from Somers Town were its three proposed squares. Two of them were to be crescents facing Hampstead Road; one of the crescents was to form an eastern continuation of Mornington Crescent on the Southampton estate.[70] The third and largest square was formed by the widening of the northward extension of Euston Grove. This square, which after many transformations became the present Ampthill Square, constituted the central feature of the proposed development. Here, it may be assumed, Stead expected the houses to be the largest and the inhabitants the most respectable on Figs Mead. It was therefore particularly important to protect this part of the estate from contamination from Somers Town to the east. He proposed to accomplish this by throwing a gate across the short street that was to connect the square with Seymour Street. The gate would be "closed both against carriages and foot passengers, so as to shut out the low popu-

69. On the plan some of the proposed streets seem suddenly to widen as soon as they cross into Bedford territory, but this probably stems from faulty draftsmanship rather than from any zeal to provide light and air; the original plan is only a rough sketch, and is not drawn to scale.

70. Harrington Square, built on the site of the proposed crescent, performed such a function until the late 1920s, when an Egyptian Revival cigarette factory rose from the site of the Mornington Crescent gardens.

lation of Somers Town, but capable (if it should be found desirable for his Grace's tenants) of being opened at church time to give them a convenient approach to the chapel opposite to it . . ."[71] Stead did not see his plan put into effect.[72] Late in 1834 the London steward sent a revised plan to the Duke (Fig. 50).[73] On it may be seen the right-of-way of the London and Birmingham Railway —first of the great trunk routes to reach London—running across Figs Mead, down the line of Euston Grove to a terminus just north of Euston Square. The coming of the railway was ultimately to cause great damage to the whole of the Duke's property in London, but in 1834 it seemed merely to require a change in the street plan for Figs Mead.

The principal alteration was that while the streets running north and south remained, in a general way, continuations of existing streets in Somers Town, the other streets now ran diagonally in a northeasterly direction. The principal square, shown on the map as Russell Crescent, likewise was oriented toward the northeast, rather than toward the north, as had been intended in 1826. By the new arrangement the bridges carrying the streets across the railway line could cross it at right angles. In addition, the proposed diagonal streets would follow roughly the paths already worn into the grass by persons crossing Figs Mead. Furthermore, Haedy believed that the new diagonal lines would facilitate the letting of building plots, "as it places an entire line of building more readily within the compass of a single builder's means—and it is more advantageous to a builder to take a whole line of building than a part of one, if he can do so . . ."[74]

Although Adam feared that "the Rail road will be a more serious affair than I contemplated,"[75] the fact that it would intersect the principal square on the new estate did not seem to trouble the planners. The large square would still, Haedy thought, "give character and name to the district, and . . . prevent it from being treated as part either of Somers Town or Camden Town." The surrounding streets would become identified with the crescent. "If, for instance," Haedy observed, "the crescent should be called Russell Crescent and the street to be made northward in continuation of Upper Seymour Street, Lidlington Street, then the latter, instead (as in all probability would be the case if a huge crescent or square were not made in some part of Figs Mead) of being called Lidlington

71. Note, dated November 1826, written on map by Mr. Stead.

72. In a letter to Haedy dated 11 December 1834, W. G. Adam referred to "Stead's ugly old plan."

73. "The Duke looked at your plan for our *new* town and was much pleased with it." W. G. Adam to C. Haedy, 28 November 1834.

74. This, together with the subsequent comments on the new Figs Mead plan are taken from Christopher Haedy's "Observations on the Proposed Plan for Building upon Figs Mead, 1836," unless otherwise stated.

75. W. G. Adam to C. Haedy, 26 November 1834.

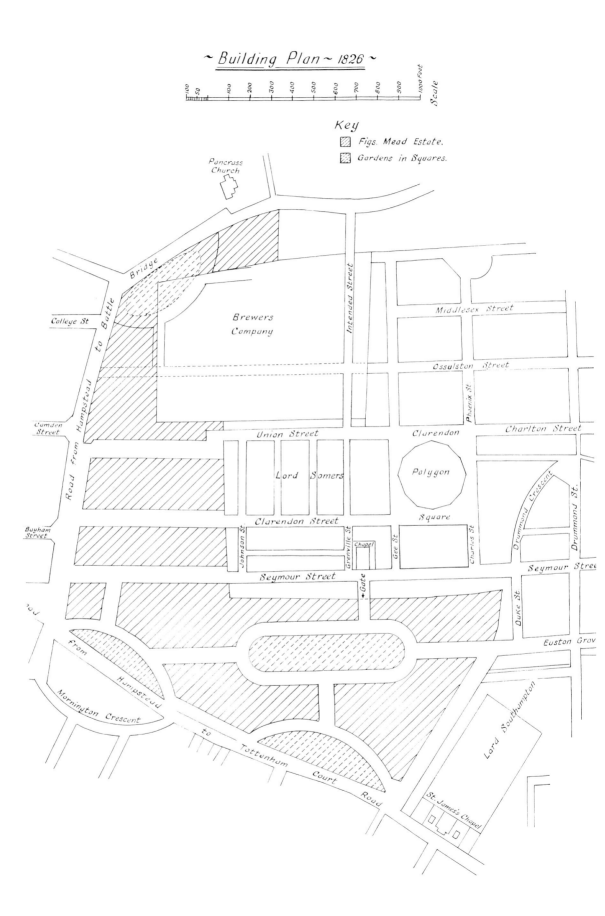

~ Building Plan ~ 1826 ~

Scale

Key
Figs. Mead Estate.
Gardens in Squares.

Pancrass
Church

Brewers
Company

Intended Street

Bridge

to Battle

College St

Road from Hampstead

Camden
Street

Buxham
Street

Middlesex Street

Ossulston Street

Phoenix St.

Charlton Street

Clarendon

Polygon

Square

Union Street

Lord Somers

Clarendon Street

Seymour Street

Johnson St.

Grenville St.

Chapel

Gee St.

Charles St.

Drummond Crescent

Drummond St.

Seymour Street

Duke St.

Euston Grov

Gate

Mornington Crescent

from Hampstead

to Tottenham

Court Road

Lord Southampton

St. James's Chapel

49. Figs Mead building plan, 1826

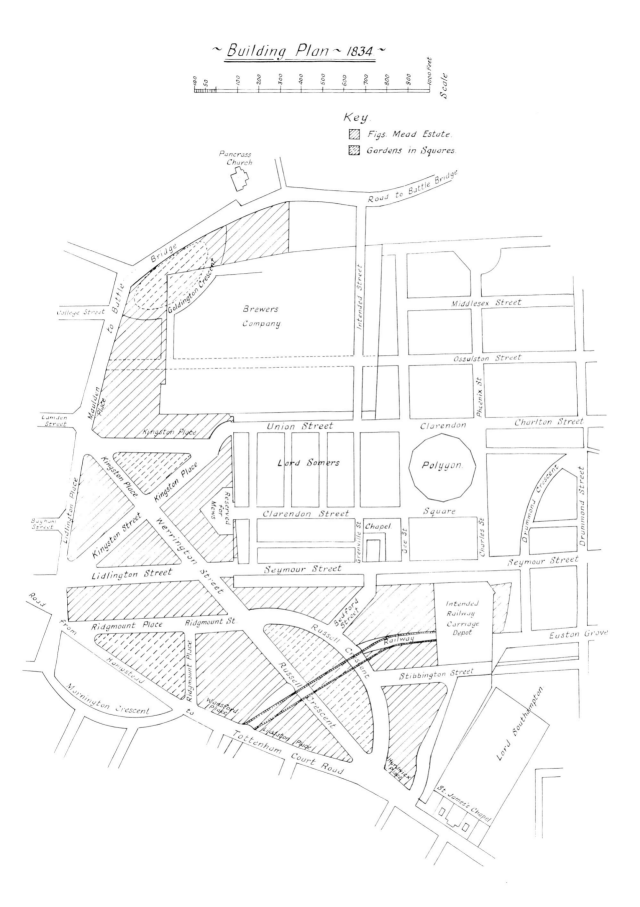

~ *Building Plan* ~ 1834 ~

Scale

Key.
Figs. Mead Estate.
Gardens in Squares.

Pancrass Church

Road to Battle Bridge

College Street

Bridge

to Battle

Goldington Crescent

Brewers Company

Intended Street

Middlesex Street

Ossulston Street

Phenix St

Charlton Street

Camden Street

Maulden Place

Kingston Place

Clarendon

Polygon.

Baynunt Street

Lidlington Place

Kingston Place

Kingston Place

Kingston Street

Werrington Street

Lord Somers

Union Street

Reserved for Mews

Clarendon Street

Square

Drummond Crescent

Drummond Street

Lidlington Street

Seymour Street

Grenville St

Chapel

Gee St

Charles St

Seymour Street

Road

from

Ridgmount Place

Ridgmount St.

Ridgmount Place

Bedford Street

Russell Crescent

Railway

Intended Railway Carriage Depot

Euston Grove

Hampstead

Mornington Crescent

Wansford Place

Russell Crescent

Stibbington Street

Lidlington Place

to

Tottenham Court Road

Lord Southampton

St. James's Chapel

50. Figs Mead building plan, 1834

Street, Somers Town, or Lidlington Street, Camden Town, would be called Lidlington Street, Russell Crescent."

By the standards of 1836 Figs Mead was inconveniently distant "from the City and the Inns of Court, and other places of business." To compensate for its out-of-the-way location, the steward advised a generous layout, with wide streets and large gardens attached to the houses. In addition to Russell Crescent and the Ridgmount Place gardens opposite to Mornington Crescent, Haedy proposed "to form an enclosed garden of the triangular space between the sides of Kingston [Russell] Place, in order to give more openings to that part of Figs Mead." As the plan stood, all of the streets, except Lidlington Street, were to "run directly into one or another of the proposed enclosed gardens." By such an arrangement there would be "no back streets, nor any of so retired a kind as to be liable on that account to be improperly occupied, and to injure the reputation of the district."

The Figs Mead development was a conscious effort to create a model suburb for the lower and lower-middle classes. Such a scheme was a new departure for the Bedford estate in London. Since 1776 it had concentrated almost exclusively on the building of first- and second-rate houses for wealthy merchants and professional men. Only in the narrow courts east of Woburn Place had new lower-class dwellings been erected; as these were to grow into one of the more notorious slums of London, they cannot be regarded as model dwellings. Neither did the decayed mansions of the once fashionable streets in Covent Garden, which were by then overcrowded tenements, result from a conscious policy of the estate to provide dwellings for the poor. But Bedford New Town was designed from the outset if not for the very poor at least for the respectable artisan and the better sort of clerk.

There is no reason to suppose that the estate would not have turned Figs Mead into an upper-class development if it had thought that it could do so with any success. The 1836 report thought it highly unlikely that speculative builders would agree to erect houses of the size of those in Russell and Tavistock squares in such a location. Nor did Haedy think it desirable that they should, "as Figs Mead would then be brought into direct competition with his Grace's estate southward of the New Road," where Cubitt had already been forced to stop building. He doubted that "tenants capable of occupying houses of that class could be obtained in sufficient numbers to occupy such houses" in both Bloomsbury and Figs Mead. He therefore concluded that the respectability of Bedford New Town would have to depend on "the size of the crescent and enclosed gardens, and the width of the streets, and the liberal manner of laying out the grounds, and the general airiness and openness of the district," rather than on the size of its houses.

Both the photographs of Bedford New Town (Figs. 53–61) and the maps (Figs. 51, 52) show how far the estate succeeded in carrying out Haedy's intentions. In most instances the area of the back garden is several times that of the house which it serves. Even excluding the large area given over to roadways, the density of houses in Bedford New Town is only twenty to the acre. The relative area devoted to actual buildings is far less than in Bloomsbury, Marylebone, or Mayfair, being in fact closer to the standards of the twentieth-century garden suburb. Such an "open and airy" layout, Haedy argued, "may attract [to Figs Mead], as tenants, many persons who now for the sake of fresh air for themselves and their families reside at Camden Town, Kentish Town, and even at Hampstead, Highgate, and other villages round London," so much farther from their places of business, "if the houses to be erected on it should be suitable to their wants and means . . ."

The houses accordingly were to be small, chiefly of the third and fourth rate of building, so as to meet the needs of "the higher class of merchants', bankers', and counsels' clerks, attorneys' managing clerks, clerks in the law offices, and persons in trade not residing where their business is carried on, and surveyors, and little attorneys, and other persons of that description, with the usual portion of medical men . . . " In the lesser streets, such as Werrington and Stibbington streets, there would probably be shops (Fig. 57); here would reside "tradesmen, for the supply of the neighborhood, with probably persons connected with the Railway and the traffic to which it will give rise, and whose employments may require them to reside near the carriage depot, or nearer than most parts of London to the depot for goods beyond Camden Town."

Recalling the difficulty Cubitt had in letting his first-rate houses in Byng Place and Tavistock Square, Haedy pointed out that in such an unfashionable quarter as Figs Mead, "it is not improbable that the builders may be unwilling to incur the risk of building [anything larger] . . . than full-sized third-rate houses. The ground plan in the margin [for a third-rate house with an eighteen-foot frontage and a depth of twenty-seven feet nine inches] allows of there being two windows in the parlor, as well as in the rooms above it . . ." Such a plan provided for "better sized back rooms than when the frontage is diminished and the depths proportionally extended."[76] Yet Haedy did not deny that, other things

76. The rate of a house, hence the structural requirements of the building acts, depended on the number of square feet of floor area as well as on its value. For a description of the provisions of the Building Act of 1774, see Summerson, *Georgian London*, pp. 125–29.

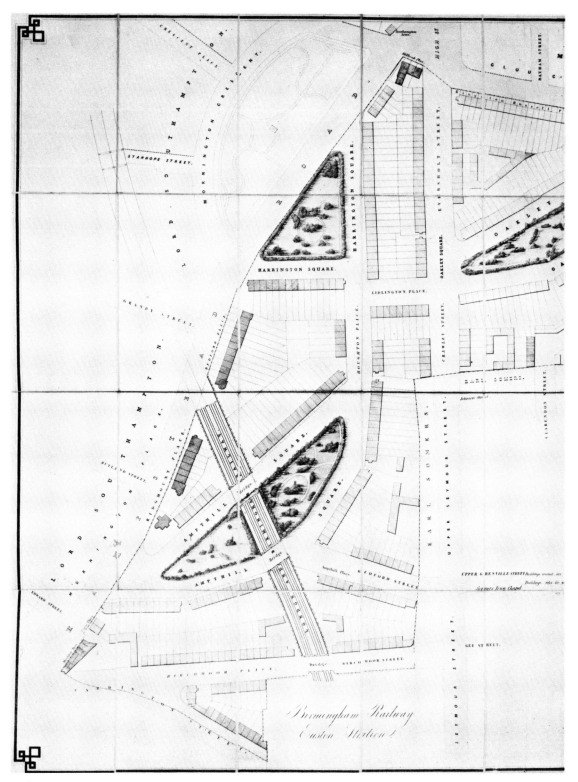

51. Figs Mead plan, 1843, western section

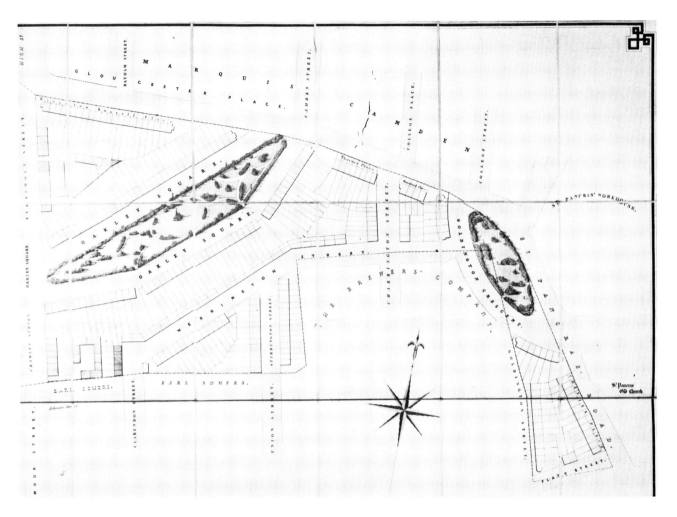

52. Figs Mead plan,
1843, eastern section

53. Werrington Street,
north side, with backs of
houses in Oakley
Square, in 1964. Note
moderate depth of
houses

54. Lidlington Place and Oakley Square, looking east, in 1964

55. Spacious back gardens of houses in Harrington and Oakley squares, from Lidlington Place, as seen in Fig. 54, in 1953

56. Goldington Crescent, in 1952

57. Original shopfronts in Stibbington Street (now Chalton Street), east side, in 1964

being equal, big houses were better than small ones, and "if the builders should be willing to build second-rate houses on parts of Figs Mead, their doing so would be preferred, but it is scarcely to be expected."

However wide the roadways, however large the gardens, however aristocratic the street names, the menace of Somers Town loomed as darkly in 1836 as it had ten years earlier. Although Haedy's report fails to mention it, one further advantage of the new diagonal street plan was that the streets of Bedford New Town would no longer, either in name or in fact, be mere continuations of the streets in Somers Town; this circumstance would help to give Figs Mead a real and separate existence and make it somewhat easier for the householders in its spacious crescents, and wide, airy streets to feel superior to the tenants of Lord Somers and Lord Southampton.

Haedy did not consider the complete separation of Figs Mead from Somers Town feasible, attractive as it might seem. For although admitting the desirability of having "as few communications as possible with Somers Town," he felt that three were unavoidable. The first, a northward continuation of Upper Seymour Street, was "necessary to keep open a direct communication from north to south . . ." The second, running between Kingston Place and Union Street, was needed to create a thoroughfare through the eastern part of Figs Mead, "without which that part would probably want the cheerfulness which would be likely to suit the tastes of the persons who [it] may be expected will occupy the houses to be built in that situation . . ." Thirdly, the Bedford Street opening was necessary "to give the inhabitants of the houses to be built west-ward of Upper Seymour Street a convenient approach to the chapel in that street, and a ready and direct way to the City, the Inns of Court," and the whole of the town to the east and south. In his 1826 plan, Stead had provided a gate to prevent through traffic between the western portion of the estate and Upper Sey-mour Street. The coming of the railway blocked the old southern outlet through Euston Grove, leaving Upper Seymour Street as the only convenient alternative.

Haedy did not plan to continue Clarendon Street onto the estate. "But," he explained, "as there will be an unappropriated piece of ground where Figs Mead joins Clarendon Street, it is proposed to reserve that piece of ground for a mews, if one should be found necessary." Stead had not provided for any mews in the 1826 plan, no doubt considering that they would be superfluous in such a neighborhood. But Haedy felt that "a few of the inhabitants . . . may keep horses, chaises, or carriages of some kind (professional men for their business, and tradesmen, for instance), and it would be inconvenient to be entirely without the means of supplying wants of this nature if they should arise." A site at the northern end of Clarendon Street would not be "inconveniently distant from any part of Figs Mead, and the access to it would be ready either through Upper Seymour Street or Union Street."

Preliminary preparations for the development were soon under way. In February 1837 the estate had an accurate map made of Figs Mead, "to serve as a working plan to enable any parts to be proceeded with in building without danger of their not harmonizing with the other parts."[77] The following year it put aside the sum of £4,000, out of £12,631 the London and Birmingham Railway paid for land on the estate, to form a building fund. The fund would pay toward the expenses involved in enclosing the squares, laying the sewers, and paving the roadways.[78]

By March of 1838 Haedy was able to report that he had received several inquiries about building sites. "The chief thing to attend to," he wrote the agent-in-chief, "will be to have good, well-built houses, that is, good of their kind. Some of our neighbors there," he observed, "have not been attentive enough to that. The choice in some degree lies between higher ground rents and badly built houses—between the present and the future." He himself was certain that the policy of the estate should be "first to secure having well-built houses, and get such ground rents as can be obtained on the terms of building such houses." In order to ensure that this was done, he proposed to draw up specifications for building agreements in cooperation with Stead and Cubitt, and to have copies lithographed for distribution.[79]

In May 1838 James Sim, one of the builders of Torrington and Woburn squares, signed a contract to build ten third-rate and two second-rate houses in Hampstead Road.[80] He started building shortly thereafter, under the supervision of the estate steward.[81] Meanwhile an animated correspondence had begun among Haedy, Adam, and the Duke on the question of street names.[82] As in Bloomsbury, they derive from titles, family names, and estates belonging to the Russell family and their connections. To advertise the new development, the

77. Bloomsbury Rental, 1837, p. 142.

78. Bloomsbury Rental, 1838, pp. 162–63. See also C. Haedy to W. G. Adam, 1 January 1838.

79. C. Haedy to W. G. Adam, 31 March 1838.

80. C. Haedy to W. G. Adam, 31 May 1838.

81. "My visits there are generally two or three times a week, to see how Mr. Sim gets on—not that I can be much of a judge of the details of building, but they don't know that, and my be-ing seen there frequently is some check upon them. I have not yet seen any thing to find fault with." C. Haedy to W. G. Adam, 3 July 1838.

82. Although the first two maps (Figs. 49 and 50) date respectively from 1826 and 1834, the street names were added at a later date. On the original maps, many names were later crossed out, and others substituted.

Bedford Office had "Russell Crescent" painted on the bridges that were to carry the roadways of the proposed square over the railway.[83]

By 1843 building on a large scale had commenced. As the map in Figures 51, 52, made in that year or shortly thereafter, indicates, the estate had introduced many alterations into the 1836 plan. Russell Crescent had become the present Ampthill Square, and Kingston Place had expanded into Oakley Square. Yet the essential qualities of Stead's and Haedy's earlier schemes remained unchanged. In his report for 1846 Haedy remarked that "to persons accustomed to observe the manner in which ground in London is commonly laid out for building purposes, and not aware how soon a neighborhood, overcrowded with houses, degenerates, unless supported by fashion (and Figs Mead has no such aid), it may seem that openness and airiness have been attained by unnecessary waste of ground, and that many more houses might have been built on the ground." But, he insisted, "that would be an erroneous opinion, for the open manner in which the ground has been laid out has given a character to it which has caused a much better class of houses to be built upon it; and the lesser number of houses built and intended to be built upon it will be of considerably greater value than a large number, crowded together would have been."[84]

Haedy returned to the same theme in his 1851 report, in which he attributed the relatively good class of houses which had been built "to the manner in which the ground has been laid out for building. A character for it had to be created," he explained, "as well as the appearance of a district distinguishable from those contiguous to it. This was effected by the formation of squares and wide streets, and avoiding an overcrowding of houses, by which an open, airy district has been formed." As a result of such a policy, nearly all the houses had been let, "and to respectable tenants, as soon as they were fit for occupation."[85]

In the building of Bedford New Town the estate was able to draw upon two centuries of accumulated experience in urban management. Building agreements were much longer and more detailed than they had been before; lists of dimensions and other specifications now occupied several pages of print. By making the contracts less general than had been the practice, and thereby leaving less to the discretion of the surveyor, Haedy hoped to improve standards of

83. "By way of establishing the existence of Russell Crescent, I proposed to have 'Russell Crescent' written on the two bridges over the railway, and, as they lie slantingly, it can be seen from the Hampstead Road. This and the laying out of the garden and planting some limes, to show its intended shape, which is done (though it is not enclosed yet with railing), will serve to show which is Russell Crescent, and what is meant by adding it to the names of the places." C. Haedy to W. G. Adam, 16 June 1838. See also Haedy's letters to Adam of 22 June and 3 July 1838.

84. Annual Reports, 2, 220.

85. 1851 Report, p. 9.

workmanship. Stead estimated that the estate's specifications would increase the cost of construction to the builder by £100 a house, only £40 of which could be got back in a higher sale price.[86] During the course of the building, Haedy made a practice of visiting Figs Mead two or three times a week. "My being seen there," he wrote to the Duke, "though only for a short time . . . tends to keep the builders up to their engagements; and they will avoid them, as I know by experience, if they can."[87] That the estate exercised architectural control as well is indicated both by the extensive collection of elevations for buildings on the new estate in the Bedford Office, and by the general uniformity of façade in the squares and terraces of Figs Mead.

Such rigid supervision was not calculated to endear the Bedford Office to the speculative builder. In order to sweeten the pill of inspection and regulation, and also to attract builders to the development, the Duke was, as in the past, prepared to give financial assistance. The estate advanced to the builders the entire cost of laying the necessary sewers and advanced to the paving commissioners the cost of forming and enclosing the three squares.[88] Its advances to the builders were in general equivalent in amount to the cost of the sewers and the vaults under the footways.[89] During the course of the development the Duke made a practice of purchasing improved ground rents at 4.5 or 5 per cent from the builders. From 1845 to 1863 inclusive the Duke made advances of this sort totaling £77,278 8s. 1d. In 1847 alone he purchased improved ground rents valued at £12,325.[90]

Haedy attributed much of the speed of the building to such loans. "If that assistance had not been given to them," he wrote in his 1851 report, "it would have taken several years to let ground for so many houses, unless the builders had been allowed to build such houses as they pleased, in which case they would have made of Figs Mead a second Somers Town, instead of a district which contrasts so advantageously with it."[91] Thus the purchase of improved ground rents was another means of increasing the landlord's control over the builder.

The first half of the 1840s saw a great burst of building activity. The leases for practically the whole of the estate apart from Oakley Square date from that period. Haedy wrote in 1844 that the letting of the property had "proceeded with unexpected rapidity." He did not expect the boom to last indefinitely. "Past experience has shown that there are cycles in building speculations in

86. C. Haedy to W. G. Adam, 31 May 1838.
87. C. Haedy to the Duke of Bedford, 15 December 1843.
88. Annual Reports, 2, 63. Bloomsbury

Rental, 1847, p. 170.
89. Annual Reports, 2, 66–67.
90. 1871 Report, 2, 16.
91. 1851 Report, p. 9.

and around the Metropolis, caused," he thought, "by the disturbance of the due proportion between the population and buildings." Booms occurred when the population increased faster than the rate of new building; depressions came about when the rate of new building exceeded the rise in population. "Causes of this kind have," Haedy recalled, "three or four times within the last half century led to a nearly total stoppage to building speculations, and the great quantity of buildings which have of late years been erected . . . may bring about one of those periodical stoppages . . ." Such a possibility made it all the more advisable to encourage, by advances of money, as much building as possible while the boom lasted.[92]

In his report for 1845 Haedy wrote that the building continued at a satisfactory rate, "and if the country should remain at peace, there appears to be good reason to expect that the whole of this ground will be built upon in a comparatively short time." He described the houses as being "better and more respectable . . . than might have been expected from the neighborhood in which this property lies."[93]

The anticipated depression materialized in 1847. Although in that year it had but slight immediate effect on the rate of building, it threatened to delay the completion of the scheme. The builders were finding it difficult both to raise money on their houses, and to find buyers for them.[94]

To help provide for the religious needs of his future tenants, the Duke in 1847 donated a site for a district church in Oakley Square, together with a subscription of £500 toward its erection. He made the grant subject, however, to certain conditions, "for guarding the inhabitants of the square from the annoyance of funerals, etc. . . ." Haedy commented on the grant that it abated "nothing from the merit of contributing thus munificently to so beneficial a work that some incidental advantage to your Grace's estate will arise from it, because you were not influenced by it in fixing the extent of your contribution. But," he pointed out, "there is no reason to doubt that a church there will prove a great convenience to your tenants . . . and will very materially tend in the completion and well-letting of the houses in Oakley Square and the streets near to it" (Figs. 59–61).[95]

92. Annual Reports, 2, 66–67.
93. Ibid., p. 171.
94. Ibid., p. 269. "The 40's saw a general decline in house production from which recovery came only in the early 50's. This rule applies rather equally to all types of residential accommodation from new dwellings intended for the homeless poor to mansions designed for magnates." Hitchcock, *Early Victorian Architecture*, *1*, 408. Cairncross and Weber, pp. 286, 292, show a peak in building activity reached in 1847, followed by a sharp fall.
95. Ibid., pp. 269–70.

58. Harrington Square, south side, in 1953

59. Oakley Square, looking east from Lidlington Place, in 1964

60. Oakley Square, south side, in 1953

61. Oakley Square, north side, in 1953

In 1852 Haedy was distressed to learn that although the church was rapidly nearing completion, nothing had been done about building its tower. "A Gothic structure deprived of the vertical character which its tower and spire would give to it," he wrote, "not only loses its beauty, but becomes a deformity, and it may be necessary . . . to prevent the disfigurement of Oakley Square to withhold your Grace's donation till the completion of the tower and spire."[96] But in his next report Haedy was able to write that the tower was in fact nearly finished.[97]

The building depression failed to dampen Haedy's optimism when writing his report for 1850. "It seldom happens," he wrote, somewhat boastfully, "that so large an extent of building ground, disadvantageously situated as regards neighborhood, and wholly unaided by fashion, has been let for building, and the buildings on all but a comparatively small part of it completed in so short [a] space of time."[98] By the end of 1851, 359 houses had been built, leaving only 49 still to be erected.[99]

Despite all the efforts of the estate the rate of building in the 1850s proved disappointingly slow. Haedy attributed it to the rise of the cost of building materials, and also—for some reason—to Free Trade.[100] Not until his report for 1856 could he write that, with the exception of a few of the interiors of the houses in Oakley Square, the Figs Mead building plan was completed.[101] And although a few houses had still to be put up in Gordon Square, for most purposes the original building history of the Bedford estate was at an end.

Structurally, Figs Mead remains much as it was in the 1850s, but it has long since lost the middle-class respectability which the Bedford Office was at such pains to achieve for it. The wide streets and spacious gardens are still there, but the classes for whom they were designed come no closer than the electric trains which carry them underneath Ampthill Square on their way to and from the northern suburbs. The present melancholy state of Bedford New Town makes it too easy to overlook the imagination and ingenuity that went into its creation. As an experiment in enlightened town planning, it was a worthy culmination for the building history which began so grandly in the Piazza at Covent Garden.

96. 1852 Report, p. 3.
97. 1853 Report, pp. 2–3.
98. 1850 Report, p. 5.

99. 1851 Report, p. 8.
100. 1852 Report, p. 3.
101. 1856 Report, p. 4.

5 The Foundling Hospital Estate

The houses on the Foundling Estate reflected the latest architectural fashions between 1790 and 1830, being built to popular taste, and at popular prices. The brick was made from local clay, of a light ochreous shade, and the estate, when first built, must have had all the brightness of a cream-coloured town in a setting of green pasture land.—London County Council Survey of London, *24* (1952)

Geographically, the estate of the Foundling Hospital represented an eastward extension of the Bedford estate in Bloomsbury. It occupied, roughly speaking, the area bounded on the west by the Bedford estate, on the south by Guilford Street, on the east by Gray's Inn Road, and on the north by Tavistock Place.[1] If less distinguished socially and architecturally than the Bedford estate, it towered above all other neighboring developments. While its houses were in general smaller and less expensive than those west of Woburn Place, the Hospital hoped by means of proper controls over the builders to create a neighborhood that would attract respectable tenants.

The systematic development of the Foundling estate as a New Town dates only from 1790. Prior to that the buildings of the Hospital had enjoyed a wholly rural situation. The trustees had purchased the site for their institution in 1741 from the Earl of Salisbury, fifty-six acres in Lamb's Conduit Fields, for which they paid £6,500.[2] Although the site was far bigger than that required for the hospital buildings and grounds, a considerable minority of the governors were opposed to letting the surplus land on building leases at all. They argued that such a policy would interfere with the amenities of the Hospital, and that any attempt at speculative building in such an inconvenient location would be doomed to failure.[3] The General Court in 1775 had considered let-

1. For the northern, eastern, and western boundaries of the estate, see John Britton's map of St. Pancras and St. Marylebone of 1837, fig. 65.
2. LCC, *Survey of London, 19* (London, 1938),
p. 25.
3. R. H. Nichols and F. A. Wray, *The History of the Foundling Hospital* (London, 1935), p. 283.

ting part of the estate on building leases, but had decided to postpone the scheme the following year (Fig. 62).[4] As late as 1792 a group of governors tried unsuccessfully in the Court of Chancery to stop the building after it had already begun.[5] (Figure 63 is a view of Queen Square in 1787, looking north onto the Foundling estate while it was still open fields.)

Whatever the misgivings of the minority, most of the governors were convinced that ground rents would provide a secure income for the Hospital. On 30 December 1789 the General Court resolved "that the general committee . . . proceed with all possible dispatch in causing . . . the ground . . . east of the walls of this Hospital, and east of Lamb's Conduit Street to be staked out and allotted according to such plan as shall appear to them to be most for the interest of this charity, in order that the same may be let on building leases."[6] The following year it appointed a committee of five governors to prepare a building plan and carry it into effect.[7]

The building committee called on Samuel Pepys Cockerell (1754–1827), the architect and the surveyor to the East India Company, to assist it in its task. On 27 December 1790 Cockerell presented them a comprehensive plan for development. He first set forth a list of criteria by which any such plan ought to be judged. To begin with, it must not interfere with the amenities of the Hospital buildings, around which there had to be preserved "such an area . . . and such spacious avenues to that area as shall secure to it (as much as is consistent with any plan of building) the advantages of its present open situation . . ." Beyond that, the plan must prove attractive to speculative builders, or "adventurers," who alone could put it into effect.[8]

Cockerell did not advocate the creation of a homogeneous neighborhood, such as the Bedford estate to the west was then promoting. Rather, the Foundling estate ought to "comprise all classes of building from the first class down to houses of twenty-five pounds per annum," but arranged so as to prevent "the lower classes interfering with and diminishing the character of those above them . . ." There must be "such principal features of attraction in the plan as

4. General Court, *3*, 187 (10 May 1775); 204 (24 April 1776). Figure 62 gives an idea of the sort of building scheme that the governors had in mind in the 70s. The principal feature of the plan was a long garden square running along the entire eastern boundary of the Hospital grounds, with a few short, subsidiary streets connecting it with the rest of the town.

5. Nichols and Wray, pp. 282–83.

6. General Court, *4*, 10.

7. Ibid., p. 25 (30 June 1790).

8. Building Committee, *1*, 8–9. See also Summerson, *Georgian London*, pp. 166–69, and the LCC *Survey of London*, *24* (London, 1952), pp. 25–50, for discussions of the building of the Foundling estate, in both instances based largely on the minutes of the building committee.

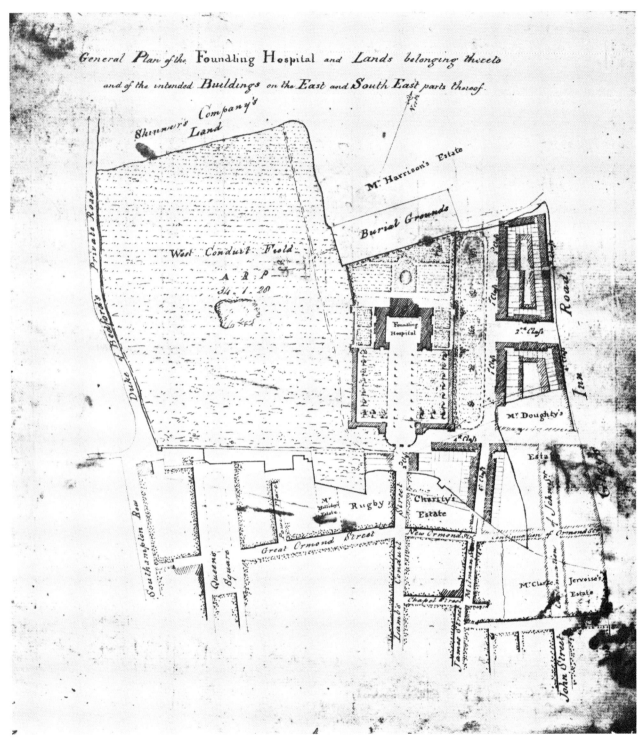

62. Foundling estate building plan, c. 1775

63. Queen Square in 1787, looking north onto Foundling estate before it was laid out for building

shall not be too great for a due proportion to the whole, but yet sufficient to draw adventurers to the subordinate parts . . ." The "principal features" would help maintain the character of the whole of the estate. Furthermore, "the style of the buildings at the several boundaries [ought to] be (in order to ensure success to the intermediate parts) as respectable as possible, consistent with their situations and with prudence in the adventurers." Cockerell advised that the streets in general be continuations of streets on adjacent estates, in order that "the great lines of communication through the town may be kept as open as possible." Finally, the plan ought to be "capable of a gradual execution, and . . . each part [should be] . . . complete in itself, and not depend for its success . . . upon the execution of the others."[9]

The principal feature to the east of the Hospital was to be a square, with first-class houses and an enclosed garden planted with grass and shrubbery. Houses to the north and south would be of the third class of building. Those in Gray's Inn Lane were to be of the fourth class, "and so built as to be capable of conversion into shops hereafter at a moderate expense, when the thoroughfare becomes more frequented."[10]

Cockerell estimated that the whole estate would produce ground rents amounting to at least £4,000 a year, and that the rents for the southeastern and eastern sections, with which his preliminary plan dealt, would approximate £900.[11]

The Hospital and its grounds would inevitably form the center of any plan. They did in fact set the tone of the entire estate, just as Bedford House did for the Bloomsbury estate. If Cockerell felt that the houses surrounding the Hospital should be of a sort to raise its character, he relied equally on the Hospital to raise the character of the surrounding houses.

Although the building committee accepted Cockerell's scheme, the General Court rejected it in favor of one which the secretary of the Hospital, Thomas Merryweather, had drawn up (Fig. 64). It did not differ in essentials from Cockerell's; like his, its central features were the two squares adjoining the Hospital grounds. It also called for an extension of Queen Square all the way to the northern boundary of the estate, and a semicircular street north of the Hospital; neither idea was in fact carried out. (See Figure 65 for the street plan actually put into effect.)

James Burton, then at the beginning of his career, had already proposed to

9. Building Committee, *1*, 9.   11. Ibid., p. 11.
10. Ibid., p. 10.

take the whole of the western part of the estate on a ninety-nine-year lease for £1,400 a year, agreeing "to erect in the principal streets substantial, uniform, well-finished houses of the first or second rate . . ." To that end he sent the building committee "two sketches of plans for such buildings, either of which (or any other which on a further consideration may be mutually approved)" he would agree to execute.[12] The Hospital rejected the proposals, both because it considered £1,400 an inadequate rent and because it felt that it was not "for the interest of the corporation to let any considerable quantity of ground to any one person."[13]

Meanwhile the Hospital had begun negotiations with landlords of adjacent estates for the exchange of pieces of land—in order to facilitate the laying out of building lots—and for agreements as to street openings. Of these, the most crucial were those leading westward onto the Duke of Bedford's private road, giving access to the fashionable quarters of the town. In a preliminary letter to Henry Holland, the Duke's surveyor, Cockerell argued that the northern and southern openings—now Guilford Street and Tavistock Place—onto what was then being developed as Southampton Terrace would be "mutually advantageous," giving the Bedford estate access to Queen Square and the area eastward toward Gray's Inn, "which will also improve the quarter of Bedford Square, now an angle of the town without thoroughfare." While he admitted that "the intermediate openings," which became Bernard and Great Coram streets, would benefit the Hospital estate more than the Bedford estate, he believed that they would "contribute to enliven and consequently improve and increase the value of the Duke of Bedford's line of building . . ."[14] The Bedford Office was not convinced by such arguments, and in 1795 the Foundling Hospital granted the Duke land valued at £1,800 along its western boundary in return for the openings.[15]

In 1791 Cockerell had prepared "general principles of regulation . . . in respect to height, materials, and substance for the buildings to be erected . . ."[16]

12. Building Committee, *1*, 6 (28 December 1790).

13. Ibid., p. 15. In a letter otherwise enthusiastic about the financial rewards to be had from letting out the Foundling Hospital's land on building leases, Robert Bromley of the Fitzroy estate had two years earlier advised Dr. White "on no account [to] let either the whole, or large portions, of ground intended to be built on, to one man at one time. The mischiefs of this I have seen abundantly, and it neither expedites buildings, nor brings as much profit, as a different procedure" (18 April 1788).

14. "Proposal for exchange of ground between his Grace the Duke of Bedford and the Foundling Hospital for the mutual improvement of their respective estates. June 1794." In London County Record Office.

15. See below, pp. 88–89.

16. Building Committee, *1*, 19 (27 May 1791).

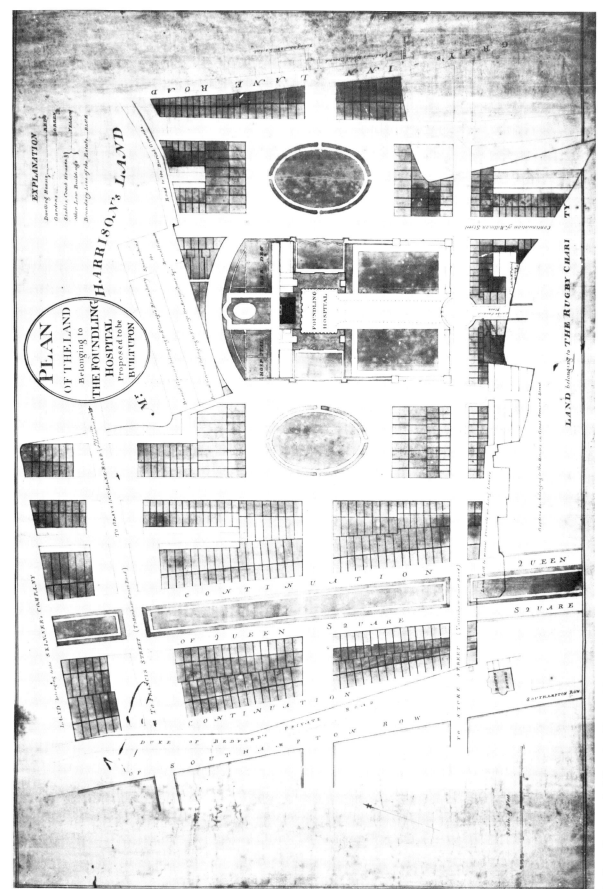

64. Foundling estate building plan. Thomas Merryweather, 1792

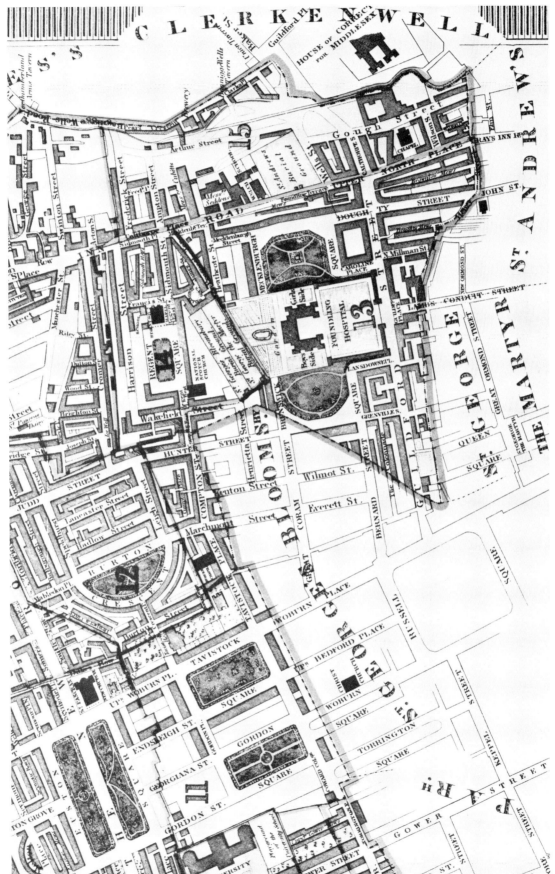

65. Detail from John Britton's map of St. Pancras (see Fig. 2), showing streets on Foundling estate, 1837

The following year the General Court adopted Merryweather's plan for Brunswick Square on the west side of the hospital.[17] It also empowered the building committee "to carry on at the expense of this corporation such sewers, drains, and roads for the use of the projected building as may be necessary, stipulating with the respective tenants for repaying such proportions thereof respectively as they may think reasonable."[18] In fact, except for the sewer in Guilford Street, most of the early sewers on the estate were laid by the builders themselves.[19]

By this time the building committee had begun to approve articles of agreement with James Burton, Henry Scrimshaw, and other contractors. Although the Hospital had rejected Burton's original proposal, it later accepted a succession of more limited ones, and before long, he had become the principal contractor on the estate.

Between 1792 and 1802 Burton was responsible for the construction on the estate of 586 houses, with a gross value estimated in 1823 at £296,700.[20] He dominated its building far more than he was to dominate the larger Bedford estate development, on which he was responsible for only 336 houses.[21] In 1807

17. Burton wrote on 22 December 1794 to Dr. White that he thought "it would be received by the D[uke] of Portland [from 1793 President of the Hospital] as a compliment if the west square was to be called by the name of *Rockingham*." Burton himself was "much more partial to that" than to Brunswick, "*as a better foundling name*." The late Marquis of Rockingham had been one of the governors of the charity.

18. General Court, *4*, 58 (28 March 1792).

19. "The Foundling Hospital estate was leased for the builders to make sewers, the [Holborn and Finsbury] Commissioners having no control over them. When they were made, these persons applied to the Commissioners for leave to communicate with the existing sewers; the Commissioners then exercised their authority by saying, 'No; these sewers are inadequately built; therefore we will not suffer them to communicate.' . . . The inhabitants, of course, applied for relief, and ultimately the directors of the Foundling Hospital came to the Commissioners. The answer was, 'Gentlemen, you have suffered these sewers to be made by builders in a very improper way; therefore we cannot suffer them to communicate, for we shall have them to rebuild in the course of two or three years.' . . . It was at length agreed that the whole of the sewers on the . . . estate should be surveyed; those that

were good should be allowed to stand, and the Commissioners would take to them; those that were not, should be rebuilt. . . . The Foundling estate adopted that method, and the whole of that estate is now drained as well as any other part of the division." Samuel Mills, representing the Holborn and Finsbury Sewer Commissioners. Parliamentary Papers, State of Large Towns and Populous Districts. R. Com. mins. of ev., p. 128; 1844 [572] xvii.

20. Dobie, p. 148. Of these, only 29 were first-rate houses, 159 were second-rate, 172 were third-rate, and 226 were fourth-rate. Their estimated annual rental including ground rents in 1823 was £36,540.

21. Ibid. His houses on the Bedford estate, erected between 1798 and 1803, had in 1823 an estimated gross value of £299,400. Their estimated rental, including ground rents, was £32,240 per annum. The social contrast between the Foundling and Bedford developments is reflected in the fact that on the latter estate Burton built 132 first-rate houses, 43 second-rate houses, and only 8 third-rate houses. He admittedly built 153 fourth-rate houses on Bedford property, but these were almost certainly all located in the courts and narrow streets east of Russell Square and Woburn Place, along the boundaries of the Foundling estate.

Cockerell was to pay tribute to Burton's contribution to the success of the development in glowing terms:

Mr. Burton is the one individual (under the attention of the five gentlemen who composed the original building committee, and I hope I may add my own labors and exertions) to whom your excellent charity is indebted for the improvement which has taken place on the estate. All that has been done by the other builders is comparatively trifling and insignificant. Without such a man, possessed of very considerable talents, unwearied industry, and a capital of his own, the extraordinary success of the improvement of the Foundling estate could not have taken place.

Mr. Burton has expended above £400,000 for the permanent benefit of the property of the Hospital. Great part of this he has done personally; the other part he has done by builders engaged under him, whom he has supplied with money and materials, secured by mortgage, or receiving his compensation in what are called carcass or profit rents, and has still heavy mortgages subsisting on unfinished buildings.

By his own peculiar resources of mind, he has succeeded in disposing of his buildings and rents, under all the disadvantages of the war, and of an unjust clamor which has been repeatedly raised against him; and at the same time those gentlemen who have speculated in purchases upon the estate with any degree of prudence, as many have done, have not had cause to repent of their speculations.

The measure of letting a large portion of land to such a man as Mr. Burton was, I conceive, founded in prudence, and is justified by the event. Where several builders are all original contractors, the delay or insolvency of one thwarts the efforts of the whole; and builders with small capital never proceed with the same confidence and spirit as where they act under the guidance, and with the aid of such a man as Mr. Burton, who while he watched over and was interested in the success of the whole, was ready to come forward (and he has done it in a great variety of instances, and in some with considerable inconvenience and loss) with money and personal assistance, to relieve and help forward those builders who were unable to proceed in their contracts; and in some instances he has been obliged to resume the undertaking, and to complete himself what had been weakly and imperfectly proceeded in.

Weighing these circumstances liberally and candidly, if gentlemen will reflect how impossible it is that all the parts of the buildings which cover the Foundling estate should have been equally free from defects, and if they will consider the magnitude and extent of what Mr. Burton has done, and appreciate correctly its deficiencies, and then examine the variety and situation of the persons he has been obliged to employ, they will rather be surprised that the whole has been completed so perfectly and unexceptionably as it now is, than complain of a few trifling imperfections.[22]

Burton had already taken the block running from the south side of Brunswick Square to the north side of Guilford Street when in December 1793 he agreed to take the whole of the ground between Guilford Street on the south and Bernard Street on the north, from Brunswick Square to the boundary of the Bedford estate.[23] In 1795 he contracted to build the west side of Brunswick Square, and all of the ground to the west as far as the Bedford estate; he also took 177 feet along the west side of what became Hunter Street; for the whole he agreed to pay ground rent rising to a total of £560 per annum.[24] In addition he enclosed and planted the gardens in Brunswick Square.[25]

Before the building of the east side of Mecklenburgh Square in 1810 the Foundling Hospital made no attempt to impose a formal architectural pattern on any group of buildings in the manner of Bedford, Russell, or Tavistock squares. Cockerell did insist on a general uniformity of façade for the houses built under his supervision, but no one—he, Burton, or the other contractors—saw fit to ornament the estate with dramatic classical compositions.[26]

In December 1792 the building committee gave directions to the Hospital's

22. Pamphlet addressed *To the Governors and Guardians of the Hospital for the Maintenance and Education of Exposed and Deserted Young Children: Assembled in General Court* (London, 1807), pp. 24–27. Hereafter cited as "Cockerell, 1807 Pamphlet."

23. Building Committee, *1*, 52–53.

24. Ibid., pp. 71–72, 74.

25. General Court, *4*, 154 (30 March 1796).

26. The building minutes relating to the articles of agreement for the south side of Brunswick Square state that "the general arrangement of the fronts of the square [is] to be settled by Mr. Cockerell," but Cockerell did no more than insist on a general decent uniformity. Building

Committee, *1*, 43 (29 November 1792). Although larger than most of those on the rest of the estate, the houses in Brunswick Square have little architectural distinction. The most that Malcolm could say for them in 1802 was that they were "all of the same height, though of unequal breadths." He did praise, however, "the views from the west side of the square," showing, "through a number of trees, the distant range of buildings beyond the verdant slope at the New River Head, Pentonville, with St. Mary's steeple, Islington, and, between other trees, the white colonnade of the hospital, its gravel walks, and grass plats." Malcolm, *Londinium Redivivum*, *1*, 6.

solicitor to prepare a paving bill for the estate.[27] The resulting Act (34 Geo. III, cap. 96) provided for a paving commission, half of whose members were to be governors of the Foundling Hospital; the other half were to be elected by the ratepayers on the estate. Their powers resembled in general those of the paving commissioners on the Bedford estate.

Building had not been long in progress before the governors began to worry about the possibility of shoddy materials and poor workmanship. They suspected—not without justification—that the builders would not live up to the specifications of their contracts unless they were carefully watched. Cockerell assured the building committee that he had from the beginning "considered it as my particular duty to attend the execution of the works and buildings there, and am usually there every Tuesday, as well as at all other times when the business of the estate requires my attendance."[28] Despite his supervision, the building minutes are filled with reports of vaults falling in, walls collapsing, and bricks deemed substandard; some at least of the governors were disturbed by what they considered a negligent laxity on Cockerell's part.

In March 1796 John Keysall, a member of the building committee, in company with "a gentleman of great knowledge," inspected the buildings then going up. He found the bricks "not sufficiently burnt, nor the clay well-tempered . . ." There were not, he thought, "sufficient bond timbers in the buildings to hold them together, [and] therefore the walls will be apt in settling to give way and separate, which must prove very injurious." He blamed the Hospital surveyor for "not giving the attention he ought in inspecting the whole progress of the work, for which he is to be so amply paid."[29]

The building committee thereupon commissioned George Dance, Jr. (1741–1825) and James Lewis (1751?–1820), the architects, to make a survey of the buildings on the estate. Dance and Lewis reported that some of the bricks were of poor quality, and "ought not to be used in any party or external wall whatever." In addition they thought some of the timbers "too slight." Despite such faults they concluded that "the state and general conduct of these buildings in other respects are much upon a par with the state and general conduct of buildings erected by speculators in various parts of the Metropolis and its vicinity. Those who build for their own occupation," they pointed out, "may reasonably expect such buildings as we fear is not practicable to obtain from speculative builders . . ." Agreeing that in theory it would be wise "to restrain

27. General Court, *4*, 79.   29. Ibid., p. 106.
28. Building Committee, *1*, 60 (26 Mar. 1794).

and regulate the conduct of the work by agreements founded on the most minute description of the dimensions and quality of every part of the building," they held that "experience has shown that such restrictions would materially impede the letting of the ground."[30]

In March 1796 the building committee recommended that the Hospital invest a maximum of £5,000 in "profit rents," or improved ground rents.[31] Cockerell had urged the measure, both as a profitable investment of the Hospital's funds and because he believed that nothing could so effectively promote the progress of the building "as assisting the builders with money, either on the security of the buildings erected, or by the purchase of the profit rents . . ."[32] The General Court accordingly authorized the practice.[33]

The development was by the middle nineties visibly taking shape. The first leases to be granted after the commencement of the building scheme were in Guilford, Millman, and Doughty streets in 1793.[34] By the end of 1797 Guilford Street was finished. The leases in Lansdowne Place all date from 1794, while those in Caroline Place date from 1797 to 1804. Grenville Street was completed between 1794 and 1796, as was the south side of Brunswick Square.

By 1797 the original rapid rate of construction had slowed down. The war with France, by raising the prices of building materials and tightening the credit market, had seriously affected the building industry. To make matters worse for the Foundling estate, Burton was taken seriously ill during the period. In December 1797 the building committee recommended that his peppercorn rent for the ground to the west and northwest of Brunswick Square be extended for another year.[35] Shortly afterward the General Court agreed "to liquidate what is due from Mr. Burton for his part of the sewer [in Guilford Street?] and in other respects not exceeding the sum of £1,000 by a purchase of profit rents at seventeen years purchase."[36]

Cockerell urged the governors to continue extending peppercorn rents and granting loans during the difficult wartime years, as the best way "to accelerate the progress of the buildings . . ." A less liberal policy might easily "check the spirit of enterprise which has been shown on the Hospital estate in so unex-

---

30. Ibid., pp. 132–33 (10 December 1796). For Dance and Lewis, see Colvin, pp. 165–68, 366–67.
31. Building Committee, *1*, 104.
32. Ibid., p. 97.
33. General Court, *4*, 150–51 (30 March 1796).
34. Information as to the granting of building leases is all taken from the Foundling Hospital Estate Book. Since a building lease was not granted until the carcass of the house was erected,

the date of the lease (granted at the time of one of the quarterly meetings of the General Court) is the best evidence for the date of the house. The standard form of lease required that the premises be completely finished, ready for occupation, by the end of the following year.
35. Building Committee, *1*, 139.
36. General Court, *4*, 204 (28 March 1798).

ampled a manner." He held up the example of an estate that had been unable to extend peppercorn rents or grant loans to builders during the American war, where the property had in consequence "remained to this time uncovered, and has suffered more than the present value in fee simple." The success of the building development on the Bedford estate had, he believed, been due to a large extent to the loans and extensions of peppercorn rent. "I do not believe Bedford Square could have been completed without those means having been exercised; and without the great increase of that neighborhood," he concluded, "the Hospital lands would not have produced half the rents they have done."[37]

After hearing Cockerell's report, the General Court ordered the general committee to begin redeeming the land tax on as much of the Hospital estate as it thought expedient.[38] But despite such willingness to encourage its builders, the limited financial resources of the Hospital prevented it from equaling the scale of the Duke of Bedford.

In April 1799 Burton asked to be excused from his contract to build along the south side of what was to become Great Coram Street. The building committee acceded to the request, reducing his rent by £210. The governors thought it would be "imprudent to proceed in any erections" on the south side of that street, since "neither the northern side . . . nor any adjoining buildings . . . [are] in a course of progress at present, nor likely to be so for three or four years . . ." Under such circumstances, "the beginning of any erections there would," as Burton had argued, "produce a ruinous and prejudicial effect upon the estate; and interrupt what is of the utmost importance at present, the completion of the buildings already begun upon the other parts of the estate."[39]

By 1800 Burton's period of retrenchment was over. Not content with contracting, in that year, to build on a large portion of the Bedford estate, he also began negotiations for taking more chunks of the Foundling estate. He offered in December 1800 both to resume his contract for the south side of Great Coram Street and to take the ground on its north side as well, for a total of £310 per annum. He likewise proposed to build on an enlarged plot of land on the west side of Hunter Street.[40]

Earlier that year Charles Mayor agreed to take the north side of Brunswick Square for a rent rising to a total of £260 per annum in the fifth year.[41] By April 1800 he had produced a sketch of the elevation of the houses for Cocker-

---

37. Ibid., pp. 225–26 (26 December 1798).
38. Ibid., p. 227.
39. Building Committee, *1*, 148–50 (27 April

1799); 152–54 (15 June 1799).
40. Ibid., pp. 189–90.
41. Ibid., pp. 155–56, 158–59, 161, 163.

ell's approval. The surveyor found them "perfectly regular, and very nearly corresponding with the south side already erected." On 19 April the building committee gave its formal assent.[42] Both the west and north sides of the square were built during the year.

Bernard Street dates from 1796 to 1802, while Coram Street was built between 1800 and 1804 (see Fig. 66). Everett Street (today the southern end of Marchmont Street) dates from 1801, while Wilmot Street (now the section of Kenton Street south of Coram Street) was finished in 1802 (see Fig. 67). Kenton and Marchmont streets proper (i.e. north of Coram Street) were completed between 1806 and 1809. The leases in Tavistock Place were granted between 1800 and 1805, while its eastern extension, Compton Street, took from 1807 until 1819 to be completed. Henrietta (now Handel) Street dates from 1803 to 1808, Hunter Street from 1801 to 1812. Wakefield Street, bordering the Harrison estate, was built between 1819 and 1823.

In January 1802 Cockerell laid before the governors a building plan for the land lying east of the Hospital. It provided, as had Merryweather's, for a street running north of the Hospital buildings connecting Brunswick and Mecklenburgh squares. Cockerell proposed that houses be built along the northern side of the connecting street, which would be called Brunswick Place. He argued that the ground, "if left entirely unbuilt upon, would render it lonely for passengers, could only extend to the Burial Grounds [of St. George, Bloomsbury and St. George the Martyr, on the northern boundary of the estate], and would expose them and the inferior and irregular buildings which will probably be built northward of them to the view from the respectable quarters already established on the Hospital estate . . ." The only alternative would be to enclose the ground as an ornamental garden at great expense. He concluded by remarking on the "uncommon spirit and skill" that had characterized the general building development in the recent years, and on the "degree of unexampled success . . . whereby the neighborhood has become exceedingly in request for persons of general and great respectability . . ." He urged the necessity of keeping alive such a spirit, and encouraging the builders "by communications, by openings, by decorations, and by every other aid which may occur."[43]

Shortly thereafter Cockerell reported on the state of the buildings, and reflected on the role of the landlord in housing developments. There were, he estimated, about 2,900 feet of open frontage on the western part of the estate, and 1,700 feet on the eastern section, together with roughly 300 feet in Brunswick Place. Depending on the "facilities which may be given to the builders

---

42. Ibid., pp. 166–67.   43. Building Committee, 2, 14–16.

. . . in opening every possible access to the several parts, and upon their own enterprise and talents . . ." the ground rents for the unlet frontage, exclusive of Brunswick Place, might be estimated at £1,500.

> The unexampled rapidity with which the buildings have been carried on westward of the Hospital may be attributed to the plans adopted for the streets and squares giving free and direct communications between all parts of the estate; to the line of Guilford Street extending through the whole of the south boundary; to the main sewers and pavements being very early completed; and to the character and very extraordinary capacity of the great and general undertaker of the buildings on that side, uniting the whole under one interest, and completing at his own risk and expense every general work necessary to combine and give success to each line of street, in which he has been wisely aided by the liberal conduct of the Hospital.

Having stressed the value of "communications" in general, he turned to a discussion of the value of Brunswick Place in particular:

> The comparatively slow progress of the buildings on the east side is manifestly owing to the want of general communications extending from respectable quarters to that side, and nothing can so strongly point out the necessity of opening the intended communication north of the Hospital, which should be made in a direct line between the squares as expressed in the building contracts, rather than in the circular form designed by the plan originally adopted by the Hospital. It may be made most advantageously by keeping the roadway on a plane level, and by elevating the garden within in the form of a terrace, the inside of which being planted and ornamented with low shrubs would make an agreeable boundary to the garden, and conceal the road without excluding the current of air from the opening left towards the north.
>
> I am of opinion that if this northern communication was immediately formed, the ground in the east [i.e. Mecklenburgh] square would let very advantageously and speedily, and unless it is made I do not think *good* houses in that square can answer to builders at all, until some other respectable buildings are erected and a neighborhood formed on the lands adjacent, which cannot be expected, if ever, for very many years to come.

I cannot suggest any *other* practicable means to further the progress of the buildings more than a perseverance in the liberal conduct hitherto pursued by the Hospital in giving every possible facility to the undertakers and the operations; and in accepting fair and moderate terms from persons of character and responsibility inclined to adventure their capital, industry, and skill in the concern, thereby creating a joint interest in promoting its success (without which no such great undertaking can be effected advantageously), and ultimately increasing the Hospital estate beyond all former expectations of its value.[44]

In March 1803 the building committee advertised in the morning newspapers that the Hospital was prepared to receive proposals for ninety-nine-year building leases of all parts of its estate not already taken. Builders were requested to inquire at the secretary's office in the Hospital, "where plans of the ground may be seen, or at Mr. Cockerell's office, Old Burlington Street, where the elevation may be seen and the conditions and further particulars may be known."[45]

The undercurrent of distrust and suspicion of Cockerell that can be discerned from time to time in the building minutes burst into the open in 1805. In that year three members of the building committee, Michael Heathcote, William Harrison, and Anthony Van Dam, formed themselves into a select committee of investigation. With a series of reports they succeeded in undermining the confidence of many of the governors in the competence of their surveyor. In March 1805, on their recommendation, the building committee rejected a proposal of James Burton to take a piece of land north of Tavistock Place, on the ground that the rent he offered was too low. The select committee argued that while at the beginning it might be expedient to accept moderate ground rents in order to attract contractors, the ground rents should be raised once the development became a success. Also on its advice, the building committee resolved that in the future its approval, in addition to that of the surveyor, would be required for the elevations of all buildings on the estate. It further decided that future building agreements would specifically prohibit the erection of unauthorized streets, alleys, passages, or back buildings. "It is notorious," the select committee reported, that "when left to the discretion of the builders, much of the ground is covered with improper tenements, such as to invite the lowest orders of inhabitants, that disgrace so fair a plot of ground."[46] The com-

---

44. Ibid., pp. 31–35 (27 March 1802).   46. Ibid., pp. 127–34.
45. Ibid., pp. 95–96.

mittee had good reason to insist on additional safeguards: it had already discovered the existence of a potential slum on Burton's ground near the western boundary of the estate.[47] Although Cockerell refused to admit that the Hospital's interests were affected, the mean courts leading off Little Coram Street were before long to become a squalid reproach to the governors of the charity.

The second report of the new select committee included a charge that the building materials in many of the houses were "shamefully bad, and not agreeable to the Building Act."[48] The surveyor replied that the building materials were not "inferior to such as are used in speculative buildings in general." The Building Act, Cockerell reminded the committee, did not regulate the quality of materials. Like Dance and Lewis in 1796, he argued that "if a weight and strength of character equal to what is required for private and individual use had been insisted upon in buildings erected upon speculation in time of war and great public expense, they would not have advanced to one-fourth of the extent they have reached; the builders would long ago have been ruined, and the Hospital estate have been a spectacle of unfinished and desolated carcasses."[49]

In January 1807 Heathcote, Harrison, and Van Dam again condemned the quality of the bricks, mortar, and timber being used. Several houses had, they said, fallen in because of shoddy materials, "and they also impute much mischief to the want of a proper person to superintend the buildings according to the terms stipulated in their contracts."[50] The building committee thereupon appointed Joseph Kay (1775–1847), a pupil of Cockerell, as inspector of the buildings on the estate.[51]

The following week it resolved to recommend to the next quarterly General Court that it replace Cockerell with Thomas Spencer as surveyor.[52] In the meantime it relieved Cockerell of all practical responsibility and appointed Spencer, together with James Spiller (d. 1829), the architect,[53] to inspect the houses going up and report on their condition. Spencer and Spiller began by condemning six houses in Kenton Street as unsound and in danger of falling in. The committee thereupon ordered the builder to take down the houses at once and rebuild them.[54] The following week the building committee, again on the recommendation of Spencer and Spiller, informed Charles Mayor, who was building along the east side of Hunter Street and the north side of Henri-

47. Ibid., pp. 112–13 (23 April 1804).

48. Ibid., p. 152 (5 June 1805).

49. Ibid., pp. 161–62 (21 October 1805).

50. Ibid., pp. 223–24.

51. Ibid., p. 228 (24 January 1807). For Kay as an architect, see Colvin, p. 332.

52. Building Committee, 2, 229.

53. Spiller was the surveyor to the Royal Exchange Assurance Company. See Colvin, pp. 564–65.

54. Building Committee, 2, pp. 248–49 (21 March 1807).

etta (now Handel) Street, that his bricks were unsound, that his mortar was "improperly compounded," and that he would "proceed at his peril."[55]

The General Court refused to dismiss Cockerell, but he remained without any real power or responsibility, while Spencer and Spiller continued their investigations.[56] On 22 April they submitted to the General Court a lengthy denunciation of Cockerell, from the beginning of his association with the Hospital.[57] Even Joseph Kay, his pupil, found fault with the quality of the buildings, particularly with respect to the bricks and mortar.[58]

In June Cockerell retaliated with a long report to the General Court, which was subsequently printed. Quoting the findings of Dance and Lewis in their report of 1796, he repeated his conviction "that if I had pressed the builders to the extent of the power I possessed under their contracts, most of them must have failed, and the Foundling estate have been left in the condition of those estates at Bath, Bristol, and other places where from the effects of the war . . . whole acres still remain in a state of ruin and desolation."[59] He pointed out that the cost of many building materials had nearly doubled—that of timber nearly quadrupled—since the building contracts had been written.[60] He cited the examples of the Bedford, Grosvenor, and Portman estates, on which a lighter character of building had been practiced since the start of the war, and "with which the buildings upon the Foundling estates are at least upon a par."[61]

After concluding the defense of his own conduct and that of Burton and the other builders, Cockerell turned to his attackers. Spencer, he reminded the Court, was the agent of Mr. Harrison's adjoining estate. "The fact of the best buildings erected on that estate not being superior to some of those so illiberally condemned in . . . [Spencer's] reports, and of his having permitted other buildings to be erected on the edge of the Foundling ground of so mean and inferior a quality as not only to discredit the estate, but even to injure the adjoining property, may," he wrote, "be easily ascertained . . ." He charged that Spencer had been given to understand that his appointment as surveyor of the Foundling estate would depend on the number of defects he could find in the buildings.[62]

Cockerell reminded the governors that the estate had been obliged in 1795 to grant land valued at £1,800 to the Duke of Bedford in return for the four

55. Ibid., p. 255.
56. General Court, 5, 117 (1 April 1807).
57. Ibid., pp. 119–23.
58. Building Committee, 3, 29–32 (23 May 1807).
59. For the effects of the financial panic of 1793 and the war on the building in Clifton, Bristol, see Bryan Little, The City and County of Bristol (London, 1954), p. 233.
60. Cockerell, 1807 Pamphlet, pp. 15–16.
61. Ibid., p. 28.
62. Ibid., pp. 38–41.

openings onto his estate. He estimated "the increased value of the Hospital estate from the acquisition of those openings . . . at near ten times that sum." In 1807 both the Skinners' Company and Mr. Harrison were negotiating for entrances from their estates onto the Foundling land. "The buildings on the Skinners' Company estate are proposed to be respectable," he observed, "and will therefore unite very well with those on the estate of the Hospital . . ." Mr. Harrison's buildings, on the contrary, were "of a character to discredit and injure any property which is connected to them." The Skinners' Company was prepared to pay for the privilege of openings onto the Foundling estate.[63] Mr. Harrison was attempting to gain similar openings "as a thing of course, and without any payment on his part to the Hospital." Spencer, Cockerell implied, was furthering Mr. Harrison's plans by means of his position on the Foundling estate.[64]

On the first of July the General Court, having read Cockerell's report, ordered the building committee to discontinue the services of Spencer and Spiller.[65] Cockerell remained as surveyor until the following April, when he resigned. The building committee thereupon appointed Kay to succeed him. Cockerell offered his services gratuitously in the future, either directly to the committee, or through Mr. Kay, whenever they might be needed.[66]

In July 1808 the building committee ordered that the Hospital pay for the completion of the sewers running along Hunter Street and Cox Street (later Compton Street, now part of Tavistock Place).[67] Two years later it decided that the remaining sewers on the estate should be built at the expense of the Hospital in the first instance, instead of at the builders' as had been the practice.[68]

Kay was as convinced as Cockerell had been of the desirability of a street to connect the two squares. While admitting that it would slightly interfere with the privacy of the Hospital buildings, he pointed out that "as provision is intended to be made to prevent a general communication with Gray's Inn Lane by Heathcote Street it is not very likely to be much used (at least for carriages) except for intercourse between the two squares . . ." On the other hand, he was convinced that "the extension which this design would effect of the ornamental character of the two squares, by giving them in some degree the effect of unity

---

63. In November the Skinners' Company paid £1,500 for two openings—continuations of Hunter and Marchmont streets—onto the Foundling estate. The two landowners agreed that for at least 200 feet north and south of the boundary, no houses were to be less than second-rate. Building Committee, 3, 84–85 (15 Nov. 1807).

64. Cockerell, 1807 Pamphlet, pp. 41–43.
65. General Court, 5, 133–34.
66. Building Committee, 3, 133 (9 April 1808).
67. Ibid., p. 153.
68. Ibid., p. 239 (14 July 1810).

in one very large square, and the erection of such a range of buildings . . . would certainly form a very handsome termination to the building plan of that part of the estate . . ." Furthermore, "by shutting out the present dead wall to the burying ground and the back fronts of the buildings rising on Mr. Harrison's ground," the street would contribute "to the cheerfulness of the whole quarter and certainly enhance the value of the ground remaining to be let on the east side of the Hospital . . ."[69] Despite such arguments the General Court rejected the plan and Brunswick Place was never built.[70]

The last of the principal features of the estate plan to be realized was Mecklenburgh Square. The location of the eastern square was unavoidably awkward. Not only was it the part of the property that lay farthest from the relatively fashionable Bedford estate, but the Hospital grounds cut it off from all easy communication with the west. It had convenient access only to Gray's Inn Road and the undesirable neighborhoods to the east. The proposed road cutting through the Hospital grounds was chiefly designed to remedy the isolation of Mecklenburgh Square. Without such a road, the reluctance of builders to erect expensive houses in the square is understandable.

As early as 1796 Joseph Astey had agreed to construct houses for eighty feet along its south side, provided that the Hospital formed and enclosed the square within seven years.[71] By 1805, although Astey's assignee, Benjamin Hornby, had begun to build, the square remained unenclosed.[72] In May 1809 Hornby complained that although the house at the southwestern corner of the square had been finished for nearly two years, and that he expected to complete the adjacent house within two months, "from the general doubt expressed . . . as to the time when if ever the square will be formed and planted, I have good reason to believe if I am driven to sell the property it will be at a loss of not less than one thousand pounds . . ."[73]

Shortly thereafter the committee ordered the treasurer to begin the necessary works, at a cost estimated at £1,100.[74] In September 1809 Thomas Penthrin applied for the rest of the south side of the square.[75] In the same month the committee accepted the proposal of George Payne—who, like Penthrin, had previously taken ground in Compton Street—to take the whole of the east side of the square for £400 per annum.[76]

69. Building Committee, *4*, 20–21 (13 April 1811).
70. General Court, *5*, 225 (24 April 1811).
71. Building Committee, *2*, 169–71.
72. Ibid., p. 172.

73. Building Committee, *3*, 183.
74. Ibid., p. 188 (1 July 1809).
75. Ibid., pp. 195–96.
76. Ibid., pp. 229–32.

66. Coram Street, north side, and Marchmont Street, west side, in 1963. James Burton et al., c. 1800–09

67. Wilmot Street (now Kenton Street), looking south into Bernard Street, in 1963. James Burton, c. 1802

68. Mecklenburgh Square, east side, in 1982. Joseph Kay, 1810

69. Aerial view of Foundling estate, looking east, in 1950. Open space in upper center is site of former Hospital, now playground. Russell Square in lower right-hand corner

The east side of Mecklenburgh Square, the leases for which date from 1810 to 1820, was the one feature of the Foundling development comparable to the more ambitious squares on the Bedford estate (Fig. 68). Reminiscent of the Adam blocks in Fitzroy Square, it gave a needed theatrical touch to an estate whose architecture elsewhere seldom rose above the level of decent mediocrity.

While there is doubt as to the identity of the designer of many of the unified façades on the Bedford estate, there is no doubt that Joseph Kay was responsible for the design of Mecklenburgh Square. In October 1810 he informed the general committee that "the houses now erecting on the east side of . . . [Mecklenburgh] Square form the southern division of a regular design that I have made for that side of the square, and are executing from correct figured working plans, elevations, and sections that I have furnished to the builders for that purpose." The governors were themselves more interested in the bricks, mortar, and timber going into the houses than in questions of aesthetics, and Kay devoted most of this and later reports on the square to assuring them of the substantial character of the buildings. He was providing for close supervision over the builders, and promised the governors that when the houses were finished they would be "worthy to rank higher, in public estimation, than any speculative buildings in that quarter."[77]

Despite Kay's repeated assurances, the governors remained uneasy about the quality of materials and workmanship of the houses going up. By the late spring of 1813 the uneasiness had brought forth an open attack on their surveyor, similar to those his predecessor had so often received.

Kay replied to the various charges with bitterness. He pointed out that "in times like the present, and to one at all concerned for the proper performance of its duties, and the maintenance of his professional character," his was "an arduous and anxious task." He reminded the general committee "how entirely the carrying on of the buildings by the persons taking ground is vested in the discretion of the surveyor," and how the surveyor required the confidence and support of the governors. No surveyor, he insisted, would ever be able to say "that the building contracts have been to the letter of them fully complied with . . ." But he assured the committee that "the general spirit" of the contract had been complied with, "as to their design, their rate of building, and the substance required by those rates; and in the progress of them I paid as much attention as possible to the materials employed, and though not in all respects with the effect I could have desired . . . it ought to be rather a subject

77. General Committee Minutes, 31, 33. (Hereafter cited as General Committee.)

of surprise that what has been done could under the circumstances have been effected at all, than of complaint that it has not been better done." He insisted that the buildings were the best that could be expected "from such builders, and in such times . . ."[78]

Kay ended by observing that it would "add to the respectability and give an air of completion to that part of the estate, as well as promote the success of the large property that has been embarked upon it, if some measures were decided upon for erecting the proposed bar at the end of Heathcote Street, with a small lodge or some other indication of an entrance to the Hospital estate from Gray's Inn Lane Road."[79] If Mecklenburgh Square could not be given easy access to the fashionable west, it could at least be protected from the unfashionable east. Located at the eastern end of Heathcote Street, the gate kept Mecklenburgh Square free from the low and noisy traffic of Gray's Inn Road throughout most of the nineteenth century.[80] In 1821 the Hospital gave Kay eighty guineas as remuneration for his architectural design.[81]

The last part of Mecklenburgh Square to be built was the north side. Kay prepared plans and elevations for these houses, as he had for the eastern block. Yet in January 1824 the secretary reported irregularities in the dimensions and decoration of two of the houses, "which seem to have been a departure entirely from the original design."[82] Kay said that he had noted the variations in the height of the roofs the previous December, and had ordered the builders, Wolcott and Browning, to alter them to conform with the adjoining roofs. The irregularity of the cornice and fascia he believed unavoidable and past remedy. Part of the ground on the north side had been taken by Thomas Weeding, a member of the building committee, and part by the John McGill who built much of Upper Bedford Place and Woburn Place.[83] Weeding had employed

78. General Committee, 32, 255–56.

79. Ibid., p. 257.

80. Paving Commission Minutes, 4, 324. Another gate on the estate, located at the eastern end of Henrietta (now Handel) Street, was permanently closed to stop traffic going to and from the cemeteries of the parishes of St. George the Martyr and St. George, Bloomsbury. When the parishes were attempting to establish a right-of-way to the cemeteries in 1806, Cockerell warned, "It must be evident that such a measure will seriously affect and lessen the value of the Hospital estate by leading all the melancholy processions of those populous parishes through the principal and most improved parts of it, and therefore that every effort should be exerted to check, and if

possible prevent the use of that entrance altogether." Building Committee, 2, 210–11 (20 December 1806).

81. Building Committee, 4, 245. Kay had delayed presenting his "statement of charge for the architectural design of the fronts of those buildings, and for designing and laying out the ornamental area of the square," until the east side of the square was completed. By that time he felt "well assured that the general success of the speculation has been materially promoted by the adoption of the ornamental disposition of these buildings . . ." Ibid., pp. 240–41 (10 February 1821).

82. General Committee, 37, 157–58.

83. See above, p. 57.

McGill to build Weeding's houses as well as his own. Kay "furnished correct and correspondent drawings for the fronts of these buildings . . . showing the heights of the several stories, which were intended to have ranged throughout. I find," he reported, "that some increase of height, of which I was not aware, has been given to those at the western end [on Mr. Weeding's ground], particularly in the chamber story . . ." McGill blamed the variations on Weeding's directions, "as he frequently interfered during the progress of the work. The situation and design of the cornice and fascia itself was also varied on his suggestion."[84]

Richard Vanheythuysen, the Hospital's solicitor, gave the builders notice to make the necessary alterations to render the houses conformable to the surveyor's elevation.[85] The builders refused to make any changes whatever. On the advice of Vanheythuysen that it would prove difficult and expensive to force them to alter the houses, the general committee decided to let them remain as they were.[86]

In December 1826 the General Court approved the last three building leases on the north side of Mecklenburgh Square, and thereby brought to an end the original building history of the estate. It resolved that the building committee remain in existence, authorized "to take such measures as they may consider expedient for rebuilding, if necessary, or upholding the buildings of this estate, according to the covenants of the respective leases, and for maintaining all boundaries, ways, and watercourses in respect thereof . . ."[87] As a matter of fact, the building committee died a natural death shortly thereafter; its last recorded meeting took place 17 March 1827.[88] The business of managing the completed estate now fell principally to the general committee, together with the Hospital's surveyor, solicitor, and secretary. (Figure 69, an aerial view of the estate in 1950, gives some idea of its general appearance.)

For all its pitfalls, the initial stage of town planning was probably the easiest and the most immediately satisfying. The planner did not have to worry about fitting his ideas into an existing street pattern, since there wasn't any: the open fields that he was to transform into a new town were the nearest thing to a *tabula rasa* that he was ever likely to find. If the area to be dealt with was extensive enough, the planner really could hope to determine the nature and character of the new quarter.

84. General Committee, *37*, 169–70 (11 February 1824).
85. Ibid., p. 174.
86. Ibid., pp. 178–79 (25 February 1824).
87. General Court, *6*, 176–77.
88. Building Committee, *5*, 42–45.

But who was the planner? Was he the steward or surveyor of the landlord, or was he an independent building speculator, such as Burton or Cubitt? From the building history of the Bedford and Foundling estates, it would seem that the answer varied with circumstances. The design of Bedford Square clearly originated off the estate; it is equally certain that the surveyor of the Foundling estate himself designed the east side of Mecklenburgh Square and imposed his elevations on the builders.

Both James Burton and Thomas Cubitt seem to have been responsible for the façades of the houses erected under their supervision, subject to the approval of the ground landlord. They, too, proposed what size and quality of houses they intended to build, again subject to the freeholder's approval. But there is little to indicate that the various "building plans" that each submitted to the Bedford Office or the Foundling Hospital did more than propose the kinds of buildings to be erected on an already existing street plan. There is no question that the governors of the Foundling Hospital themselves, together with their own surveyor, were wholly responsible for planning the street pattern and general character of that estate. There is less clear evidence with respect to the street plan of the adjacent Bedford estate, but the implication is that it originated, at least in its broad outlines, within the Bedford Office. Certainly the later development in Bedford New Town originated with the Duke's steward and surveyor and remained throughout under their control and direction.

Both estates were reasonably successful in seeing their building plans put into effect. Both introduced modifications in their original schemes, partly in response to demands from builders or at least from attempts to hasten the building and ensure its success. The architectural and structural provisions of the building agreements were followed to a greater or lesser extent depending on circumstances. Sir John Summerson has commented on the structural superiority of Cubitt's buildings on the Bedford estate to those put up thirty years earlier by Burton.[89] Cubitt, unlike Burton, did not have to contend with the inflated prices of building materials brought about by the French wars; one should not judge Burton too harshly as a jerry-builder, despite the unfortunate later history of some of his property.[90] The failure, or at best limited success, of serious attempts by the Bedford estate to enforce building agreements in Keppel Street, and of the Foundling estate in Mecklenburgh Square, shows the limitations that existed on the power of any ground landlord.

89. *Georgian London*, p. 192.   90. See below, pp. 129–39.

And yet the Dukes of Bedford and the governors of the Foundling Hospital could look back on the building history of their estates with some degree of satisfaction. The Bloomsbury estates showed the results of conscious town planning in a particularly striking manner. If they contained no examples of great architecture, neither did they contain any buildings that would offend the sensitive eye.

When the streets and squares north of Great Russell Street were new, Londoners looked upon them with approval and even pride, if not with undue enthusiasm. Thomas Allen wrote in 1833 that "the grandest features in the northern quarter of the town are to be found on the estates of the Duke of Bedford and the Foundling Hospital. Here several magnificent squares have been built, or are now in progress; together with many respectable leading streets."[91] A few years later James Grant was "struck with the aspect of elegance and comfort" which the squares in Bloomsbury presented.[92] W. Weir, in 1844, regretted that the squares in that part of London were "all modern and middle-class, and devoid of associations to tempt us to linger in them," yet admitted that all of them were "comely, and some elegant." The combination of Brunswick and Mecklenburgh squares with the Hospital and grounds in between he considered "very striking and interesting."[93]

If a later generation was to call Bloomsbury dull, it could not accuse it of lacking dignity. Designed as a haven of respectability for the moderately well-to-do, it acquired a population of families as dignified and unexceptionable as the houses they occupied. One need not accept Isabella Knightley's view that life was positively unsafe away from the neighborhood of Brunswick Square to admit that few parts of late Georgian London provided a more satisfying compromise between the openness of the country and the bricks and mortar of the town. The setbacks which the two estates met should not obscure the splendor of their achievement in giving London one of its most delightful neighborhoods.

But if town planning was to be something more than the creation of an agreeable network of streets and squares, it could not afford to abandon its operations once the original building scheme was achieved. To be successful, a town plan required continuous vigilance on the part of some supervisory authority. The forces of decay and degradation set in as soon as the houses were

91. Thomas Allen, *A New History of London, Westminster and the Borough of Southwark* (4 vols. London, 1833), *3*, 25.

92. James Grant, *Sketches of London* (2 vols. Philadelphia, 1839), *1*, 15.

93. W. Weir, "The Squares of London," in Charles Knight, ed., *London* (6 vols. London, 1841–44), *6*, 199.

completed, and from that time until the leases expired the principal duty of
the estate office was to preserve the buildings as close to their original state
as possible. Once the leases fell in, the ground landlord might introduce dramatic changes: pull down buildings, cut through new streets, alter the very
nature of his property. But for the first ninety-nine years the most he could
hope to do was to maintain the estate in accordance with its original plan. Even
that was easier in theory than in practice.

III *PRESERVING THE NEW TOWNS*

6 Gentility Maintained

The exertions of our fathers in the general improvement of houses and streets have left us little to do. . . . Repairing-leases contribute greatly to the handsome appearance of the houses; everything is in order.—Malcolm, Anecdotes of the Manners and Customs of London during the Eighteenth Century (1810)

For the first few years after the completion of a building plan the ground landlord could ordinarily afford to relax. If the original plan was a good one, if it attracted desirable tenants to the estate, he would probably not think it necessary to engage in active interference. Yet if a landlord persisted in a policy of laissez-faire, the best of town plans could crumble and decay, the best of New Towns become the worst of slums.

Apart from some inevitable physical deterioration, population movements, as well as changes in fashion or economic conditions, could make a once-respectable neighborhood decline into squalor and wretchedness. Urban blight is not unique to the twentieth century. It has always been far easier to lay out a pleasant neighborhood than to keep it that way, far easier to maintain its character than to restore it once it has declined.

In theory, the extensive powers that a building or repairing lease gave the ground landlord ought to have enabled him to maintain indefinitely the original character of his estate. In the typical lease, the lessee agreed that he would "at his . . . own proper costs and charges well and sufficiently repair, uphold, support, sustain, maintain, tile, slate, glaze, lead, paint, pave, purge, scour, cleanse, empty, amend, and keep the . . . premises . . . and all pavements, walls, fences, pipes, gutters, waters, watercourses, privies, sinks, drains, sewers, wy-draughts, and appurtenances belonging . . . thereto . . . with all manner of . . . necessary reparations, cleansings, and amendments whatsoever, when and so often as need or occasion shall require . . ."

The lessor or his agents or workmen could at any time "enter . . . the . . .

premises . . . to view, search, and see the state and want of the reparations thereof . . ." After their inspection they might give the lessee written notice "to repair and amend the same within the space of three calendar months . . ." Failure to comply with the notice would give the lessor the right to recover the possession of the house.[1]

In leases granted later, the lessee had also to agree to "paint all the outside wood, cement, stucco, and ironwork . . . three times over with good oil color once in every leap year, and also in the last year of the term hereby granted," and paint the inside walls every seven years.[2] The landlord ordinarily encouraged or required all the tenants in a street to paint at the same time, and to use the same colors in the interests of uniformity.[3]

In upper and middle-class neighborhoods, the ground landlord could assume that self-interest would make the tenant keep his house in reasonable repair, at least until the last few years of the lease. But the same self-interest might also lead to a more insidious form of decay: the conversion of a dwelling house for professional, commercial, or even industrial purposes. While such conversion might benefit the individual tenant, it could cause great damage to the rest of the estate.

Leases in the more important streets might therefore provide that the houses could only be used as gentlemen's private residences, and that no trade whatsoever be carried on. For streets with fewer pretensions the lease would ordinarily include a list of forbidden occupations. The standard form for repairing leases in use on the Bedford estate in the 1850s forbade the following:

> Brewer, baker, sugar baker, publican, vintner, victualler, butcher, slaughterer, cowkeeper, chimney sweeper, tripeseller, poulterer, fishmonger, cheesemonger, fruiterer, herbseller, coffeehouse keeper, coffee-

---

1. Quotations from a Portman estate building lease dated 9 October 1824 for houses in Church Street, St. Marylebone, in the Portman Office, London.

2. Printed form of Portman estate business lease, in use in 1896. "I may observe that the . . . lessee under modern leases has a painting covenant which the old lessee had not . . . (I do not mean on this estate specially, but generally throughout all the metropolis) . . ." Frederick W. Hunt, surveyor of the Portman estate, TH, p. 597; 1888 (313) xxii. He dated the change to stricter covenants as "within the last 30 or 40 years." Covenants tended during the 19th century to grow increasingly specific in requirements.

3. Although details varied from estate to estate, leases usually followed a standard pattern: "Mr. Baumann: Of course, you always insert in your leases covenants providing that the lessee shall pay the rates, taxes, insurance, and repairs, and that he shall not carry on any trade or business without the consent of the freeholder, or any trade which may be a nuisance to his neighbors? —Francis Edwards [surveyor of Evelyn estate in Deptford]: Those are the universal covenants." Ibid., p. 470; 1887 (260) xiii. For the provisions of repairing leases on the Northampton estate, see HWC, p. 47; 1884–85 (4402-I) xxx.

shop keeper, cookshop, distiller, dyer, pawnbroker, goldbeater, tanner, brazier, brass founder, ironfounder, diesinker, lacquerer, working smith, working tinman, farrier, dealer in old iron or in bottles, rags, bones, marine stores, dogs, birds, timber, wood, second-hand clothes, ready-made clothes, second-hand books, second-hand shoes, prints, or carica-tures; pipeburner, boneburner, boneboiler, melting tallowchandler, soapboiler, blackingmaker, undertaker, mason, bricklayer, plasterer, carpenter, sawyer, coffinmaker, trunkmaker, boxmaker, working printer, working bookbinder, working hatter, or working cooper, or . . . any noisy, noisome or offensive trade or business whatever . . .

The form further stipulated that the premises could not be converted into or occupied as chambers without the consent of the Duke or his agents. They might not be "used or occupied as or for a school, seminary, or college of any kind, or as or for a madhouse or billiard room or . . . for public concerts, music, or balls, or . . . for a shooting gallery, police office, police station, spunging or lock-up house, sheriff's office, or tax office, or . . . for betting or gambling . . . or . . . for a public office of any kind . . ." Nor could they be used as "a brothel, house of ill fame, or place of resort for lewd or disorderly persons, or . . . for a hospital, infirm-ary, dispensary, or institution of any kind, or . . . for a shop or place for the sale of coals, potatoes, wines, spirits, ale, beer, or ready-dressed provisions without such consent . . ."

Leases granted for premises intended from the outset for commercial pur-poses ordinarily contained special covenants designed to prevent such a use from interfering with the comfort or sense of decorum of neighboring tenants. One such covenant which the Duke of Westminster included in his leases to butchers in Mount Street in the 1880s brought forth an angry paragraph from Frank Banfield, the journalist, in one of a series of articles he wrote for the *Sunday Times* on the great landlords of London:

It might be expected that, as the terms of the ground landlord are so sufficiently onerous as regards building and ground rent, there would be no hard covenants to hamper a man in the conduct of his business. Butchers in Mount Street, however, will be in future under a dis-ability which, in the eyes of their trade, may seem a serious one. They have been compelled in their leases to sign away the right to hang car-casses outside their shop-windows on a rail. The current of air thus obtained does the meat no harm, and in the morning, when the butcher is busy, it gives him more room inside to move about and attend to his customers. He and his *confrères* have a profound faith in the trade benefits to be derived from what is known as a good display, and they argue that any stipulation which prevents them from giving full advertisement to their business in the old-fashioned style inflicts on them injury and loss. The powers that be do not see the thing in this light, and frown sternly upon the very suggestion to bring "a slovenly, unhandsome corpse between the wind and their nobility." A butcher remarked feelingly on this subject: "A row of clean, white carcasses is rather a taking and pretty object," and Mount Street would, perhaps, have been none the worse if the monotony of its southern *façade* had been broken by the raw material of the roast beef of Old England swaying in the breeze.[4]

Since failure to comply with any of the provisions could result in his being ejected from the premises, it would seem at first glance that the tenant was wholly at the mercy of the landlord. This was not so. It should not be assumed that because a lease gives a certain power to the landlord, he will in fact exercise that power. Henry Trelawny Boodle, the agent for the Westminster and Northampton estates, told the Royal Commission on the Housing of the Working Classes that landlords had less power than laymen might suppose. "Looking at a lease as it stands," he pointed out, "the proviso for re-entry seems to enable the landlord to eject the tenant if he commits any breach of covenant whatever; but practically that is not the case, and in fact no well-disposed landlord would attempt such a thing." Recent legislation[5] required the landlord to give a tenant written notice of any breach of covenant, and enabled the courts to stop an action of ejectment at any time. While protecting the tenant from a despotic landlord, it also meant, as Sir Charles Dilke pointed out, "that negligent lessees, knowing that the landlord can do nothing unless he has served a statutory notice, and that after that they will have plenty of time to obey the covenants, frequently neglect the covenants until the notice is served."[6]

One of the principal objects of the Select Committee on Town Holdings was to find out whether the London leasehold system hastened or retarded urban decay. The Royal Commission on the Housing of the Working Classes had decided that it encouraged the growth of slums. Particularly where leases had only a few more years to run, the Commissioners thought that decay and degradation were inevitable under the London system. They based such con-

4. Frank Banfield, *The Great Landlords of London* (London, 1890), pp. 60–61.

5. Lord Cairns' Conveyancing and Law of Property Act, 44 and 45 Vict., cap. 41.

6. HWC, p. 42; 1884–85 (4402-I) xxx.

clusions chiefly on their investigation of the Northampton estate in Clerkenwell. Here, certainly, covenants had not been systematically enforced, and here
had developed one of the most deplorable slums in London.

The evidence brought before the Commissioners showed the estate to be
characterized by overcrowding, inadequate sanitation, insufficient ventilation,
and generally poor repair. Two years later, after serious attempts at improvement by the Northampton estate, the Home Secretary found the conditions
still unsatisfactory. Of 475 houses in the parish that he had inspected, 294 had
water closets without water supply, 52 had water closets with defective plans
or apparatus, 32 had defective cisterns, 106 lacked dustbins or had only defective ones, 32 had defective gullies and sinks, 10 had defective drains, and
117 had defective paving in the yards. In addition he mentioned "a large
number of dirty and dilapidated houses, particularly the houses formerly occupied by one family, but now let out in tenements."[7]

The building leases of the property dated for the most part from 1815 and
1818. Although they contained the covenants usual at that time, they did not
prohibit further building on the premises.[8] In any event, the estate had done
nothing to prevent the erection, around 1831, of cheap tenements over the
courts that lay behind the original houses.[9] By about that time the older houses,
intended for single families, were also being converted into tenements, again
without interference from the ground landlord.[10]

While the leases lacked specific covenants against either new building in
the courts or overcrowding, they did contain provisions for keeping the property in decent repair, and these were flagrantly violated. Lord William Compton, son of the Marquess of Northampton, admitted to the Commissioners
that the property would have been kept in a less deplorable state had the
covenants been stringently enforced.[11] Boodle admitted "a certain amount of
blame," three years later, in not giving the estate close enough supervision, and
"in trusting the middlemen."[12]

With the growing agitation to provide better housing for the poor, of which
the formation of the Royal Commission was symptomatic, the Northampton
estate began to pay closer attention to its property. As a result of more systematic inspection and a more thorough enforcement of repairing covenants,

7. Parliamentary Papers, Report by D. Cubitt Nichols, Esq. on the Sanitary Condition of
the Parish of Clerkenwell, p. 5; 1886 [C. 4717]
lvi. Although the Marquess of Northampton was
the principal ground landlord in the parish, the
investigation did not confine itself to his estate.

8. HWC, p. 43; 1884–85 (4402-I) xxx.
9. Ibid., p. 36.
10. Ibid., p. 33.
11. Ibid., p. 36.
12. TH, p. 339; 1887 (260) xiii.

its appearance had improved noticeably by 1884. Thomas Jennings, chairman
of the sanitary committee of the Clerkenwell parish vestry, whose evidence was
mainly critical of the management of the estate, admitted that it was taking
steps to remedy the situation. "Very great alterations and improvements are
taking place undoubtedly, I believe owing to the efforts of Lord William
Compton," he reported. "I can see from the condition of the places I visited
last week as compared with the condition of the places when we visited them
last autumn that very great changes have taken place."[13]

Three years later Howard Martin, a surveyor, told the Committee on Town
Holdings that the Northampton estate compared favorably with much of the
nearby freehold property. "Repairing covenants have been enforced," he insisted, "and there is not the slightest doubt that owing to the operation of those
repairing covenants, where they have been enforced by the Marquess' agents,
the cottages on that estate, as a rule, are in a far better condition than cottages
in the surrounding properties." He was even able to praise the conditions in
the courts. "It is a most astonishing thing, under the circumstances, to go over
that district and see how respectable the occupants of those houses are," he
maintained, "and certainly those houses are in a fair condition as a rule, having
regard to age and situation."[14]

But the estate itself doubted that it could effect any significant improvement
while the existing leases continued in force. Although Boodle toured the estate
"several times in the year," and a clerk in his office went through it on his way
to work "nearly every day of his life, and the surveyor goes there when in-
structed, and my instructions are to look after those houses as far as possible,"
Boodle was not satisfied with the result. "Where you have many houses of the
poor, and they do so little to help themselves and keep the houses clean, it is
impossible to make them perfect."[15] The chief difficulty, he thought, was that
the occupying tenant was rarely himself the lessee, but merely rented from
a middleman. And although the ground landlord could mitigate certain evils
"by insisting upon repairs and sanitary improvements," the real responsibility
lay with the lessee. The freeholder "can insist upon the covenants being observed, and those covenants are sufficiently comprehensive if the middleman
will only observe them. . . . There is the difficulty; we find that they are so
very unscrupulous. There are few who observe their covenants properly."[16]

The middleman, or "house-jobber," who often held the lease of large blocks
of house property which he sublet on weekly tenancies, emerged as the villain

13. HWC, p. 92; 1884–85 (4402-I) xxx.   15. HWC, p. 119; 1884–85 (4402-I) xxx.
14. TH, p. 103; 1887 (260) xiii.   16. Ibid., p. 46.

of the investigation, condemned by ground landlord and reformer alike. "I have heard it stated over and over again, and I believe it to be true," said Boodle, "that if a man hardens his heart, and treats his fellow-creatures like brute beasts, and crowds them in like pigs, this system of farming houses is the most remunerative thing possible." Pointing out that "it is a thing that [ground] landlords do their best to check," he argued that middlemen would be even more powerful if they possessed the freehold of their tenements: "They know how they can grind down the poor. There would be nobody over them except Parliament and the reformed vestries or municipalities, or whatever they may be eventually." He had little faith in their good intentions. "In one sense the prosperity of your tenants is your own prosperity, or ought to be," he thought; "but I am afraid all [the middlemen] care about in the matter of 'interest' is merely to screw as much as they possibly can out of their tenants."[17]

As a result of such evidence, the Royal Commissioners concluded that "there is an indisposition on the part of landlords to avail themselves stringently of the provisoes in their leases for re-entry and for the troublesome and costly process of ejectment of tenants in case of breach of covenant . . ." They pointed out that although "the terms of the leases provide that the tenant shall keep the house in repair . . . the stringent conditions of the leases fall into disuse; the difficulty of personal supervision of the property is apt to grow greater, and the relations between the ground landlord and the tenant who occupies the house grow less and less." The great number of people having leasehold interests in a single house often "causes the greatest doubt as to who is the person . . . to execute repairs or to look after the conditions of the premises. This is especially the case when building has taken place for which no trace of sanction can be found on the part of the ground landlord," as took place on the Northampton estate, "the erections under such circumstances being often crowded on gardens or courts, the preservation of which would have been for the sanitary benefit of the existing houses."[18]

A supplementary report by ten of the seventeen members of the commission went further, declaring that "the system of building on leasehold land is a great cause of the many evils connected with overcrowding, unsanitary buildings, and excessive rents." The evidence of Lord William Compton and Henry Trelawny Boodle in particular contained "strong condemnation of the whole system of building on leasehold tenure." They therefore argued "that legislation favorable to the acquisition on equitable terms of the freehold interest on the

17. TH, p. 340; 1887 (260) xiii.   Rep., p. 21; 1884–85 (4402) xxx.
18. Housing of the Working Classes. R. Com.

part of the leaseholder would conduce greatly to the improvement of the dwellings of the people of this country."[19] The reluctance of the Northampton estate to enforce the covenants in its building leases—along with the fact that those leases were not in themselves as stringent as they might have been—provided the exponents of leasehold enfranchisement with some of their most telling arguments. The wretched slums of Clerkenwell seemed inescapable proof that the London leasehold system was itself an evil. By breaking up the great landed estates in London and other towns they hoped to do away with one of the fundamental causes of urban decay.[20]

The Select Committee on Town Holdings did not content itself with examining the practices of a single estate, but took evidence with respect to many other large properties not only in London but throughout England, Wales, and Ireland. Their findings were more conflicting than those of the Royal Commission had been.

Some witnesses suggested that on many estates restrictive covenants were dead letters. Charles Harrison, one of the chief exponents of leasehold enfranchisement, did not believe "that the ground landlords very much interfere with the covenants to repair, so long as you pay the ground rent, until it comes towards the end of the term."[21] John R. Bourne, in his report for 1877 to the Duke of Bedford, defended such a policy:

> To be constantly interfering with lessees, even within authorized powers, is impolitic. Under newly granted building leases the value of the leasehold is greater than that of the freehold, and even under a twenty-one years repairing lease the lessee has always a margin of estate sufficiently valuable to be marketable and worth preserving. Self-interest may therefore be relied upon to largely influence the lessees in properly keeping and making the best use of their property, and this especially when coupled with the knowledge that a constant superintendence is being exercised.[22]

Francis Edwards, surveyor of the Evelyn estate in Deptford, admitted that he was "not too particular" about enforcing covenants. "Every now and then" he would take notice of the state of repair on the estate, "but we do not want to be

19. Ibid., p. 59.

20. For an account of the leasehold enfranchisement movement, see D. A. Reeder, "The Politics of Urban Leaseholds in Late Victorian England," *International Review of Social History,* 6 (1961), Part III.

21. TH, p. 335; 1886 (213) xii.

22. 1877 Report, 2, 2. Shirley Foster Murphy, the medical officer for St. Pancras, told the Royal Commissioners that the estates in his parish did little to enforce repairing covenants until the leases were about to expire. HWC, pp. 68–69; 1884–85 (4402-I) xxx.

objectionable, and intrude upon people unduly."[23] Edward Bailey, one of the trustees of the Portland Marylebone estate, said that it was quite common for tenants—shopkeepers in particular—to make minor alterations in their premises without first getting the landlord's consent, although they were legally forbidden to do so. Other estates, he thought, were even more lax in this respect: "I think you may say where there are gardens, and so forth, in front, you constantly see shops thrown out over them without the consent of the freeholder." On the Portland estate such a flagrant violation of the lease would not be permitted, "because we keep up a general supervision of our estate for the benefit of neighbors."[24]

Several witnesses spoke of the expense and difficulty of getting an action of ejectment through the courts. Charles Harrison referred to cases in which the court of chancery refused to enforce a covenant against a particular lessee because it considered that the neighborhood had so changed in character as to make such enforcement unreasonable. "Now that," Harrison argued, "is an illustration of a great number of those large London estates. They have started out with a particular scheme and a particular covenant. They have broken through those over and over again, and the result of it is, that on the big estates it is hardly possible to enforce a covenant where they are broken through."[25] Howard Martin, a surveyor and builder, commented on the notorious unwillingness of juries to deprive a tenant of his leasehold interest no matter how flagrantly he had broken the covenants.[26]

Other witnesses insisted that despite such difficulties landlords could and did enforce their covenants.[27] George B. Gregory, treasurer of the Foundling Hospital and at one time a member of the Town Holdings Committee, reported that he had found that lessees would usually comply with notices to repair without the landlord having to resort to legal proceedings. "In the case of the Foundling estate," he went on, "we have had expense in enforcing covenants for repair. The process is a somewhat cumbrous one and an expensive one, but we have done it."[28]

Frederick Cooper, a builder working in Beckenham, reported that the ground landlords in that area were "very strict" about enforcing covenants; one of them sent a surveyor on weekly inspection tours to see that they were lived up to. With respect to the periodical painting of the houses, "we have a specification

23. TH, p. 474; 1887 (260) xiii.
24. Ibid., p. 456.
25. Ibid., pp. 335–36; 1886 (213) xii.
26. Ibid., p. 99; 1887 (260) xiii.

27. See, for instance, the testimony of Edward Ryde, ibid., pp. 370–71; 1886 (213) xii.
28. Ibid., p. 173; 1887 (260) xiii.

to work to, and in that specification the color of the paint, and the time of painting, and various other things, is [sic] especially dictated by the surveyor."[29]

Although Charles Harrison denied that repairing covenants were ordinarily
enforced, he criticized some estates, notably that of the Bishop of London in
Paddington and the Crown estate in Regent's Park, for enforcing too strictly the
covenants against alterations, thereby preventing tenants from making improvements in their houses. On the Eyre estate in St. John's Wood, he charged,
"it is very difficult very often to obtain a release of the restrictive covenant against
carrying on schools. I have known of and have had property through my hand,"
he asserted, "in regard to which we have been compelled to refuse an eligible
tenant in all other respects, simply from our inability to obtain a license to carry
on a school, although there are a great number of schools in the district . . ."[30]

Probably the most unexceptionable generalization on the subject was made by
Edward Ryde, the surveyor and builder. The covenants, he said, "are very strict
in themselves, and they are more or less looked after, depending upon the way
in which the estate is managed." On the whole he thought that leasehold property in London was kept in better condition than comparable freehold property. "I think I could point to many ground landlords," he said, "who have
looked after and seen that their property has been maintained, and I think I
may speak from a pretty general knowledge of property round about London.
In some parts, no doubt, there has been neglect," he admitted, "but I think,
generally speaking, the property has been fairly well maintained."[31]

Repairing Covenants: The Bedford Estate

Both the Bedford and Foundling estates made serious and consistent efforts
to enforce the provisions in their leases. They found, however, that the forces
which were undermining the integrity of their original plans were too powerful
to be stopped by restrictive covenants. The whims of fashion, the tide of Irish im-
migration, the London and Birmingham Railway, and the determination of
Bloomsbury residents to take lodgers proved ultimately too strong. But however
limited the success of the two estates in maintaining their original character,
vigorous and continual enforcement of covenants did save Bloomsbury from
the fate of Clerkenwell.

The history of the Bedford estate from the late seventeenth century onward
has been one of creeping decline. The decline did not show itself in statistics of

29. Ibid., p. 318.   31. Ibid., p. 315.
30. Ibid., pp. 332–33; 1886 (213) xii.

annual income; the Duke inevitably profited from the general increase in land values in central London. It took place instead in the less tangible realm of fashion and bourgeois respectability.

By the early eighteenth century the noble occupants of the town houses in Covent Garden were moving westward toward the newer squares and streets of St. James's and Mayfair, and, to a lesser extent, northward into Bloomsbury. By the early nineteenth century parts of the Covent Garden estate were practically slums. The Bedford Office made sporadic, ineffectual attempts to arrest the decline, enforcing repairing covenants and insisting on substantial repairs or rebuilding whenever leases fell in. Such measures slowed the decline but could not halt it. During the middle nineteenth century the Bedford estate adopted a more vigorous and imaginative policy toward Covent Garden, where it embarked on a program of large-scale redevelopment. Having abandoned hopes of restoring its old residential character, it determined instead to transform it into the commercial center it has since become.

Bloomsbury had different problems. Except for a small area east of Woburn Place, it never threatened to turn into a slum. Instead it presented the Bedford Office with the task of preventing, or at least discouraging, the conversion of dwelling houses into private hotels, boarding houses, institutions, offices, and shops. Bloomsbury suffered in the nineteenth century from the same westward march of fashion that had so dramatically lowered the character of Covent Garden in the eighteenth. If the decline proved neither so sudden nor so great as it had in Covent Garden, the explanation lies in the more efficient techniques of estate management that the Bedford Office was by then employing.

Bloomsbury had started to decline before the close of the eighteenth century. It had never, since the seventeenth century, enjoyed anything like the social prestige of the neighborhoods of Pall Mall, Piccadilly, and Grosvenor Square. Despite the mansions in Great Russell Street and the noblemen's houses in Bedford Square, Bloomsbury had long ceased to be a center of fashion when, in the late 1790s, the fifth Duke determined to pull down Bedford House and move to Arlington Street. The fact that from 1800 the Duke of Bedford ceased to live on his own London estate indicates the force of the *Drang nach Westen* that characterizes the history of fashionable London.

For a comparison one is driven to Turner: "Stand at Cumberland Gap and watch the procession of civilization, marching single file—the buffalo following the trail to the salt springs, the Indian, the fur-trader and hunter, the cattle-raiser, the pioneer farmer . . . Stand at South Pass in the Rockies a century later and see the same procession with wider intervals between."[32] Standing at the Piazza in Covent Garden, Berkeley Square, and Queen's Gate in the eighteenth, nineteenth, and twentieth centuries one could have seen an analogous procession: the nobleman, followed by the wealthy merchant, the professional man, the charitable institution, the solicitor's office, the shop—all moving inexorably westward.

The process was not very far advanced in 1800, and the new streets that grew up on the site of Bedford House and its grounds easily attracted inhabitants of the first respectability. Russell Square, Dobie wrote in the 1830s, "has, from its first formation, been a favorite residence of the highest legal characters; and here merchants and bankers have seated themselves and families, the air and situation uniting to render it a pleasant retreat from the cares of business."[33] In 1844 a writer characterized the inhabitants of Bloomsbury as "the aristocracy of the City and the Inns of Court." The proximity of the British Museum and the new London University had attracted "the scientific section of London literary men" to the neighborhood. "The wealthy," he wrote, "who had no particular ambition of belonging to the first fashion, have long been attracted to this quarter by its proximity to the open fields . . . A society is here formed," he concluded, "which already rivals that of the west end, as the noblesse of robe and the rich fermiers-general rivaled in anterevolutionary France the high aristocracy."[34] (Figures 70 and 71 give an attractive picture of Bedford Square in 1851.)

Yet as early as 1830 the demand for houses of the first rate in Bloomsbury had noticeably diminished. The difficulties experienced by Cubitt in finding tenants for his houses in Tavistock Square and the long delay in the completion of Gordon Square both exemplify the general decline. In January 1832 auditor W. G. Adam predicted a fall in the Middlesex receipts for the year, due in part to "the change that seems taking place in the fashion as to the places of residence . . ."[35] His successor, Christopher Haedy, wrote to the Duke in 1840 about the problems raised by "the disposition which exists to move westwardly." He believed that "the great struggle not infrequently is between men in business and their wives and daughters. Their convenience would keep them here within easy reach of their places of business, but their wives and daughters would give the preference to a more fashionable residence at the west or

32. Frederick Jackson Turner, *The Frontier in American History* (New York, Henry Holt and Co., 1921), p. 12.

33. Dobie, p. 171. In an earlier decade Russell Square had been the address of both the Sedley

and Osborne families, and here Becky Sharp began her social career.

34. Weir, "The Squares of London," in Knight, *London, 6,* 199.

35. 1831 Report.

70. Bedford Square, east side, looking south, 1851

71. Bedford Square, east side, looking north, 1851

72. White Hart Street, Covent Garden, north side, in 1898.
Pulled down 1902

73. Shops in Everett Street (now Marchmont Street), looking
south into Bernard Street, in 1963

northwest ends of the town."[36] The problem was how to thwart the wives and daughters in their evil designs.

To make matters worse, tenement houses were establishing themselves on all three of the Bedford estates. By February 1886 the steward reported that, excluding houses let in part as chambers or furnished apartments, there were 395 tenement houses on the London estate. Of these 135 were in Bedford New Town, 140 in Bloomsbury, and 120 in Covent Garden. On all three estates they occupied the lesser streets and courts; Goldington Crescent, Bedford New Town, which had three lodging houses, was the only square included.

The disproportionate number in Bedford New Town—where they were four times as common as in Bloomsbury—indicates the rapidly falling character of that neighborhood, despite the excellence of its original plan. The steward suggested that the respectable families which had once occupied most of Bedford New Town had moved to the suburbs. Their houses thereupon gradually fell "into the category of tenement houses, the Duke's lessees finding it necessary to bend to the altered circumstances."

In the squares and principal streets of Bloomsbury the houses were either in separate occupation or sublet as "furnished apartments," not as unfurnished rooms. "The portions of the Bloomsbury estate in which the tenement houses are found," the steward observed, "are chiefly those that are affected by the commercial influence, and where the size and consequent rent would make impossible a separate occupation by a single family of the working class." The tenements were almost without exception either east of Woburn Place or south of Great Russell Street. Little Russell Street alone had twenty-one.

In Covent Garden the tenement houses were chiefly to be found in the courts off Drury Lane, or in their immediate vicinity. Most of their leases had been "granted in contemplation of the premises being used as tenement houses—the situation being in the very heart of a neighborhood densely populated by the laboring classes. The sites of these houses," remarked the steward, "if not used for manufacturing purposes, would always be occupied by buildings let out in separate tenements." The tenements varied in character from that of "perfect respectability through all the grades down to the level that is reached in White Hart Street, Drury Lane" (Fig. 72). Their occupants varied from the "well-to-do working, trading, and lower middle-class people" to the "poorest of day laborers, hucksters, etc."[37]

---

36. C. Haedy to the Duke of Bedford, 25 May 1840. See also Davis, "University Site," pp. 94–103, for a discussion of the social decline of Bloomsbury in the nineteenth century.

37. London Reports, 2, 51, 54–55 (18 February 1886).

In order to combat the decay, the Bedford Office, during the nineteenth century, grew gradually more despotic and at the same time more enlightened. The control it exercised over its property grew steadily in intensity and increasingly systematic. The passion for facts, for tables, for statistics, for exhaustive surveys resulted in volumes of annual reports that grew ever larger and more detailed.

Before 1815 there were no periodical summaries of developments on the Bedford estates beyond the inevitable rentals and account books. The chief agent kept in touch with the stewards of the scattered estates and with the Duke by means of personal visits, and by frequent letters dealing with day-to-day occurrences and problems. By the middle nineteenth century new methods, of which Jeremy Bentham himself would have approved, had imposed themselves on the old informally paternalistic pattern. Systematic donations to approved charitable institutions and the building of schools, churches, and model cottages had replaced the older, more indiscriminate charity to the poor on the estates. Every item of expenditure, no matter how trivial, on every one of the Duke's estates and in each of his households was now carefully accounted for. Elaborate annual tables listed the number of fires lit on each floor of Woburn Abbey every month, the consumption of wines and spirits in the servants' dining room at Belgrave Square, and the housekeeper's wages at Norris Castle, Isle of Wight. Surveys and inspections of every conceivable sort produced long reports, replete with statistics.[38]

The greater emphasis on inspection, reports, and control affected the London estates as much as the country property. An urban landlord could not possibly exercise over his tenants as much power as a rural landlord. There could be no sort of personal relationship between landlord and tenant in a city like London. Yet the Bedford Office was able to practice a kind of institutionalized paternalism even in dealing with its tenants in London.

Such paternalism served to protect the Duke's tenants from one another. A single house in a state of decay or converted into a place of business could damage an entire street. In working to protect the Duke's reversionary interests, the Bedford Office inevitably enhanced the value of the leasehold interests as well.

Over the years the leases grew gradually more strict, as the Duke's agents added new and more rigid covenants. In the seventeenth century the leases had not even prohibited the conversion of houses into shops.[39] By 1776 the estate had established a policy of prohibiting all business in its new developments

---

38. David Spring, *The English Landed Estate in the Nineteenth Century*, pp. 26–34, attributes many of these changes to the initiative of the seventh Duke, who succeeded to the title in 1839.

39. Gladys Scott Thomson, *The Russells in Bloomsbury*, pp. 43–44, 178.

north of Great Russell Street. Where it did permit shops to exist, it kept them under control by means of restrictions in the licenses it granted.

A report from James Gubbins, the estate surveyor, to John Gotobed, the solicitor, dated 16 November 1797, in relation to a proposed bookshop in Covent Garden, illustrates the policy which the estate was trying to pursue. Since the house in question had for some time been used as a shop, Gubbins thought that there could be no objection to letting it to a bookseller. "As to the other question whether it would be prudent to permit sales of books by auction, contrary to the restrictions in the Duke's leases," Gubbins advised that it be permitted, "if no abuse is made of it, such as keeping porters and men at the door to invite in customers, or selling anything but books." He further observed that it had "become a general practice amongst booksellers of selling books by auction," giving as an example Messrs. Leigh and Southby of York Street, Covent Garden: "they are people of respectability, and are the means of bringing trade to the neighborhood by the genteel attendance on their sales."

But trade was not to be of the sort which might offend the other tenants. Thus on 26 January 1804 Thomas Pearce Brown, an associate of Gotobed, wrote to a tenant to warn him against opening a poulterer's shop. Other tenants had complained to the estate office, "and it being a trade always excepted in the leases, and certainly a very offensive one, it leaves us no option," wrote Brown, "but to oppose it in the first instance, and it will be our duty to serve an ejectment as soon as it is attempted to be opened, and which we must certainly do."

Sometimes the estate inserted the license in the lease itself. Thus a twenty-one-year repairing lease in 1805 omitted the word "butcher" from the list of prohibited trades. The lessee on his part promised "within twenty-four hours after killing any sheep, lamb, hog, or beast [to] remove all the blood and offal from and well and sufficiently cleanse the said premises."[40]

The estate did not object to trade or manufacture in Covent Garden, or in the streets of southern Bloomsbury, so long as it was not productive of nuisance. The important streets of northern Bloomsbury and all of the squares were quite a different matter. The Bedford Office fought long and vigorously to preserve Bloomsbury as an eastern outpost of the Gentleman's Private Residence. The danger was not so much conversion into shops as the alteration of houses into private hotels, boarding houses, and solicitors' offices.

At first the threat came not from offices and institutions but from tenants subletting parts of their houses. A sign advertising chambers in a house at the corner of Russell Square and Keppel Street in the late 1820s caused the Duke's

40. Abstract of Leases (1799–1805), fol. 364 (25 March 1805).

auditor to lose all control over his punctuation: "Such an application would degrade the estate," he wrote. "How can it be prevented if possible it must I am quite alarmed at it."[41]

Adam was justified in his alarm. By the middle of the century many of the large houses in Bloomsbury had been illegally converted into private hotels. During the 1850s and 60s the Bedford Office engaged in a good deal of litigation to force its lessees to discontinue the operation of such hotels. Bloomsbury today demonstrates that in the long run it was a losing battle.

What one steward described as "the lodging house dry rot" proved impossible to eradicate. In December 1890 A. R. O. Stutfield, the steward, reported increasing concern over the problem of boarding and lodging houses. For many years their number had, "notwithstanding many warnings and occasional legal proceedings, been constantly on the increase, until at the present time it may be said that some streets are almost entirely occupied by persons carrying on these businesses." In other streets, such as Montague Place and Upper Woburn Place, the evil was "of comparatively recent growth, and might by the adoption of stringent measures be checked." He recommended that "as regards the boarding houses it would be advisable to select one or two of the most flagrant cases, and that application should be made for an injunction to restrain the occupiers of the houses in question from carrying on that business." He suggested "that the knowledge that stringent measures for enforcing the covenants were being taken in certain portions of his Grace's property . . . [might] operate as a wholesome check to the spread of a disease which, unless stopped, will, it is to be feared, bring about the deterioration of the whole estate."[42]

The estate's policy toward boarding houses was not inflexible. By 1892 Stutfield had come to regard Montague Place as a lost cause. The circumstances of the street had altered, he explained in his report. Two of the old residents had died, and more houses had fallen into the hands of lodging-house keepers. While not recommending action against them, he did not advise that they be granted licenses, since, he pointed out, "these houses so frequently deteriorate (especially towards the end of a lease) that it is well to keep the slight hold over the occupants which is afforded by the provisions of the existing leases."[43]

Prior to the latter part of the nineteenth century, the estate systematically inspected leasehold property only when the leases were about to expire; at that time the surveyor always made a careful examination in order to prepare the schedules of dilapidations. By 1878, when the leases of a great deal of Blooms-

41. W. G. Adam to C. Haedy, 11 July 1828.   43. Ibid., pp. 275–76 (10 November 1892).
42. London Reports, 2, 134–35 (11 Dec. 1890).

bury were running out, the Duke's steward had grown concerned over the condition of property on the estate. The deterioration in some of the mews in particular was, he wrote, "so great as to have become almost a scandal." While few parts of the estate were then comparable to the notorious Abbey Place,[44] there were sections which might "rapidly fall into a condition as bad unless prompt measures are taken to prevent it." He proposed that the Duke's rights of entry and inspection be exercised, "in the first place upon those parts (and isolated houses) that are in the worst condition, and afterwards to have the whole estate surveyed in sections, so as to bring each section under periodical inspection of more than a mere superficial character." Nothing less would suffice, he thought, to "preserve the character and condition of the estate." He was prepared to meet the expected opposition and ill will with firmness and tact, and observed that "the temporary evil may well be encountered for the sake of the permanent good." Much as he disliked legal proceedings, he would not hesitate to advise them, "if they became necessary to arrest the deterioration of any section of the estate. If the course above indicated had been in use in the Bedford Office during the last quarter of a century," he concluded, "such a condition of things as that which exists in Little Coram Street and elsewhere would not have been possible, and the adverse criticism both public and private to which the estate has been subjected would have been spared."[45]

The report for 1879 mentions an inspection of Torrington Mews, followed by notices to repair; the following year the Bedford Office sent a number of informal notices with respect to paint and external repair to lessees in Bedford New Town.[46] But the estate seems not to have persisted in its new policy, for in 1894 the steward's report again suggested that a system of periodical surveys of the whole estate be inaugurated. Stutfield deplored the tendency of lessees to shirk their responsibilities for repairs by selling their lease seven or eight years before it expired to anyone who would buy it. A purchaser under such conditions, he remarked, was not likely to "take a very exalted view of the responsibility he is undertaking . . ." Under such circumstances, "houses which have for years been systematically neglected and wastefully used come in hand at the expiration of their terms in a state bordering upon ruin, and the last owners of the leases are found to be people against whom it would be useless to take any legal proceedings." The Duke therefore approved a recommendation that in the future surveys be made at intervals during the last twenty years of a long

44. See below, pp. 137–43, for a discussion of Abbey Place and other slum property on the Bedford estate.

45. 1878 Report, 2, 1–2.
46. 1879 Report, 2, 4; 1880 Report, 2, 3.

lease, and eight years before the expiration of a twenty-one-year or shorter lease.[47]

If the Bedford Office was unable to maintain Bloomsbury as a wholly residential district, it has been fairly successful in making it look residential even when it isn't. If there were to be offices in Bloomsbury, the estate saw to it that they were offices of the most respectable sort. If the new tenants would insist on making a "show of business," the estate saw to it that the show amounted to no more than a neat brass plate beside the front door. Even if the street or square was wholly given over to solicitors' offices and institutions, the Bedford Office saw to it that the houses continued to look like gentlemen's private residences. Bedford Square today indicates how successful such a policy can be.

Enforcement of Repairing Covenants: The Foundling Estate

Like the Bedford estate, the Foundling Hospital hoped to safeguard the reversionary value of its property by preserving the status quo. Where this was impossible the Hospital, too, tried by compromises and strategic retreats to limit change and control its speed and direction. For a variety of reasons the Foundling Hospital was less successful in preventing the decay of its part of Bloomsbury than was the Bedford Office of its part. Neither did it wholly fail; the governors were able to preserve their estate as a peninsula of gentility surrounded on three sides by poverty and squalor. All, that is, except for a few stubborn courts and mews toward the western boundary, which resisted all conventional attempts to raise them to a level of decency.[48]

During the building of their estate, the governors of the Hospital were intensely interested in seeing that the builders adhered strictly to the specifications in their contracts. If they did not feel deeply about the aesthetic qualities of the new buildings, they did on the question of structural soundness. A house need not necessarily be a work of art; it had to be substantially built. The great battles between Cockerell and Kay on the one hand and their enemies on the

47. 1894 Report, pp. 140–41.

48. As a means of demonstrating the differing death rates in different classes of streets, the Registrar of Births, Marriages, and Deaths in the district of Gray's Inn Lane divided streets in the area into four main categories. The highest, occupied by "merchants and professional gentlemen," consisted exclusively of streets on the Foundling estate: Mecklenburgh and Brunswick squares; Guilford, Heathcote, and Bernard streets, and Lansdown Place. In the second, occupied by "respectable tradesmen and lodgers, not over crowded," he included Compton Street. The only street on the Foundling estate which he included in the category, "laborers, costermongers, and poor mechanics," was Compton Place. Parliamentary Papers, State of Large Towns and Populous Districts. R. Com. mins. of ev., p. 254; 1844 [572] xvii.

other all revolved, ostensibly at least, around questions of the structural qualities of the houses.

Once the houses were finished and leased, the burning interest in matters of structure and durability died down. For the first few years most of the houses were too new and too respectably inhabited to show any flagrant signs of decay. Yet in the 1830s the discovery of the existence of a miniature slum that had grown up in certain of the courts on the western part of the estate roused the governors from their complacency. Here the problem of disrepair was linked with problems of drainage, water supply, overcrowding, and crime. So squalid were the courts and alleys that ordinary methods—inspection, and the rigid enforcement of covenants—proved insufficient to put down the nuisances. Ultimately the solution came only with the demolition of the tenements and the rebuilding of the sites. But for decades the courts leading off Little Coram Street illustrated, quite as vividly as the worst parts of the Northampton estate, the limitations of the London leasehold system.

But the greater part of the property seemed to require little attention. As long as the larger houses continued to be gentlemen's private residences, the governors were reluctant to exercise their rights of inspection elsewhere than in the courts and mews. Not until 1840 did a special committee recommend that the surveyor "be required to inspect or cause to be inspected frequently the property of the estate, and make reports . . . of any and all breaches of covenants . . . and the then state of the property . . ."[49] The surveys were at first superficial. "I presume," wrote Kay in his first quarterly report, "that . . . it is not intended to enter upon internal surveys, except where the exterior may indicate any necessity for such examination, nor upon inquiries as to present occupations long continued, unless upon a representation by adjoining tenants, or actual observation of nuisance or inconvenience arising therefrom."[50]

Over the next two decades the reports of the surveyor show an increasing attention to the condition of the houses on the estate. Notices to repair were no longer confined to courts and mews. The surveyor's final report for 1856 listed no fewer than one hundred and one premises.[51] Yet despite the attention paid by Kay and his successor Henry Currey in seeing that the lessees carried out the stipulated repairs, the character of the estate declined. In 1827 the estate paving commissioners received a petition from thirty-four inhabitants in Hunter Street which indicated that the neighborhood was even then not characterized by perfect decorum:

49. General Committee, 45, 357.
50. Ibid., 46, 23 (6 January 1841).

51. Ibid., 54, 178–80.

Hunter Street . . . has become the common walk of the lowest prostitutes, who congregate at the doors and under the windows of the inhabitants, and make use of such indecent and improper language that
the wives and daughters of the inhabitants cannot but hear it while
sitting in their parlours and drawing rooms; and frequently grossly in-
sult the visitors of the inhabitants and the female domestics, and are
altogether such a nuisance that it is now exceedingly unpleasant to
reside in the street. It also causes several of the houses to remain unlet,
and must ultimately occasion a considerable depreciation in the value
of the property belonging to the Hospital.[52]

The commissioners similarly learned in 1845 "that loose and disorderly women
frequented both Brunswick and Mecklenburgh squares at late hours of the
night, to the great annoyance of the householders."[53]

In July 1863 John Brownlow, the secretary of the Hospital, tried to assess the
causes of the creeping decay. A great deal of it, he thought, had been inevitable:
"Neighborhoods have their rise and fall, and depend for the character of their
occupation very much on fashion or caprice." Yet if depreciation was unavoidable, "it is the more desirable every means should be taken to make this depreciation as gradual as possible, and to offer as many checks to its decline as
may be convenient . . ." One way to retard the decay, he believed, was by "the
appointment of necessary officers to watch and control it . . ." To supplement
the activities of the surveyor, he recommended that the Hospital employ "a
person of lower caste, such as a resident inspector of nuisances . . ."

Something of this sort had in fact existed before 1855, when the Metropolis
Management Act brought to an end the estate paving commission. The Foundling estate commissioners had employed both "a surveyor of pavements and a
beadle—the latter perambulating the estate every day, and both . . . in constant
communication with the secretary [of the Hospital]—their headquarters being
at his office." Under such a system, "the secretary received instant information
of nuisances and breaches of the covenants of the leases, and was thus enabled
. . . to act promptly for their removal or remedy." Since 1855 no such system of
continuous inspection had existed, with the result that "the constantly recurring nuisances and breaches remain for the most part unchecked, which has

52. Foundling Estate Paving Commission Minutes, 5, 292.

53. Ibid., 8, 166. Three years later they reported "that disorderly persons are in the habit
of frequenting the northeastern angle of Brunswick Square, and the northwestern angle of
Mecklenburgh Square for immoral purposes."
Ibid., p. 352 (8 June 1848).

produced invidious comparisons with the management of a neighboring estate by no means complimentary to that of the Hospital."[54]

In 1865 a committee of governors came to similar conclusions. They deplored, as was customary, the state of Compton Place and the courts leading off Little Coram Street. They noted the large number of businesses being carried on without proper licenses. They considered the problem of the general decline of the estate. "The natural deterioration of house property as the leases advance towards their termination, and the low character of a large portion of that on the Hospital estate (inviting as it does occupiers driven out of other districts by the improvements in progress there) calls," they argued, "for increased vigilance on the part of those whose ultimate interests, as trustees, will materially depend on the condition of the property when it shall fall into their hands."[55]

The surveyor and solicitor agreed that the wretched condition of the back courts and alleys, as well as "the short terms now unexpired of some of the leases," made increased supervision essential. They recommended that the governors appoint an assistant to the surveyor, who could devote his whole time to inspecting the state of repair and occupation of the buildings.[56] In December 1865 the General Court agreed to the appointment of an inspector, who was to "perambulate the estate . . . and report weekly in a book to be laid before the [general] committee any irregularity or apparent breaches of the covenants of the leases, or any other matter he may think deserving of notice."[57] The committee elected William S. Wintle to the new office.[58]

Wintle's appointment at once intensified the processes of management. Every week the general committee—or simply "the committee," as it was now called—read his report and proceeded to recommend or oppose a license, an order to repair, or any other actions that the inspector suggested. The number of licenses granted—mostly no doubt regularizing breaches of covenant that had been long ignored—and of notices to repair increased remarkably.

In April 1872, on the resignation of Brownlow, the governors appointed Wintle to succeed him as secretary.[59] The new secretary continued to carry out his duties as inspector. Not until December 1892 did the General Court appoint another inspector, John B. Chubb, to assist Wintle.[60] Chubb gradually took

---

54. General Committee, 57, 436–38. The "neighboring estate" was of course the Bedford estate. The estates to the north, east, and south of the Foundling Hospital were by then little more than slums.

55. Ibid., 59, 150–53.

56. Ibid., p. 227 (16 September 1865).

57. General Court, 8, 99–100.

58. General Committee, 59, 327 (3 February 1866).

59. Ibid., 63, 17.

60. General Court, 9, 201.

over more and more of the surveyor's duties, and in 1899 the Hospital dispensed entirely with Henry Currey's services.[61]

Business and Residential Zoning: The Foundling Estate

One evident flaw in the original building plan of the Foundling estate was its wholly residential character. Except for the Hospital itself, the estate was to consist exclusively of streets of single-family houses served by stables and coach-houses in the mews. Although Cockerell's 1790 plan contemplated the building of houses in the Gray's Inn Road which could be easily converted into shops, it made no provision for the building of shops in the first instance.[62] Unlike many earlier developments, the Foundling estate had no market. Neither did it, in its original form, include anything in the nature of a shopping or business center. On paper, at least, it was to be a dormitory suburb and nothing more.

Such a situation could not last long, despite the covenants against trade in the leases. Before long, tenants in the lesser streets began applying for permission to convert their houses into cheesemongers', butchers', coal and potato merchants', or bakers' shops. In most instances the governors were eventually forced to grant the requests.

The wastefulness of building a private house only to have it immediately converted into a shop is evident, even when it is remembered that in the eighteenth century shops did not differ much in point of structure from private houses. The process of conversion inevitably brought angry protests from neighboring householders, who had moved into the street on the assumption that it would retain its residential character.

The governors, too, wanted the estate to retain as nearly as possible its original form. But the absence of shops and the overabundance of private houses made some sort of change necessary. The problem was to make it take place in an orderly fashion. The surveyor and the governors had to decide first of all in which streets they would permit shops and which streets should remain unsullied by trade. In addition, they had to decide which trades were so noxious that they had to be excluded altogether from the estate. Once they had agreed on a rational policy toward licenses for trade and business, they had to enforce that policy, and this was most difficult of all.

As early as 1802 the building committee was granting licenses to tenants in Millman Street to use their premises as a public house, in one instance, and a

---

61. General Committee, 77, 64–65, 70.

62. Building Committee, *1*, 10 (28 December 1790).

greengrocer's shop, in another. According to Cockerell, such alterations were "not contrary to the original intention of other builders in that street, who have found the houses suitable for shops . . ." He advised the committee against licensing "the cobbler's stall, or any other encroachment upon the front line of the street."[63] In 1808 the building committee acted to prohibit the holding of public auctions in a house in Great Coram Street.[64]

In April 1809 George Payne and Thomas Penthrin, who had contracted to build second-rate houses in Cox (later Compton) Street, asked permission "to build the said houses for respectable shops . . . as we have had a great many applications for shops in that street, and as there are a great many private houses at present not let, we are induced to think that it will be a general good." Their request was not granted.[65]

Two years later James Smith was denied permission to convert his house in Compton Street into a shop. Kay observed "that as that street has always been considered as intended for private houses only, and many purchases have been made of leases from the builders upon the idea of its continuing so, such permission cannot be granted without some degree of injustice to those purchasers . . ." He laid down the general rule that "unless by a general concurrence of the persons interested in the property of the street, it would not be right to admit the principle of making any alteration in its present character . . ."[66]

The committee did not object in principle to shops in streets of a lower order than Compton Street. It had, for example, granted permission for a butter and cheesemonger's shop and a milliner's shop in Kenton Street.[67] It also permitted shops in Upper Marchmont Street.[68] By 1811 the general committee had evolved a flexible zoning policy. Kenton and Marchmont streets were to become shopping streets. Great Coram and Compton streets were to remain entirely residential. The dividing line ran roughly between streets consisting chiefly of second-rate houses and those consisting of third-rate or smaller houses.

Such considerations continued to guide estate policy throughout the century. In July 1849, recommending the denial of an application to convert two houses in Great Coram Street into shops, Currey observed that "as the immediate locality is at present composed of private residences, I do not think it would be desirable to sanction such a conversion." He advised that "permission for shops . . . be confined to certain localities, such as Everett, Wilmot, Marchmont, and

63. Ibid., 2, 43–44.
64. Ibid., 3, 119.
65. Ibid., p. 181.

66. General Committee, 31, 172–73 (26 June 1811).
67. Ibid., p. 11 (12 September 1810).
68. Ibid., p. 238 (6 November 1811).

Kenton Streets, which are at present principally occupied by parties in trade, and where no objections are likely to be raised by owners of adjoining property."[69] (See Figure 73 for shops in Everett Street.)

It was not easy to guide the proper trades into the proper streets. No matter how strongly the landlord was determined to maintain a given street as a street of gentlemen's private residences, he would fail unless enough private gentlemen were willing to live in the street. The alternative to shops then became not private houses but empty houses. Furthermore, a tenant might choose to ignore the terms in his lease prohibiting trade, and defy—often successfully—the attempts of the landlord to enforce the relevant covenants.

The general committee had to back down on its policy for Compton Street as early as 1812, when it authorized one of its tenants to convert his house there into a shop.[70] Having granted one license, it could not consistently refuse to grant others, and before long Compton Street joined the lowly Marchmont and Millman streets as a shopping area.

The granting of business licenses often brought on a flood of protests from neighboring householders. The minutes of the general committee are filled with tenants' angry letters complaining about nuisances committed by other tenants. In many such cases the governors declined to interfere. Only when the nuisance was flagrant and the offense obvious did the committee resort to legal action. And even when it did successfully achieve an action of ejectment, it ordinarily came to an understanding with the erring tenant, by which he would be permitted to retain his lease in return for abating the nuisance.

The Hospital realized that it could not be too demanding of its tenants. Mr. Currey, in April 1855, reported that "the trades and businesses professed and shown to be carried on [in Henrietta—now Handel—Street] are of the lowest description. The street," he observed, "has much depreciated, and the owners are induced to admit of such tenants as the only means of letting their property." One of the private tenants in the street had written to complain about the situation, explaining that he had "purchased his house on the faith of the covenants in the leases prohibiting any public show of business . . ." The surveyor recommended that the Hospital attempt to enforce the covenants, but was afraid that the result might be that the houses would "either stand empty, or become occupied by even a more objectionable class of tenants, in which case it may be desirable to consider whether the whole street should not be permitted to be converted into shops as the lesser evil of the two."[71]

69. Ibid., *50*, 421.   71. Ibid., *53*, 311.
70. Ibid., *32*, 126–27.

On 31 January 1816 the general committee read a memorial signed by twenty-seven tenants, protesting the granting of a license for a butcher's shop at the corner of Hunter and Henrietta streets. "The value of our situations as private residences," they predicted, ". . . will be greatly depreciated by your admission of a nuisance which is not suffered in many of the most inferior streets of the metropolis, and is consequently incompatible with a respectable neighborhood."[72] The governors had not in fact granted a license at all, but took no action.

It later developed that another butcher's shop had appeared one block north, and was making an illegal show of business not only toward Compton Street—in which trade was elsewhere permitted—but on the side facing the more respectable Hunter Street as well. Still worse, the proprietor was slaughtering animals on the premises. The general committee thereupon ordered the lessee to discontinue all show of business toward Hunter Street and to stop the slaughtering.[73] The only response was a letter from the butcher, Mr. Dare, informing the governors that he had taken premises in Compton Mews, "with a view of converting them into a private slaughter house." The governors informed him that, "should he persist in his intention, the committee will proceed to inquire upon what authority he has opened a butcher's shop upon this estate."[74]

On 17 July the committee read a letter from Edward Brown of Hunter Street, asserting that "Mr. Dare still continues not only to make a show of business towards Hunter Street, but also to slaughter meat; sheep and lambs are continually driven into the premises, and yesterday I saw two calves driven into the shop." The family of Mr. Cartwright in Hunter Street, Brown continued, "have found the smell and vapor arising from the warm blood very offensive . . ."[75] In September Dare having removed all the causes of the objections of the neighborhood to his business, the general committee granted him a license, prohibiting slaughtering and any show of business toward Hunter Street.[76] The following month Mr. Brown wrote again to complain "of the manner in which Mr. Dare the butcher keeps his blinds in the window next Hunter Street."[77] The committee sent a notice to desist, and the complaints ceased.

One of the more protracted struggles to preserve a street from the pollution of trade began late in 1822, when a tenant of a Joseph Evans began to convert the house at 1 Heathcote Street into a bakery. The other inhabitants of the street immediately complained to the general committee.[78] The committee or-

72. Ibid., *33*, 395–96.
73. Ibid., p. 439 (17 April 1816).
74. Ibid., p. 448 (1 May 1816).
75. Ibid., *34*, 17.

76. Ibid., p. 50.
77. Ibid., p. 70 (16 October 1816).
78. Ibid., *36*, 415 (6 November 1822).

dered the solicitor to take the necessary measures to prevent the establishment of the bakery.[79] The building of the gate at the east end of Heathcote Street, cutting off easy communication with the Gray's Inn Road, had given it a fair degree of respectability, which the governors were determined to maintain.

Evans and his tenant long defied the efforts of the Hospital to close the bakery. In June 1823 William Whitelaw, the sub-lessee of one of the houses in the street, wrote to protest. "The houses," he reminded the committee, "are all tenanted by persons of great respectability, several of whom have paid premiums for the purchase of their leases . . ." His own tenant, Mrs. Harrison, had warned him that if the annoyance of the bakery was not speedily removed, she would move out of the house. "Mrs. Harrison truly states that it is not merely the nuisance of the shop and the disagreeable smells proceeding from it and the oven by which she is annoyed, but she finds herself much disturbed by the house being let out in lodgings, particularly to that class of persons who alone generally lodge at a baker's shop." Whitelaw estimated that the shop would lower the value of his own house by at least £20 annually.[80]

The governors eventually instituted proceedings of ejectment. In July 1825 the Hospital solicitor reported that Evans had forfeited his lease of nine houses in Heathcote Street and Gray's Inn Road. On his agreeing to reinstate the bakery as a private house and pay £200 toward the legal costs of the Hospital,[81] the governors dropped the proceedings, and allowed Evans to retain his lease.[82]

Such instances were dramatic but exceptional. Where there were no serious complaints, the Hospital was usually quite willing to grant licenses for respectable trades in all but the most important streets. In December 1832, recommending a license for a chemist's shop at the corner of Great Coram and Kenton streets, Kay observed that it was "desirable for the general interest of the property to give encouragement for the establishment of respectable houses of business in similar situations, when it can be done under proper limitation . . ." The house in question had been empty for five years, "and in the present depressed state of house property, particularly in private houses, there seems but little chance of its being let except in the manner now proposed . . ." He thought the altered occupation would prove "highly respectable, being for the residence of a medical practitioner, who has resided on the estate in Marchmont Street for many years."[83] He knew of no objection by the neighborhood and had no intention of making a personal inquiry to find out if there were any. "Such voluntary

79. Ibid., p. 426 (20 November 1822).
80. Ibid., 37, 56.
81. Amounting in all to £274 11s. 8d.

82. General Committee, 37, 471.
83. One wonders if it might have been Mr. Wingfield.

interference on my part might," he feared, "occasion fancied and groundless objections to any alteration whatever . . ."[84]

However lenient it might be elsewhere, the Hospital was always particularly loath to grant licenses for innovations of any sort in the two squares. In February 1868 the committee rejected an application to let chambers in a house in Brunswick Square. Currey advised that although "in certain portions of the estate such approbation might not be objectionable . . . a distinction should be drawn between the squares and the streets, and . . . it would not be desirable to introduce the business element into the best residential portions of the estate."[85]

In 1888 the committee, bowing to the inevitable, resolved to permit the exhibition of "board and residence" notices on all parts of the estate except in Brunswick and Mecklenburgh squares.[86] It was not unalterably opposed to lodging houses in Brunswick Square, so long as they were managed unobtrusively. In February 1892 it granted a license to a lessee in Brunswick Square "to let apartments, but not to make any show of so doing by cards, brass plate, or otherwise."[87] Not until September 1909 did the committee approve in principle of boarding houses in Mecklenburgh Square, and even then it insisted that there be no show of such occupation.[88]

84. General Committee, *41*, 316–17.
85. Ibid., *60*, 388.
86. Ibid., *71*, 369.

87. Ibid., *73*, 225.
88. Ibid., *81*, 537.

7 *Leasehold Slums*

Close to the splendid houses of the rich . . . a lurking place of the bitter-
est poverty may often be found. So, a short time ago, on the occasion of
a coroner's inquest, a region close to Portman Square, one of the very
respectable squares, was characterised as an abode "of a multitude of
Irish demoralised by poverty and filth."—F. Engels, The Condition of
the Working Class in England (1845), trans. W. O. Henderson and
W. H. Chaloner (Oxford, Basil Blackwell), 1958

The experience of the Bedford and Foundling estates would seem to confirm the
inconclusive findings of the Committee on Town Holdings about the effect of
restrictive covenants on the appearance and condition of London. While it is
probably true that Bloomsbury would have sunk farther and faster had it not
been for the efforts of the two estates, it is equally true that street after street
intended for gentlemen of the highest respectability and their numerous families became instead streets of private hotels, solicitors' offices, greengrocers'
shops, students' hostels, and institutional headquarters.

The shabby gentility of latter-day Bloomsbury represents only a partial failure of estate management: private hotels and greengrocers' shops must, after all,
exist somewhere. The existence of a slum, on the other hand, represents a failure of the community as a whole, a problem different in kind as well as in
degree from the natural deterioration of a middle-class neighborhood. As such,
it required a different sort of treatment. Landlords tended to deal with slums as
if they were simply extreme cases of deteriorating neighborhoods. But techniques which were successful in middle-class streets proved powerless to inhibit
the growth of slums.

What made slums particularly resistant to control, either by ground landlords or by local authorities, was that the occupants were neither legally responsible for nor financially capable of maintaining their residences in proper condition. The leaseholder—the "middleman" or "house-farmer"—was legally
obliged to carry out necessary repairs, but in practice was either unwilling or unable to do so. If he was a large-scale owner of slum property, he would not him-

self have to live in such circumstances: his own comfort would not suffer from neglected repairs. If he found it possible to get tenants to pay weekly rents for substandard accommodation, he would have little economic incentive to improve the standard. Usually the worst slum landlords were not the big ones but the small investors, possessing perhaps a single tenement house in which they themselves might live, and simply not having the capital to keep it in decent repair. The situation of both kinds was essentially the same whether they were leaseholders—as they usually were in London—or freeholders—as was more common in many provincial towns.

Certain conditions conducive to slums were beyond the control of either the leaseholder or the occupant, but not of the ground landlord or the local authority. The openness of the layout of the quarter, the adequacy of the drainage, the state of the paving, the nature of the water supply could in many instances mean the difference between working-class comfort and a slum. The local authority or the freeholder could sometimes intervene to introduce improvements, particularly with respect to drainage and ventilation. The cholera epidemic in the early 1850s shocked local authorities and ground landlords alike into taking action to improve drainage and sanitation wherever they had been most flagrantly neglected.

The gradual revelation by royal and parliamentary commissions and by individual investigators of the shocking conditions to be found in the slums of London and other large towns made the "slum landlord" a figure of general detestation. It is unfortunate that the English language does not distinguish between the landlord who lets out house property on building or repairing leases and the landlord (often a lessee or sub-lessee of the other kind) who lets out rooms on weekly tenancies. Of the latter it might sometimes be said that he profited from the misery of the slum dwellers; of the former it was never true.

The ground landlord did not and could not profit from slums on his estate, any more than the community as a whole did. By causing physical deterioration, by frightening away respectable tenants, by making the estate a less desirable place to live, slums inevitably ate away at the reversionary value of his property. When the leases expired, slum conditions would mean that he could expect lower rents on any new lease, either because of the poor condition of the premises or to compensate the new lessee for the extensive repairs which would be needed. More likely, the property would have to be pulled down and rebuilt, and the freeholder would not receive improved rents at all but only new ground rents. And if, as often happened, he chose to let the former slum property to a model lodging house company, he would ordinarily content himself with ground rents at much less than the value of the land on the open market.

The attitudes of the big landowner toward the slums on his estate were essentially the same as those of the community at large. Both, as the nineteenth century progressed, recognized slums as a social cancer, evil in itself and a danger to the moral and economic health of the community—or the estate, depending on the point of view. The methods of the ground landlords in dealing with slums paralleled those of the public bodies. Both engaged in fact-finding surveys, which uncovered the same evils: overcrowding, physical deterioration, poor sanitation, immorality. Both tried to remedy the evils by issuing orders to repair or to desist from specific nuisances. Both found such orders frequently ignored. Both ultimately found it necessary to acquire effective ownership of the slum property, through purchase, condemnation, or the falling in of the lease, in order properly to rebuild the premises, or more often to demolish them and re-develop the site. Both ground landlord and public body acted from motives which combined, in varying proportions, philanthropy with enlightened self-interest.

It could be argued that the existence of a slum indicated a flaw in the original building plan. Districts of well-built houses equipped with proper sanitary facilities and fronting on wide streets might decline in character—as Bloomsbury and Bedford New Town did—in spite of everything that the ground landlord could do. Yet proper estate management was able to prevent them from sinking below the line that divides squalor from decency. But a neighborhood of poorly constructed buildings crowded around unsanitary alleys and courtyards would quickly become a slum and resist all but the most heroic efforts to raise it from such a state. Both the Duke of Bedford and the Foundling Hospital found that it was far easier to prevent a respectable neighborhood from becoming a slum than to turn a slum into a respectable neighborhood.

The size of a house was a less important factor than its situation. The mansions on the Covent Garden estate had become cheap lodging houses at a time when undeniably middle-class families were living in the third-rate houses of Bedford New Town. The best insurance against slums seemed to be to lay out the property with wide streets and extensive open spaces, and prevent builders from constructing courts and alleys on the vacant ground behind the houses. Once the neighborhood was properly laid out and built upon, the landlord had to continue to guard against the erection of mean tenements on any vacant ground, and to see that the stables and coachhouses in the mews remained stables and coachhouses. If in addition he was reasonably vigilant in enforcing repairing and occupation covenants, the neighborhood—although it might sink in value—would not become a slum. And the poor, who insisted on living in slums, would not appear to embarrass or annoy his more respectable tenants.

In the summer of 1827 Joseph Kay reported to the general committee of the Foundling Hospital that a number of the "small inferior buildings in back situations are in a very defective state, chiefly owing to their original bad construction."[1] The buildings he referred to were soon to constitute the most serious nuisance on the Hospital estate, if pockets of squalor, misery, and disease can be called by so mild a term.

The squalid courts and narrow streets that lay around the boundary between the Bedford and Foundling estates were among the less admirable contributions of the speculative builder to the Bloomsbury scene. They demonstrated the limitations of the management of both estates, growing up as they did without proper supervision, sometimes without the estate offices knowing of their existence until it was too late.

In April 1804 the building committee of the Foundling Hospital discovered that there were "some improper buildings erecting in Coram Place, Chapel Place, and Russell Place east of Little Coram Street," on land let to James Burton.[2] Cockerell agreed that they were "of a very small and slight character . . ." Yet, since Burton had taken the ground "for the purpose of any useful buildings, workshops, or other occupations (not noisome) but without any obligation to build thereon at all, and as he is under articles to build substantial houses on the surrounding ground next the public streets," the surveyor did not believe "the interests of the Hospital to be affected thereby," and had not "taken any notice of them in their progress."[3]

There were two slum districts on the Foundling estate. The one lay at the western boundary, between Tavistock Place and Bernard Street. The other was north of Compton Street, on land taken by George Payne. A letter from Payne in 1809 describes his difficulties in letting the coachhouses and stables he had built north of Compton Street. Instead of continuing to build them as required by his contract, he proposed to erect "some respectable fourth-rate houses . . . with a restriction on my part not to build higher than the stables already built, nor to make any back windows so as to annoy the inhabitants in Compton Street or Hunter Street North . . ."[4] The building committee agreed to the proposal. Kay remarked that he did not think "that the principle of objection to the annoyance in general arising from smaller houses to those of a better class sur-

1. General Committee, *38*, 390.
2. Building Committee, 2, 109.
3. Ibid., p. 113.
4. Ibid., *3*, 201.

rounding them would in this instance very strongly apply . . ." The houses in Compton Street were in any event "not of a class likely to be injured by the mere approximation of such buildings, if the occupancy of them is prevented from creating annoyance."[5]

Payne's difficulty in finding tenants for his stables was not unusual. Both the Foundling and the Bedford estates had overestimated the demand for stable accommodation, and both found that their mews tended, more quickly than any other type of property, to degenerate. The Foundling Hospital provided far more houses for the more prosperous classes than turned out to be justified. Too many houses were too large for their situation. Not enough gentlemen of the standing of Mr. John Knightley chose to live in the airy streets near Brunswick Square. Too few of them kept carriages to justify the accommodation offered in the mews. As a result, each mews became a potential nuisance, for the day was far distant when a mews could be considered a fashionable address. Improper occupation of mews premises was a chronic concern of the Hospital throughout the nineteenth century. When converted into tenements, they often approached the conditions of squalor of the courts leading off Little Coram Street. (See Figure 74 for a typical mews on the Bedford estate.) As early as 1818 the clerk and surveyor of the Foundling estate paving commission were reporting that "the mews are more generally occupied by poor families carrying on little trades, and by profligate and destitute persons, than as stables."[6] On surveying the mews, they found that "in many instances the buildings are in a neglected and ruinous state . . ."[7]

The Hospital soon regretted the inattention that had permitted a slum to develop. The worst buildings were in Compton Place, which Payne had built in 1809 (Fig. 75). In August 1823 the inhabitants of Compton Street were complaining "that great riots have been committed by the inhabitants of Compton Place, (who are chiefly Irish) . . ."[8] The houses in Compton Place were, Kay observed in 1830, "from the nature of their construction and occupation . . . liable to constant wear and dilapidation, and never have been or are likely to be maintained in a state of complete repair." The inhabitants were "chiefly of the working class and not the more disreputable description. Some inconvenience may occasionally arise from a tenantry of this description," he remarked, "but

5. Ibid., pp. 204–05 (18 November 1809). It is hardly necessary to comment on the limitations of a sort of town planning that deprived the lower orders of windows in order to preserve their betters from annoyance.

6. Paving Commission Minutes, *4*, 97.

7. Ibid., p. 105 (7 May 1818).

8. Ibid., *5*, 21.

74. A typical mews: Keppel Mews South, looking east, in 1900. Pulled down 1901

75. Compton Place and neighboring courts

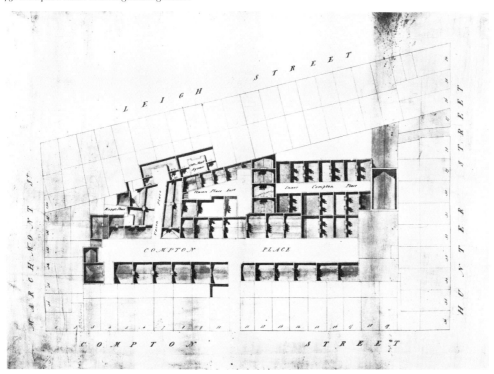

76. Little Coram Street, west side, in 1895. Pulled down 1896

77 (below left). Duke's Court, looking west from Drury Lane, in 1898.
78 (below right). Crown Court, east side, in 1899. Pulled down 1901

it should be also remembered that some advantage is derived to the trade of the neighborhood in the supply of so considerable a number of persons." He advised against active interference, but proposed to continue his visits of inspection to encourage repairs and make "the lessees aware that this attention . . . is given to their proceedings."[9]

Inspection and encouragement proved insufficient. In April 1833 the clerk of the estate paving commission complained to the general committee of the filth that had accumulated in Compton Place, owing to the absence of any system of drainage.[10] The Hospital thereupon agreed to pay the Holborn and Finsbury commissioners of sewers to construct a sewer.[11]

Early in 1835 the lessees and tenants in Compton Street officially protested to the governors about conditions in Compton Place.[12] The following June the general committee recommended that actions of ejectment be brought against the lessees for breach of the repairing covenants.[13] On 22 December Richard Vanheythuysen, the Hospital's solicitor, reported that he had obtained judgment against one of them, a Mr. Hinton, and all but one of his undertenants. The day before, the sheriff had taken possession of the premises.[14] The Hospital proceeded to take down several of the houses early in 1836.[15]

The governors offered to return the greater part of his property to Hinton on a new lease at £20 per annum.[16] Meanwhile it effected a number of improvements in the houses at a cost of £164.[17] In October 1837 the General Court approved the granting of a seventy-one-year lease of ground in Compton Place to the Metropolitan Police, who proceeded to build a police station there.[18] It was hoped that the addition would have a salutary effect on the behavior of the inhabitants.

But on 8 May 1839 the committee received a letter from a tenant in Compton Street reporting "that the nuisances formerly complained of by him in Compton Place, and which were to a considerable extent remedied by the interference of the governors of this Hospital, are recurring . . ."[19] The secretary referred the letter to Police Inspector Jenkins, at the Compton Place station, who replied that the complaint "of there being riots in that place is wholly without foundation . . ." He asserted "that Compton Place is inhabited by a better

9. General Committee, *39*, 445–46 (3 February 1830).

10. Ibid., *41*, 404–05.

11. Ibid., *42*, 13–15 (19 June 1833).

12. Ibid., pp. 432–36.

13. Ibid., *43*, 28–29.

14. Ibid., pp. 156–57.

15. Ibid., pp. 167, 247.

16. Ibid., p. 314 (24 August 1836).

17. General Court, *6*, 385.

18. Ibid., pp. 408–09.

19. General Committee, *45*, 65.

class . . . than formerly—that occasionally disturbances may arise, as in the best regulated streets, but they are put down immediately."[20]

Conditions deteriorated during the next decade despite a succession of countermeasures from the Hospital. In April 1844 Kay presented a detailed account of the slum property on the estate to the general committee. Neglect and dilapidation, he found, characterized the whole of Russell and Coram places. "At the period of the general amendment of the sewage of that part of the estate and drainage of these buildings," he recalled, "the whole were respectably maintained and apparently well occupied." At some more recent date they had "become occupied by an inferior class of tenants, committing constant destruction of the property . . . and . . . causing annoyance and deterioration of the neighborhood." Although the reforms of 1835–36 had temporarily raised the level of respectability in Compton Place, by 1844 a "general deterioration of the occupancy" had taken place, and the buildings were again in a state of such neglect as to require "more urgent measures than a mere notice to repair . . ."[21] But for the moment the Hospital contented itself with giving such notices to the lessees.[22]

Mr. Owen, a tenant in Great Coram Street, wrote later in 1844 to complain of the "vast number of the lowest class of people" living in the courts behind his house "who, from their continual disturbances cause considerable annoyance to the respectable portion of the district, so much so that several persons have left the neighborhood in consequence, and many others have declared their intention of doing so."[23]

In August 1845 the general committee referred a letter from another tenant, "complaining of assemblages of low and mischievous persons," in Great Coram Street, probably coming from the nearby courts, to the estate paving commissioners.[24] Two months later a group of inhabitants of Great Coram Street presented a memorial complaining of the "Irish paupers . . . [from the courts] assembling before the houses of the memorialists, particularly on Sundays."[25]

By the end of the year Kay was able to report that the buildings in Russell, Coram, and Marchmont places had been repaired, and the objectionable occupants removed, "and that under due precaution as to the tenants for their future occupation, they can now be maintained in a respectable and satisfactory state, and that the legal proceedings in respect of them may be abated." A number of buildings in Compton Mews that had fallen down were rebuilt, but other

20. Ibid., pp. 73–74 (15 May 1839).
21. Ibid., 47, 456–58.
22. Ibid., 48, 22–23.

23. Ibid., p. 70.
24. Ibid., p. 379.
25. Ibid., p. 442.

premises there still needed repair. In Compton Place and the adjoining courts, "no degree of improvement has taken place . . ." in spite of notices to repair.[26]

Meanwhile the surveyor had begun a systematic program of inspection of the mews and courts throughout the estate, leaving notices to repair and advising the solicitor to start legal proceedings wherever necessary. Although effective elsewhere, such methods failed in Compton Place and its neighboring courts. In November 1847 the general committee ordered the solicitor to begin proceedings to eject the lessees of Compton Place and the adjoining Poplar Court. "The present deteriorated condition of the buildings," Kay reported, "arises chiefly from the nature of their occupation; nor could the substantial amendment of them be undertaken to any efficient purpose without the entire removal of their present occupants being first effected." He recommended that the buildings be pulled down and "suitably remodeled for the residence of tenants of a respectable description." The existing dwellings were crowded into a confined area, totally lacked back ventilation,[27] and suffered from unsound brickwork. Their woodwork was "decayed and rotten . . . the glass . . . extensively broken, and some of the sashes entirely removed. All the roofs require painting and repairs, and in many instances the leadwork has been entirely removed. The plastering of the ceilings and walls . . . is falling down . . ." The drains were defective, "and the most noisome and dangerous effluvia is consequently perpetually occasioned to the peril of the tenants and neighborhood, and there are now several cases of severe disease. This is enhanced by the deficient supply of water, and its not having been laid on to many of the houses . . ."[28]

On 7 December, shortly after writing the damning report on Compton Place, Joseph Kay died, after more than forty years of service to the Foundling Hospital.[29] He was succeeded by Henry Currey, who continued Kay's policies as surveyor virtually unaltered.[30]

Compton Place continued to vex Currey, as it had his predecessor. In December 1848 the new surveyor reported to the General Court that some of its houses had been repaired. The leaseholders of "some of the most wretched houses, namely those in King's Court and the upper part of Compton Place," had proposed to have them pulled down "and the ground allotted as gardens or yards to the adjoining premises."[31] The three houses at the west end of Compton Place along with the whole of King's Court were demolished in 1849. The oc-

---

26. General Court, 7, 105–07 (31 December 1845).
27. See above, pp. 129–30.
28. General Committee, 50, 14–15.

29. Ibid., p. 24.
30. Ibid., p. 39 (24 December 1847).
31. General Court, 7, 178.

cupants of the remaining houses, which were once again repaired, were "of the same objectionable character as before."[32]

Late in 1852 Currey reported that Compton Place and Poplar Place were "again in the same neglected and dirty state, and it would appear useless to enforce further repairs; for all trace of those recently executed has disappeared, from the nature of the occupation."[33] Shortly thereafter, the Hospital, having decided that it could achieve lasting improvements only by regaining full control of the houses, bought up several of the leases in Compton Place, Compton Street, and Poplar Place. It then relet the property in small parcels on condition that certain improvements would be carried out.[34]

Elsewhere, complaints as to the unsanitary, overcrowded, and disease-ridden courts continued to appear in the Hospital records with monotonous regularity. In 1849 a subcommittee reported to the estate paving commissioners that the state of the drainage on the property left much to be desired:

> In most of the inferior courts and places of the estate, the drainage from the houses is defective, arising in some instances from their want of connection with the main sewer, and in others from the foul state of the drains where such connection exists. We also find that some tenements are without any watercloset convenience whatever, and in others that there are privies common to the inhabitants of several distinct dwellings. We further find that the gullies in several parts of the estate emit mephitic vapour by reason of their not being trapped.[35]

Each complaint resulted in a new inspection and report by the surveyor, and in new notices to repair, but in no permanent improvement.

In January 1857 the medical officer of St. Pancras suggested a permanent solution: the purchase of all the leasehold interests, followed by the demolition of the buildings. On their site could rise model lodging houses, the great new enthusiasm of the Victorian philanthropist.[36] Currey agreed that lesser measures would be futile. "Though the governors have the power to enforce the repairing covenants . . . they have," he pointed out, "no means of compelling any alterations or improvements in the construction of the dwellings, and until that is done I fear they will continue to be a nuisance to the neighborhood."[37]

The Hospital was unsuccessful in its attempts to induce the lessees to sell their interests, and so had to be content with serving the usual repairing notices.[38]

32. Ibid., p. 188 (28 March 1849).
33. General Committee, 52, 322.
34. Ibid., 71, 460 (11 January 1889).
35. Paving Commission Minutes, 9, 2 (8 November 1849).
36. General Committee, 54, 201–02.
37. Ibid., p. 211 (7 February 1857).
38. Ibid., pp. 315–16 (23 May 1857).

The surveyor and solicitor later remarked in a joint report, "It is just possible that by taking the parties by surprise some of the premises might be found so much out of order as to entitle the Hospital to a verdict in an action of ejectment for breach of covenant, but," they regretfully concluded, "it would scarcely be right in a charitable institution to take that advantage. Upon notice being given they immediately repair."[39]

In July 1858 Currey reported that the mews property was growing dangerously dilapidated, and that Compton, Poplar, Chapel, Marchmont, Coram, and Russell places were in as bad a condition as ever: "All trace of any cleansing and repair which may be executed disappears in the course of a few months."[40]

A deputation from the sanitary boards of St. Pancras and St. George, Bloomsbury, came to the Hospital late in 1863 to point out the increasingly unhealthy conditions in the courts.[41] Dr. Hillier, the medical officer for St. Pancras, submitted an extended indictment. In the period from 1856 to 1863 the death rate in the parish as a whole had been 23 per 1,000. In Compton Place it had been 27 per 1,000; in Poplar Place, 33 per 1,000. The death rate for children under 5 in 1862 and 1863 had been 14.5 per cent in Compton Place, 9.1 per cent in Poplar Place; the rate for the parish was 8.5 per cent.

The housing conditions he described were such as to make it surprising that his vital statistics were no grimmer. "The staircases," he reported, "are narrow and dark; the rooms are small and low; under the stairs is a damp, dirty, and offensive privy. . . . The water tank is close to the privy and its contents are . . . charged with effluvia from it. There is no back ventilation . . . Each room is occupied by a family. The passages and rooms are out of repair and very dirty." The low level of the houses made drainage difficult.

However appalling the conditions, Dr. Hillier realized—as the Hospital had learned through years of frustrating experience—that it was easier to make reports than to effect improvements. The sub-lessees who were "the only parties against whom the sanitary authorities can take legal proceedings are men of no substance or position, so that it has been found impossible to get from them any radical improvements, or even enough to keep the houses out of a state of palpable nuisance."[42]

Dr. Hillier suggested once again that the Hospital buy up the leases, tear down the houses, and erect model dwellings in their place. Conferences between the Hospital solicitor and surveyor and the parish authorities ensued, but it soon developed that neither the Hospital nor the parishes had the necessary

39. Ibid., p. 379 (15 August 1857).
40. Ibid., 55, 106–07.
41. Ibid., 58, 104.
42. Ibid., pp. 119–20 (23 January 1864).

funds for any radical scheme of improvement. The Hospital thereupon reverted to its customary practice of serving notices to repair, and the evils of the squalid courts continued unabated.[43] Simpson, the solicitor, and Currey estimated that the buildings would have to be inspected every three months if they were to be maintained in even a tolerable state of repair.[44]

The 1870s finally saw the beginning of a vigorous program of demolition and redevelopment, but the initiative came from outside the Foundling Hospital. In the summer of 1872 the St. Giles's Board of Works obtained a legal order for the demolition of the whole of Russell Place and Coram Place. Later that summer the Peabody Trustees applied to purchase the freehold of Coram, Russell, Marchmont, and Chapel places, together with a portion of Little Coram Street.[45] After some hesitation the governors agreed to sell the property for £5,400.[46]

In December 1882 the Hospital sold the remainder of its slum property in the Little Coram Street area to the Metropolitan Board of Works for £3,337. The Board proceeded to buy up forty leasehold claims at a further cost of £8,145 16s. It then handed over the property to the Peabody Trustees, who built on it and on their own adjacent property eight blocks of model dwellings, accommodating 840 persons.[47]

In the meantime the St. Giles's District medical officer had made a formal complaint about the condition of houses in the Colonnade, a mews running behind the houses in Bernard and Guilford streets. The secretary made the usual communication with the lessee, who promised to require his tenants to carry out the necessary repairs.[48] Apparently he was not successful: in January 1884 the vestry of St. Pancras condemned property both in the Colonnade and in the long notorious Compton and Poplar places. On learning of its action, the committee ordered the solicitor to write to each lessee "in the strongest possible terms . . ."[49] Shortly afterward the St. Pancras vestry gave notice that it would within three months pull down certain of the houses in Poplar Place and Compton Place as unfit for human habitation.[50] It then bought up the leasehold interests, which it later surrendered to the Hospital.[51]

In 1888 the Hospital entered into a building agreement with Messrs. Dover Wood and Co. for the construction of artisans' dwellings on the vacant ground

43. Ibid., pp. 269–70 (16 July 1864).

44. Ibid., *59*, 225–27 (16 September 1865).

45. Ibid., *63*, 100–01 (27 July 1872); pp. 134–36.

46. Ibid., *64*, 370–71 (20 February 1875).

47. General Court, *8*, 454–55. LCC, "Housing of the Working Classes Committee," *The Hous-*

ing Question in London (London, 1900?), pp. 151–54.

48. General Committee, *67*, 234–35 (24 September 1880); p. 239 (1 October 1880).

49. Ibid., *69*, 69 (11 January 1884).

50. Ibid., pp. 116–17 (29 February 1884).

51. Ibid., *71*, 459–61 (11 January 1889).

in Compton and Poplar places.[52] The firm proved unable to carry out its contract, and in October 1891 the Hospital granted another building agreement to a Mr. Woodrow. He contracted to build workshops and stables on the vacant ground according to plans approved by the Hospital surveyor, laying out a minimum of £2,000.[53] Woodrow proved equally incapable of fulfilling his agreement, and in 1895 the governors agreed to let the vacant land in Compton Place and Poplar Place to Messrs. Hilder and Edge, for the construction of "stabling and a mineral water manufactory."[54]

Earlier in the decade the governors had accepted an offer from a Mr. Hinton to take down the whole of the houses in the Colonnade and clear the site for £880.[55] By this time the original leases were beginning to fall in, and the Hospital took advantage of the opportunity to pull down and rebuild a number of the mews on the estate. In 1907 the leases of the eighteen remaining houses in Compton Place would expire, and enable the Foundling Hospital to eliminate the last traces of its small but embarrassing slum.

Nearly a century of honest effort had demonstrated the difficulty of combating slums by invoking leasehold covenants. Perhaps if the building leases had been more rigorously drawn, the outcome would have been different. But proper building agreements and leases would not have permitted such property in the first place. Enforcing covenants could help maintain a good building plan; it could not reform a bad one.

The Bedford estate's experience with its substandard property resembled that of the Foundling Hospital. It, too, tried to improve the conditions of lower-class tenements by enforcing repairing covenants, but ultimately solved the problem only through demolition and redevelopment.

Except for Abbey Place and the other narrow courts east of Woburn Place, the Bloomsbury estate had no slums.[56] Even its narrow streets south of Great Russell Street—such as Gilbert, Little Russell, and Silver streets—were, if undeniably lower-class in character, far superior to the streets just west and south of the estate. And although Bedford New Town sank in respectability toward the end of the nineteenth century, it was still mostly lower-middle class at the beginning of the twentieth.

52. Ibid., pp. 272, 341, 460–61.
53. Ibid., 73, 135.
54. Ibid., 75, 108–09.
55. Ibid., 73, 158 (27 November 1891).
56. "Is it not true that in St. George's, Blooms-

bury, with the exception of a very small spot called Coram Street, there is in fact no such thing as a slum?" HWC, p. 28; 1884–85 (4402-I) xxx.

The slum property in Bloomsbury, if small in extent, was in every other re-spect deplorable. Concentrated along the eastern boundary, adjoining the Foundling estate, it consisted of a series of narrow, unsanitary courts, built on land which had originally been leased by James Burton—similar in all respects to the narrow, unsanitary courts on the other side of the boundary.

The worst of the courts was Abbey Place, just west of Little Coram Street (now Herbrand Street; see Fig. 76). In October 1801 the Duke had granted a building lease to James Burton of nine houses on the west side of Little Coram Street. Some time afterward, someone—probably Burton—put up some addi-tional buildings behind the houses, thereby forming Abbey Place. Badly situ-ated, improperly planned, and poorly drained, Abbey Place followed the same pattern of overcrowding, decay, and disease that characterized the adjacent courts on the Foundling estate.

In 1869 the St. Giles's District Board of Works informed the Bedford Office that on the recommendation of its medical officer it was considering ordering the demolition of the unsanitary houses on the east side of Abbey Place.[57] As it developed, the Board's powers under the Artisans' and Labourers' Dwellings Act of 1868 were inadequate.[58]

Three years later the Bedford Office had a Mr. Trehearne survey the whole of the Duke's property in Little Coram Street, Abbey Place, and Tavistock Mews, consisting of about sixty-five houses. The steward reported that while the ideal solution would be for the estate to buy up all the leases and subleases, it had at the time no funds for such a purpose. The best he could recommend was to en-force more strictly the repairing covenants.[59]

Conventional measures proved insufficient. In November 1876 the medical officer of the St. Giles's district made another report condemning the condition of the entire area of the courts on both the Bedford and Foundling estates. Two years later the District Board decided to include the two-and-one-fourth acre plot in a large improvement scheme.[60] The Bedford estate opposed the plan, and ultimately came to an agreement with the Metropolitan Board of Works by which the Duke was permitted to deal with Abbey Place in his own way, in return for which he agreed to give the Metropolitan Board another site for the erection of artisans' dwellings.[61]

The estate proceeded to issue writs of ejectment for breaches of covenant, but only carried the actions "on to a stage at which the defendants would realize

57. London Reports, *1*, 11–12 (15 November 1869).

58. 1870 Report, 2, 2.

59. Middlesex Estate Report, 1872, pp. 7–8.

60. *The Housing Question in London*, pp. 151–52.

61. Ibid., pp. 153–54.

the Duke's generosity while leaving his Grace free to deal with the property as the circumstances made necessary." The Duke then purchased the various interests at prices "based upon the actual condition of the property and the estimated cost of restoration so as to make it fit for habitation."[62] The total cost of compensating leaseholders and demolishing the buildings came to slightly more than £1,300.[63] The steward predicted that the effect of the Abbey Place affair on the Bedford Office would be "to create such unceasing vigilance in supervision and insistence upon the observance of obligations by lessees as to render impossible any pretext for a future attack."[64]

The estate dealt with the remaining portions of Burton's slum buildings at the close of the century, when all the original leases fell in. In May 1897 Stutfield wrote that the buildings in Little Guilford Street and Little Coram Street were "exhausted and insanitary, and they should be taken down." He suggested that the opportunity be taken to widen the two streets from thirty to forty feet, and to let the sites on building leases. The ground between the new buildings and the backs of the houses in Woburn Place might, he thought, be turned into a garden.[65] The estate renamed the two streets Herbrand Street, after the eleventh Duke. Instead of letting the cleared property on building leases, it sold the whole Herbrand Street site to the London County Council in October 1898 for £40,000. On it the LCC built artisans' dwellings. At the same time the LCC purchased sites in Duke's Court and Russell Court on the Covent Garden estate for £78,400 for another housing scheme.[66]

Of the three Bedford estates in London, Covent Garden was the least satisfactory in the character of its residents. Its relatively spacious layout and many splendid features had excited the admiration of Londoners in the seventeenth century, and in its early years it was highly fashionable.[67] But by the early eighteenth century its wealthy inhabitants were moving westward into newer quarters, leaving their mansions to be converted into tenements.

Nowhere was the decay more evident than in the narrow courts that branched off from the west side of Drury Lane. Marquis Court, Russell Court, White Hart Street, and others like them constituted the worst of the Bedford estate in London (Figs. 72, 77, 78). As early as 1730, the more respectable residents of

---

62. 1879 Report, 2, 1–3.
63. 1881 Report, 2, 1.
64. 1879 Report, 2, 2.
65. London Reports, 3, 95–96 (10 May 1897).
66. *The Housing Question in London*, pp. 272–74.

67. "In 1672 . . . the then Lord Littlehampton (the 'Wicked Lord') decided to leave his castle at Courantsdair and reside at Drayneflete, whence he could more easily reach his town house in Covent Garden." Osbert Lancaster, *Drayneflete Revealed* (London, John Murray, 1949), p. 25.

Covent Garden were complaining to the Westminster Sessions that "people of the most notorious characters and infamously wicked lives and conversation have of late . . . years taken up their abode in the parish." They specified in particular Russell Street, Drury Lane, Crown Court, and King's Court as being "infested with these vile people. . . . There are frequent outcries in the night, fighting, robberies and all sorts of debaucheries committed by them all night long to the great inquietude of his majesty's subjects."[68] A century later, it could still be said that, "whatever may be the rival claims of Ratcliffe Highway and Agar Town, of Bethnal Green or Lambeth, no one will question that both the policeman and the philanthropist will find plenty to occupy their time and attention in the neighborhood of . . . the reeking courts which branch off from Drury Lane."[69]

The policy of the Bedford Office toward the Covent Garden estate during the nineteenth century aimed at the alteration of its character from a lower-class residential area to the commercial quarter that it is today. But it was far from indifferent to the conditions in which its inhabitants lived. In 1845, the year of the publication of the Report of the Commission on the State of Large Towns, on the request of the Duke of Bedford, the steward made a survey of the lodging houses in Covent Garden. He found that there were on that estate "about forty-six houses occupied by a poor class of persons, and of those eighteen by a very poor and low class of persons."[70] Except for one lodging house in Rose Street and two in Maiden Lane, all of them were located in the various courts. The houses occupied by a "poor class of persons" were in Cross Court, Duke's Court, Red Lion Court, and Marquis Court. The "very poor and low class of persons" lived in Eagle Court, New Bedford Court, and Jackson's Alley.

In 1853 the parishes of St. Martin-in-the-Fields and St. Paul, Covent Garden, embarked on an ambitious program to improve the drainage of the area. At the same time the Bedford estate began a policy of reconstruction and amendment at the expiration of leases, particularly with regard to "the reconstruction of the underground rooms or cellars occupied as dwellings, and not built in conformity with the rules . . . of the Metropolis Management Act,"[71] and the "alteration and amendment of the drains and water closets . . ."[72] Some of the works were compulsory; others were instituted on the initiative of the estate, as part of a long-range improvement scheme.

68. *Middlesex Records* (Orders of Court, Westminster, June 1730), quoted in M. Dorothy George, *London Life in the XVIIIth Century* (London, Kegan Paul, 1925), p. 83.

69. *Church Times*, 26 November 1864.

70. C. Haedy, marginal comment on letter from Duke of Bedford, 27 January 1845.

71. Section 3 of the Act, 1853.

72. 1862 Report, p. 78.

A portion of the expenditures went to improve the sanitary condition of the courts, and "to render the houses, which are very old and badly arranged, habitable . . ." In 1856 the estate began to buy up the leasehold interests of houses in Russell, Marquis, and Cross Courts; leases that fell in were not renewed, and the houses were either completely rebuilt or thoroughly repaired at the expense of the Duke. In order to ensure the success of such projects, the estate often purchased the freeholds of adjacent property that it considered was in an objectionable state of decay.[73] "As soon as the houses are completed," wrote the steward, "they are leased to very desirable tenants. By the insertion of a covenant in the leases prohibiting without consent the whole or any portion of the houses being underleased or underlet, the objectionable class of tenants who formerly were inmates of these houses are excluded from residing in these courts."[74] Where the objectionable class moved was of course not a problem for the Bedford estate.

At the request of the Duke, the steward made a detailed survey of the thirteen courts on the estate in 1884, while the Royal Commission on the Housing of the Working Classes was making its own comparable inquiries. In all, the courts contained ninety-nine houses, of which Mr. Bourne classified thirty-one as being in good repair, forty-four in fair repair, thirteen as bad, and five as very bad. The sanitation was nearly everywhere satisfactory. There was little excessive overcrowding; the density averaged about twelve persons per house, or one and one-third per room. Bourne listed a few isolated instances of severe overcrowding—such as two rooms occupied by a man and wife with their seven children—but on the whole, conditions were quite decent.[75]

The steward found "several gradations of the wage-earning class" living in the courts. Although a few carried on trades in their homes, most of the men had employment elsewhere in the neighborhood. The most prosperous, living in Crown Court and Broad Court (Fig. 78), included market salesmen, theater musicians, policemen, and printers. "The homes of these people are as a rule," he reported, "well furnished, and the houses in repair and all sanitary appliances in order." At the opposite end of the scale were Russell and Marquis courts, where there lived "market porters, shoe menders, jobbing tradesmen, and laborers, with laundresses and charwomen." There were "few if any of the absolutely destitute class, though the pinch of poverty must be felt by many directly there is sickness or want of employment." He could find neither thieves

73. 1860 Report, pp. 1–2.
74. 1861 Report, p. 110.
75. The model lodging house in Eagle Court

was far more crowded than the average. It had 179 occupants in its 76 rooms, roughly 2 1/3 per room.

nor prostitutes, but feared that both classes might shortly appear in Marquis Court, "unless sharp measures are adopted with the lessees."

The weekly rents varied from 6s. per room in Crown Court to 2s. 6d. in Russell Court. The average rent payable to the Duke was £30 a house. Considering the additional outlay on rates, taxes, and repairs, Bourne did not think that the lessees made any great profits from subletting.

There were, naturally, exceptions. In 1862 the estate had served notice on the trustees of the Drury Lane Theater, "requiring them to reinstate the houses in Marquis Court which they had suffered to fall into a very dilapidated condition."[76] The results could not have been satisfactory, for twenty years later the steward described the houses included in the lease to the theater—along with those leased by the Scottish Church in Crown Court—as the worst on the estate. The sole aim of the proprietors of the theater was, according to Bourne, "to get as much as possible out of the estate. These houses as an adjunct are all sublet, and so long as the rent is paid to the receiver there is complete indifference as to the condition of the property . . ."

In general he found the condition of the courts to be satisfactory. The comparatively few cases of poor repair resulted, he believed, from specific causes, and did not stem inevitably from the leasehold system itself. Yet "active interference on the part of the Duke's agents" would be necessary to maintain the courts in a decent state. In particular Bourne advised "that committees and corporations must be subject to the same drastic treatment that is needed by individuals."[77]

Bourne's survey showed that careful management could do much to maintain decent living conditions for the poor. Yet however rigidly the estate might enforce the covenants in the leases, however often it might rebuild the houses, the narrow, sunless courts leading off Drury Lane could never be made really attractive places to live. In 1890 the Bedford estate began pulling down all of the buildings in the courts and replanning the whole area along more open lines. As the leases for the various parts of the property fell in, the Bedford Office had the houses demolished systematically; by the beginning of the new century the courts had virtually disappeared.

Writing of one block of houses in the area that had just come in hand, Mr. Stutfield reported that while the houses in Drury Lane were "exhausted and not fit to be relet," those in Cross Court and Russell Court were "in fairly good condition, and might be kept going for a few years if it were thought desirable." Yet all of the houses were "quite incapable of affording the light and air space

76. 1862 Report, p. 81.   77. London Reports, 2, 8–11 (27 March 1884).

necessary for the poor people who crowd into them." The steward therefore recommended that the whole block be pulled down "as a commencement of the general clearance which it is desirable to carry out gradually in this neighborhood."[78]

In order to facilitate the scheme of general replanning, the Duke bought up during this period a great deal of freehold property in the area of the Drury Lane courts, as well as many leasehold interests on his own estate.[79]

In both Bloomsbury and Covent Garden, the Bedford estate came to much the same conclusion as had the Foundling Hospital: that slum property could be dealt with effectively only by demolition or complete rebuilding. The enforcement of leasehold covenants helped the situation somewhat, but could not in itself solve the problem of substandard housing. Improvement schemes, while not solving the problem for the poor as a whole, did at least raise the standard of decency within the boundaries of the estate.

78. Ibid., p. 439 (25 April 1894).

79. 1895 Report, pp. 133–35; London Reports, 3, 33–34 (20 May 1896); 124–26 (8 November 1897).

8 Guarding the Amenities

*The great landlords of England are really the rulers of principalities.
. . . They are charged with the administration of a miniature empire,
which often embraces a number of provinces, whose conditions, resources, and necessities differ as much as if they were separate kingdoms.*
—T. H. S. Escott, England, her People, Polity, and Pursuits (1885)

It would be deceptively easy to make a sharp contrast between the enlightened
landlord rigorously enforcing the covenants in his leases and thus maintaining
the character of his estate, and the unenlightened landlord permitting his tenants to do as they liked—deceptively easy because the enforcement of covenants
was only one of many factors which determined the character of a neighborhood. No estate policy could do much to change the shifts of fashion. The experience of the Foundling Hospital with Compton Place would indicate that
no number of notices to repair and actions of ejectment could do much to re-
deem an area badly laid out and badly built in the first place. At the other
extreme, there is no evidence that the Grosvenor estate was especially active in
enforcing repairing or occupation covenants in Belgravia or Mayfair; there was
no need to. Furthermore, the difficulty and expense involved in an action of
ejectment was enough to deter all but the most determined landlords in all but
the most flagrant cases from imposing the ultimate sanction on a recalcitrant
tenant. The most that can be concluded is that some landlords enforced some
covenants in some instances, and that such policies prevented some neighborhoods from deteriorating as much as they might otherwise have done.

Fortunately, leasehold covenants were not the only weapons which a ground
landlord could use to protect the value of his property during the term of a
lease. The Committee on Town Holdings for the most part overlooked the
other ways in which the owner of a great estate could exercise a benevolent
paternalism. If by enforcing covenants the landlord protected his tenants from
one another, he had other means of protecting them from harmful forces out-

side the estate. Harmful outside forces took any number of shapes. They might be cattle on their way to market; they might be empty cabs bound for railway termini. They might be poverty and disease; they might be the London County Council. Whatever the nature of the external menace, tenants tended to turn to the landlord for assistance whenever their interests were threatened.

Symbolic of the activities of the London estates to protect their inhabitants from the outside world were their many gates and bars, formidable obstructions to traffic for the greater part of the nineteenth century. They were the most obvious visible manifestations in London of the power of the ground landlord.

One of the basic aims of Georgian estate planning was to secure as many communications with the more fashionable parts of town, and as few with the less fashionable parts, as possible. For the Bedford estate, to put such a principle into practice would have required streets that led toward the City and the West End and none at all leading toward Camden Town and the other disreputable districts to the north. Unfortunately, much as the Bedford estate would have liked to ignore the New Road and what lay beyond, it would have found it impossible to do so in practice. The estate office could hardly prevent the tenants from traveling toward the north and the east. The problem was how to permit the Bedford tenants to travel to the northern and eastern suburbs, while preventing the northern and eastern suburbs from traveling to the Bedford estate. Gates barring the streets at the northern boundary provided the answer. The gatekeepers ordinarily permitted carriages, gentlemen on horseback, and pedestrians to pass, but turned back droves of cattle, together with omnibuses, carts, and other low vehicles. Such an arrangement kept the streets on the estate from becoming noisy thoroughfares. After a certain hour at night the gates were closed to all vehicles, thereby ensuring uninterrupted sleep to the residents of the protected streets.

A conference agitating for the removal of such gates in 1879 estimated that their number was "not less than 150 in the whole of the metropolis."[1] Returns made by vestries and district boards in 1866 listed no fewer than twenty-nine in the parish of St. Pancras alone. The regulations varied greatly among the different barriers. Of the seven in the parish of St. Marylebone, for example, "some . . . are described as against carts and empty cabs, except for the use of the inhabitants of the street; one as open only for inhabitants subscribing to the expense of maintaining the *gates*, and one as open on Sundays and State Festivals. The *gates* in Harewood Place, Oxford Street . . . are described as always closed,

1. *The Times*, 11 October 1879, in Mark Searle, comp., *Turnpikes and Toll-Bars* (London, Hutchinson, 1930), 2, 714.

except for the private use of the Earl of Harewood."[2]

One of the earliest of such gates stood at the north end of the Duke of Bedford's Private Road, built in the 1750s to connect Bedford House with the New Road from Paddington to Islington. Only those residents of the estate who paid a guinea deposit for a silver ticket could use the road.[3] The regulations provided that only families resident on the estate could pass through the gate; servants could do so only "in their attendance on the master, lady, or children of the family . . ." Hackney coaches, hearses, wagons, and carts were expressly forbidden. No person whatsoever could use the road from 6 P.M. until 8 A.M. between Michaelmas and Lady Day; from Lady Day to Michaelmas the gate was closed between 11 P.M. and 7 A.M. Such regulations seem to have remained in effect until the late 1820s.[4]

In 1802 Burton had suggested that they be altered to allow all carriages—but not carts, wagons, or stage coaches—to pass through. He further advised that another gate and lodge be built at the northern extremity of Bedford Terrace (the present Gordon Street) as soon as the road was completed. No other openings for carriages or horses ought, he felt, to be allowed. He pointed out that his plan would tend "to facilitate the letting of the ground by most essentially promoting the comforts and conveniences of the tenants and their *friends*—who (the latter) cannot (without an unreasonable bribe to the gatekeeper) at present find access southward but by a very circuitous route." He offered to build and maintain the two new lodges at his own expense, "on being allowed a very small toll (and that not from the persons already possessed of tickets) . . ."[5]

The five lodges and gates on the Bloomsbury estate—in Upper Woburn Place, Endsleigh Street, Georgiana Street (later Taviton Street), Gordon Street (originally William Street), and Torrington Place—had all been erected by 1831, presumably by Thomas Cubitt.[6] (For their location see Fig. 34; the gate and gatekeeper at Taviton Street are shown in Fig. 79.)

2. *The Times*, 10 February 1868, quoted ibid., 713.

3. See John Wynne to Mr. Williams, 26 February 1759, in Wynne's Letter Book (1758–65), p. 32. The Duke sometimes gave silver tickets to nonresidents as a special favor, but it was not customary.

4. A letter from W. G. Adam to C. Haedy dated 15 June 1827 refers to presumably new "private gate regulations to which the Duke agrees." Shortly afterward a new lodge was built in Upper Woburn Place, near the site of the old gate.

5. James Burton to John Gotobed, 16 October 1802. Nothing seems to have come of Burton's proposals.

6. Cubitt definitely built the last two gates—in Endsleigh and Georgiana streets—and was responsible for practically all the other great public works on the northern part of the estate, such as laying sewers, paving the roadways, and forming the squares. See the Bloomsbury Account Book for 1831.

The rules for the new gates—with the exception of the one in Upper Woburn Place—permitted "gentlemen's carriages of every description, cabs with fares, and persons on horseback" to pass through them. They prohibited "omnibuses, empty hackney carriages, empty cabs, carts, drays, wagons, trucks, cattle, and horses at exercise, or funerals . . ." The gates were closed to all traffic from 11 P.M. to 7 A.M.[7]

The Upper Woburn Place gate had its own rules. As late as 1840 the Bedford Office was issuing its special silver tickets, enabling tenants "to pass the gate . . . in carriages or on horseback, but not in hackney carriages." Haedy defended the prohibition of hackney carriages as a great protection against the "noise and bustle of the increased traffic" brought on by the building of Euston Station. The direct route to the station, then as now, passed through Upper Woburn Place, which would have got the bulk of the traffic were it not for the special restriction. As it was, the traffic was spread evenly through the other gates. "The inhabitants on the lines of the other gates complain very much of the noise and bustle of the carriages . . ." but Haedy doubted the wisdom of a universal ban on hackney carriages. He feared that such action might "endanger the existence of the gates (a most valuable protection to your Grace's estates against cattle, carts, and the stunning noise of omnibuses), for if wholly shut up, the inconvenience to the public would be so great that Parliament might be induced . . . to pass an Act to remove the gates, as obstructions to the highways in the town."[8]

The Foundling estate felt a similar need to insulate itself from its neighbors to the north and east. Along the northern boundary this was done by running as few streets across the line as was possible. In order to protect Mecklenburgh Square from the low traffic of Gray's Inn Road, the estate erected a gate at the end of Heathcote Street. The Heathcote Street gate was to a great extent responsible for attracting respectable inhabitants to Mecklenburgh Square, otherwise so awkwardly located.[9] In a letter protesting the intention of the estate paving commissioners to establish a pavior's yard in Heathcote Street, the then residents of Mecklenburgh Square stated that their "inducement to become the inhabitants" of their houses "was principally the tranquil and private nature of that part of the estate, a lodge and gates being erected at the northern entrance . . . to shut it up as a public thoroughfare and to prevent all traffic whatsoever."[10]

7. London Reports, *1*, 389 (21 May 1875).

8. C. Haedy to the Duke of Bedford, 15 August 1840.

9. General Committee, *32*, 257 (30 June 1813); 282–83 (28 July 1813).

10. Paving Commission Minutes, *4*, 324 (28 November 1822).

If Bloomsbury required protection from the contamination of Somers Town and Camden Town, the Figs Mead estate, surrounded by these slums, needed it all the more. The Bedford estate therefore set up gates at the eastern entrances to Oakley Square, and at the north end of Harrington Square. By such means, through north–south traffic was either deflected along St. Pancras Road or Hampstead Road outside the estate, or funneled down the unfashionable Eversholt or Charrington streets (Figs. 51, 52). The gates thus completed the layout of the new development, and formed an integral part of the town plan.

For the Duke's tenants the gates proved to be an unmixed blessing. In 1891 the steward wrote that houses in "gate-protected streets" were "much sought after by professional men, to whom quiet at night is an important element in the choice of a residence."[11] Even Frank Banfield was forced to admit that "many of the residents in these neighborhoods do not object to these bars and gates, for if they block the circulation of the metropolis generally, they provide a larger amount of privacy, seclusion, and quiet for the favored few."[12]

However popular they may have been with the tenants, it is not surprising that the gates caused great resentment among those who did not themselves live in protected streets. They could not but aggravate the traffic problem, and intensify noise and congestion along the streets which were unobstructed. It was obvious to everyone that the gates frequently lay across the lines of what would otherwise have been important thoroughfares. "I am a constant passenger by the Great Northern Railway," the Marquis of Salisbury told the House of Lords in 1890, "and I must say that I have never passed the *sacred Gates* in going to the Great Northern Station [King's Cross] without mental imprecations against the persons who originally set them up and the persons who have since maintained them there."[13] The difficulties of getting from Westminster to Euston, St. Pancras, or King's Cross after 11 P.M. must have been equally great for people other than the prime minister.

The ducal—or at least aristocratic—ownership of many of the barriers did nothing to enhance their popularity. As early as 1826 the *Sunday Times* was calling for legislation "to prevent the great landed proprietors who grant building leases from assuming aristocratic privilege of shutting out the public from the King's Highway, by the erection of barriers at the end of any new street. Such barriers," it insisted, "form a great inconvenience to the public at the

11. London Reports, 2, 172 (10 August 1891).
12. Banfield, *The Great Landlords of London*, p. 90.

13. *Hansard*, 17 July 1890, quoted in Searle, *Turnpikes and Toll-Bars*, 2, 724.

termination of the streets leading into the Paddington [i.e. New, now Euston] Road, and ought to be abolished."[14]

Although the Metropolis Management Act of 1855 had specifically denied the Metropolitan Board of Works the power to interfere with such gates, from the 50s onward both that body and the parish vestries saw recurrent agitation against the barriers.[15] *Punch* joined the campaign in the 80s, condemning the "Duke of Mudford" both for his gates and for the allegedly unsanitary condition of "Mud Salad Market."[16] In 1884 the Metropolitan Cab Proprietors' United Associations Parliamentary Committee presented a memorial to the Metropolitan Board of Works complaining of the "great inconvenience and annoyance" caused by the "*Bars* and *Gates* placed across the streets."[17]

Despite a vigorous opposition from the landlords and their tenants—in which the Duke of Bedford played an important part—Parliament in 1890 authorized the new London County Council to remove four gates, all of them in St. Pancras. Three of them—in Torrington Place, Gordon Street, and Upper Woburn Place—were on the Bedford estate.[18] The opposition succeeded in inserting a clause requiring the LCC and the parish vestries to lay "noiseless pavement"—i.e. asphalt or wood blocks—in the streets affected.[19] In 1893 Parliament authorized the removal of the remaining gates in London. By the end of that year the LCC was able to list fifty-five barriers in sixteen parishes, which it had taken down under the two acts.[20]

It might be argued that the demolition of the gates in Bloomsbury destroyed

14. 21 May 1826, quoted ibid., p. 711.

15. Ibid., pp. 711–20.

16. Ibid., pp. 715–16. See also *Punch*, vols. *82, 83* passim.

17. "Gentlemen engaging our vehicles frequently complain of the delay occasioned by the driver being compelled to take a circuitous route instead of being allowed to drive straight ahead, the result being, loss of temper on the part both of rider and driver. . . . Your Memorialists consider the *Gate* at [Upper] Woburn Place and the *Bar* across Gower Street particularly objectionable; the former preventing a direct line of communication between Holborn and the north eastern district of London, the latter compelling us to drive round three sides of a square block of buildings when one would suffice; moreover this *Bar* causes annoyance to the inmates of the University College Hospital, inasmuch as the pa-

tients on two sides of the building are compelled to bear the noise of the traffic." Searle, *Turnpikes* and Toll-Bars, 2, 717.

18. The fourth, in Sidmouth Street, was on the Harrison estate.

19. 1890 Report, pp. 157–59.

20. Searle, *Turnpikes and Toll-Bars*, 2, 729–30. For the Bedford estate, see 1893 Report, pp. 105–06. "Yesterday afternoon the *removal* of another *bar* across a London thoroughfare took place opposite the University College, Gower Street, when . . . Gower Street . . . [was] opened to the public vehicular traffic for ever. . . . The motion of thanks to the St. Pancras vestry for rendering Gower Street open to the public for ever was carried with loud cheers." *The Times*, 27 April 1893. Quoted in Searle, *Turnpikes and Toll-Bars*, 2, 729.

its character as an outpost of residential calm in west central London. Certainly today the cabs, trucks, and buses racing through its once secluded streets make it difficult to believe that it was once thought a gloomy, retired neighborhood. While they lasted, the gates did much to preserve Bloomsbury relatively unchanged, a Georgian anachronism in Victorian London.

Even the LCC seems to have had second thoughts on the wisdom of its policies in this respect. Its County of London Plan of 1943 suggests that through traffic be diverted from the "University Precinct, Bloomsbury," corresponding roughly to the Bedford estate. To achieve such an end it proposed to block up the entrances to no fewer than fifteen streets; certain of the proposed barriers, north of Gordon and Tavistock squares, were to be on the very sites of the old Bedford gates.[21]

The gates were conspicuous symbols of the paternalism of the London estates, but were not the only ones. It was, for instance, a continuing principle of management in the Bedford Office to keep off the estate all persons and things that might annoy a significant number of tenants. Such annoyances might be a bus route or a blacksmith shop, a lodging house or a telephone pole, a group of poor Irish laborers or a row of houses, empty and decayed. Whether the landlord tried to exclude such nuisances by invoking covenants in leases or by other means, the object was the same: to maintain the amenities of the estate at the highest possible level.

The coming of the railway, by permitting London to expand to an extent that would have been otherwise impossible, proved a great boon to the landowners of outer Middlesex and the Home Counties in general. It did not so benefit the owners of property in central London. By making available a vast quantity of new building land in the London area, the railways seriously diminished whatever monopoly the older landowners had. By making possible the garden suburb, the railways enabled the professional and business classes to combine a semirural residence with urban employment. The suburban train and the season ticket reduced the significance of Bloomsbury's proximity to the City and the Inns of Court. To make matters worse, three of the railways chose to locate their London termini virtually at the entrances to the Bedford estate, thereby depreciating its residential value. Bedford New Town suffered most of all, for the busy main line of the London and North Western bisected

21. J. H. Forshaw and Patrick Abercrombie, *County of London Plan* (London, 1943), p. 52. East-west and north-south tunnels, meeting under Bedford Square, were to be provided for through traffic.

Ampthill Square, (Figs. 51, 52), the focal point of the whole development.

The Duke of Bedford was able to insert a number of restrictive clauses into the bill (5 & 6 Wm. IV, cap. 56) authorizing the London and Birmingham Railway (later the London and North Western) to complete its line to a terminus just north of Euston Square. The Act limited the uses to which the railway might put the land it purchased from the Duke for its right-of-way through Figs Mead. Among other things, it prohibited the erection of steam engines (except, understandably, locomotives), foundries, forges, "manufactories," or breweries south of the Regent's Canal. A later Act (9 & 10 Vict., cap. 152), providing for the enlargement of Euston Station and the consequent closing of Birchmore Street, modified the 1835 Act, but required the approval of the Duke of Bedford and Lord Southampton of any workshop or forge erected at the terminus. The carriage repair shops were to be constructed "so as to occasion the least possible annoyance to the houses or property in the neighborhood."[22]

The restrictions proved irksome to the railway, and the inhabitants of Ampthill Square frequently complained to the Bedford Office of the nuisances committed by the company. In 1869 and 1884 the London and North Western obtained Acts of Parliament for alterations to Euston Station and its approaches, necessarily involving Ampthill Square. In both instances the Duke was able to secure modifications to minimize the annoyance to his tenants.[23] Yet conditions remained far from satisfactory. It would be hard to imagine one of the largest railways in England making the heavily graded approach to its London terminus either innocuous or inconspicuous.

A solution was finally reached in 1887 when the railway purchased the freehold of sixteen houses in Hampstead Road and fourteen in Ampthill Square, together with a portion of the garden of the latter, for £47,500.[24] Apart from the handsome purchase price, the solution was in a sense a surrender by the Duke to the railway, after a half-century struggle to keep it from annoying his tenants. But whatever the Bedford Office may have thought in 1835, the railway had come to stay, and no number of agreements and no amount of litigation could make it other than a nuisance to the householders of Ampthill Square.

The only certain way of preventing railways from becoming a nuisance was to keep them from being built in the first place. The Bedford Office consistently opposed all attempts to build steam underground railways through the estate. None of them ever reached the point of becoming a real threat to the quiet of

22. Sections 12 and 13.   24. 1887 Report, p. 173.
23. 1870 Report, 2, 2; 1884 Report, 2, 3–4.

Bloomsbury; how far the opposition of the ground landlord was responsible is hard to say. The estate did nothing to oppose the building in later years of tube railways, since they were located too far underground ever to prove a nuisance.

Tramways and omnibus lines were as incompatible with the atmosphere of quiet decorum which the estate was trying to maintain as were railways. The Bedford Office was generally successful in keeping bus and tram lines off its residential streets.[25] For a long time the estate was able to exclude omnibuses from Hart Street (now Bloomsbury Way).[26]

Hackney coach stands and cab ranks were another nuisance to be curbed. As early as the 1760s the Duke of Bedford was attempting to have one of the former removed from the center of Bedford Street, Covent Garden, where it was interfering with traffic and annoying the "substantial tradesmen on the west side" of the street.[27] The 1806 Bloomsbury Square Act forbade hackney coaches from standing for hire in the square or within 300 feet of it. In 1886 the Bedford Office attempted, without success, to eject the cab ranks that had just been established in Tavistock and Russell squares.[28]

During the term of a lease the landlord could ensure that the houses would appear attractive only by enforcing the repairing and painting covenants. He could take a more active role with regard to the garden enclosures. Ordinarily a committee of the residents in a square maintained the central garden, levying a rate on the surrounding houses. In some instances the landlord himself took on the responsibility. The Bedford estate and the Brewers' Company jointly paid for the formation of Goldington Crescent and its subsequent upkeep.[29] The Bedford estate itself maintained the gardens in Bedford Square after 1874 when the original leases fell in. It has also been responsible for various smaller pieces of garden area—such as those in Gower Street, Ridgmount Gardens, and Tavistock Place North (Fig. 80).

Although in theory the householders in most squares bore all the expenses of the garden enclosures, the square committees—on the Bedford estate at least—tended to turn to the ground landlord whenever any extraordinary works were required. The volumes of annual reports in the Bedford Office are filled with applications for assistance in rebuilding the iron railings, regraveling the walks,

25. There was a danger in 1871 that a tramway would run through Bedford Square. 1871 Report, p. 125.

26. See 1892 Report, p. 106.

27. Plan of Bedford Street, ca. 1765–68, with annotations.

28. 1886 Report, 2, 2.

29. For a detailed discussion of the ownership, history, and management of the semipublic garden enclosures in London, see the *Report of the Royal Commission on London Squares* (London, 1928).

or relandscaping the gardens of one or another of the squares. Such requests were rarely denied.

Occasionally the Bedford Office itself would initiate the improvements. In 1860 the Duke, disturbed by "the unsightly state of the trees and plants in the gardens of several of the squares," and mindful of "the advantage to the owner that the foliage should be in perfection when the existing leases expire," hired a Mr. Mann to inspect Russell Square. On his recommendation, the Duke ordered the expenditure of £477 on drainage, the renewal of the soil, "and replanting and . . . varying the character of the garden . . ."[30]

The estate ordinarily contributed about half of any extraordinary expenditure on a square. Thus in 1871 the steward recommended that the Duke give £40 to the Oakley Square garden committee, out of £75 that it needed for regraveling walks, drainage repairs, and fresh soil. He advised such assistance as a matter of sound estate policy, "it being for his Grace's interest that the general value of the property should be maintained, and this end being evidently promoted by strengthening the interest of the lessees themselves in it." He did not think that "the lessees should . . . be altogether relieved from occasional extraordinary expenditures," and therefore did not advise the Duke to undertake the whole expense.[31]

More significant than the expenditure on the gardens were the large sums of money spent by the Duke of Bedford for improving the drainage on his estate during the middle years of the nineteenth century. In general the Holborn and Finsbury Commissioners of Sewers undertook to build the more important sewers, while the ground landlords built the lesser ones.

In 1854 the Duke had made at his own expense sewers in Tavistock Mews, Great Russell Street, Little Russell Street, Gilbert Street, and Rose Street. The estate also was engaged at the time in a program of installing water closets in the houses on its property, and connecting them with the new sewers, as required by law. Haedy reported that while the cost had been great, the outlay had "very much raised the character of those parts of your Grace's estate on which that outlay has taken place, as well for occupation by the tenants as for their letting portions of their houses in lodgings, a much better class of persons than those to whom they could be let in their previous condition taking them and lodging in them when thus improved."[32]

In a letter to the *Lancet* that year the physician to the Bloomsbury Dispensary praised the Duke's sanitary projects, and attributed to them the mildness of

30. 1864 Report, pp. 14–15.   32. 1854 Report, pp. 2–3.
31. London Reports, *1*, 80 (20 March 1871).

the recent cholera epidemic on his estate.[33] In 1862 the annual report of the same official observed that "the absence of any general epidemic serves to testify to the high sanitary condition of the district, to the improved drainage and ventilation, and to the greater attention to personal cleanliness of the inhabitants."[34] In 1884 the medical officer for St. Pancras commented on the striking variations in the death rate in the different sections of the parish, ranging from more than 30 per thousand in some parts to a low of 9 per thousand in Bloomsbury.[35]

The need for planning when laying out a building estate was obvious and inescapable. The need to maintain an active control once the estate was built, if equally important in the long run, was less obvious at the time. To a greater or lesser extent landlords allowed many of the restrictive provisions in their leases to become dead letters, or enforced them only sporadically. Even a conscientious landlord often found it legally impossible to enforce his covenants, or found it necessary to overlook violations in order to keep tenants from deserting his estate. Certain evils—such as overcrowding—while they obviously lowered the value of the property, were not strictly speaking violations of leasehold covenants. Growing concern for sanitary requirements might sometimes demand improvements in drainage or water supply which had not been contemplated when the lease was drawn up. At the most the leaseholder was obliged to maintain the premises in something approaching their original condition, when what was often needed was nothing less than total demolition and rebuilding.

Yet leasehold covenants were enforced, on some estates more rigorously than on others, and such enforcement often slowed the process of urban decay even if it could not wholly stop it. Even the dwellings in Compton Place, deplorable though they remained, would surely have been even worse had it not been for the continuing inspections and orders to repair from the Foundling Hospital.

The difficulty was that during the term of the lease, apart from occasional expenditure on public services, the ground landlord was limited to passive and defensive measures. No estate could be better than its original plan; if that was defective, the landlord had to wait until the leases expired before he could do anything about it. The building plan might have been a good one for its own time, but have grown outdated because of changing circumstances. Here at best the landlord could hope to modify the changed circumstances, as the Duke

33. "Of sanitary regulations and improvements, it may be asserted—and our statistics bear out the assertion—that, although the epidemic was not averted by these means, yet that it was greatly divested of its fatal character." *Lancet,* 2 (1854), 426.

34. 1862 Report, p. 8.

35. HWC, p. 73; 1884–85 (4402-I) xxx.

of Bedford did in trying to stop locomotives from smoking while passing through Ampthill Square.

Not until the leases expired could the ground landlord resume a creative role as town planner. Only then did he regain the kind of power which he had when the estate was first being laid out and developed. Only then could he demonstrate the flexibility which the London leasehold system was supposed to possess.

IV *REBUILDING THE NEW TOWNS*

9 Renewal

Today, the master planner must work in four dimensions, for time has become an important consideration. The new towns must be regarded as living organisms, and the likelihood of a plan's being realized exactly in the form in which it is presented depends upon the ability of the planner to predict any future changes in the social organization and habits of the people.—Stewart, A Prospect of Cities (1952)

No town plan can be judged a success merely because it meets the needs of the generation for which it was designed. It must be one which makes possible peaceful change, organic adaptation to the unforeseen requirements of new generations. Such organic adaptation must be subject to the same rational, centralized control as the original plan itself. And since no plan can be completely flexible, it must also contain within it the possibility of its own destruction, if it should ever seem desirable to wipe out the past and start again from scratch.

The London leasehold system permitted only limited change while the leases were in effect, and the initiative for such change as was possible lay solely with the lessee. The ground landlord could not initiate any significant alterations, but could only choose between enforcing covenants and failing to enforce them. His position was wholly defensive: he could prohibit, restrain, and regulate; he could not innovate. When he granted a license, he ordinarily inserted restrictions to prevent the alterations from creating a nuisance, but the most conscientious landlord could do no more than modify the plans of his tenants.

It was only when the leases had expired and the landlord was once again in actual possession of the buildings that he could adopt a dynamic policy of change and adaptation. He might then choose either to reassert or to abandon the original plan. If he decided on the former, he would grant new repairing leases. If the latter, he would demolish the buildings and grant new building leases for their sites. Legally he was a free agent, no longer limited by the rights of subordinate leasehold interests.

Most well-managed estates felt obliged to engage in periodic schemes of demolition and redevelopment, perpetually renewing themselves. "As the old parts of the estate sink into ground rents, through the houses upon them requiring to be rebuilt," wrote Christopher Haedy, steward of the Bedford estate, in 1852, "the new parts will rise by the falling in of the building leases from ground rents to house rents, and this process will always be going on as the new parts of the estate become old and the old parts new . . ."[1] The defenders of the London leasehold system emphasized the flexibility of planning which it allowed, enabling the landlord to adapt his estate to the changing needs of the times. A freeholder of an individual building could at best try to adapt it to the changing character of the neighborhood. A large landowner could change the character of the neighborhood itself. Many of the arguments for land nationalization apply on a smaller scale to the big estate. Just as the Greater London Council could reshape London in any way it wished if it were the freeholder as well as the political authority, so the Duke of Westminster could reshape Mayfair or Belgravia in accordance with changing requirements and changing conceptions of what those neighborhoods ought to be.

Unless an estate had been badly planned at the outset and badly managed thereafter, complete demolition and redevelopment would rarely seem desirable. The landlord would ordinarily content himself with continuing and intensifying the policies which he had followed during the term of the lease. Only now he did not have to rely on the difficult and expensive process of a legal ejectment as a final sanction. For he could require the new lessee to perform as many repairs and improvements as he thought proper before giving him his lease. He could, in addition, insert more stringent covenants in the new lease than there were in the old. But while his methods differed, the process involved a tightening of existing kinds of control rather than the imposition of new types, a reaffirmation of the original town plan rather than its replacement by another one.

An intensification of control first became evident a few years before the leases fell in. As a lease approaches its end, the reversionary value to the freeholder becomes greater and greater, while the value of the lease proportionally diminishes. Therefore the lessee will have fewer selfish motives to keep his property in good repair at the same time that the landlord will be more interested than ever in seeing that he does. One of the basic charges made against the leasehold system was that lessees ordinarily allowed their property—especially in working-class neighborhoods—to fall into disrepair toward the end of the lease, since

1. 1851 Report, p. 12.

most of the benefit of any work done then would go to the ground landlord.[2] Therefore it was then if ever that a landlord would send his surveyor to inspect the premises, then that he would bombard his tenants with notices to repair. "There will always be considerable sections of the estate," John Bourne reminded the Duke of Bedford in 1877, "on which the leases are growing short or expiring, and where the leaseholder's interest is lessening or becoming onerous. On these sections more active interference is called for, both for the protection of the reversion and of adjoining lessees."[3]

Ideally the rational lessee would bear in mind his legal obligation to hand over the property at the end of the term in good and tenantable condition or pay "dilapidations" to make good any deficiencies in that respect. In 1870 Thomas J. R. Davison, then the steward of the Bedford estate, argued that the practice of assessing dilapidations induced tenants to maintain their property in better condition than they might otherwise have done:

> I think there can be no doubt that a very important principle is involved in the assertion of the claim [for dilapidations] which may be made to conduce largely to the maintenance of the repaired condition of the property.
>
> The ordinary repairing covenants in the Duke's leases are probably not more onerous than those which are usually inserted in most leases of house property, and it must be taken that all such covenants are inserted with the express object of protecting the interests of the lessor and of the reversioner, and returning at the end of the term a sound and repaired property which has been properly cared for and upheld, and diminished in value only to the extent of fair wear and tear. These obligations necessarily represent diminished rental value, and as contrasted with a money rent may be termed "rent in kind"— the pecuniary equivalent of which if not rendered during the term should be required in the shape of a payment for dilapidations at the termination of the lease.
>
> It will probably in the majority of cases be preferred to pay the "rent in kind" rather than in the dilapidations—and when it is found that the obligation in one shape or another must be recognized, the

2. See esp. Housing of the Working Classes. R. Com. Rep., p. 59; 1884–85 (4402) xxx. For a more favorable estimate see TH, pp. 316–17; 1886 (213) xii.

3. 1877 Report, 2, 3.

repairing covenants will receive closer attention and the condition of the property *qua* repairs will be improved and maintained.[4]

John Bourne later defined a dilapidation to the Town Holdings Committee as "a default, a neglect, a breach of covenant, as much as the non-payment of rent would be."[5] Viscount Folkestone, a member of the committee, agreed: "It is the fault of the tenant if there is a claim for dilapidations; if he forces his sub-tenants week by week, and month by month, and year by year to keep the property in proper repair and stick to the terms of the contract, there would be no dilapidations at the end of the lease."[6]

That outgoing tenants almost invariably were liable for dilapidations indicates that they seldom fully lived up to the letter of their repairing obligations. "Strictly speaking," Bourne told the committee, "dilapidations do accrue at the end of every lease."[7] Although Hunt of the Portman estate had "met with houses where there were none at all," he admitted that tenants almost always were liable for dilapidations.[8]

The estates did not always demand their full legal rights in this respect. Hunt estimated that on the Portman estate he claimed dilapidations in only about half the cases where the tenant was liable.[9] "As a matter of practice, in dealing with questions of that sort," the steward of the Bedford estate told the committee, "there is an amount of discretion used, but you can hardly say there is any general rule laid down either one way or the other. . . . You act according to circumstances."[10] It was, for instance, customary to waive claims for dilapidations where it was felt that the tenant was unable to pay. In other cases, after a heated exchange of letters between landlord and tenant, they would compromise on a smaller sum than that originally set.

Although the outgoing tenant had the choice between doing the necessary repairs and paying the sum of money, he almost invariably chose the latter. Bourne explained that "the sum of money is always calculated at a much less amount than it would cost him to do the work. It is the rarest thing for a man to make good his dilapidations by actual work."[11] Hunt suggested that tenants preferred paying the lump sum "to avoid the trouble and expense . . . almost turning him out of the house sometimes . . ."[12]

The occupying tenant would be more likely to keep his house in good repair if he knew that he would be granted a new lease when the old one expired.

4. London Reports, *1*, 69–70 (26 November 1870).

5. TH, p. 567; 1887 (260) xiii.

6. Ibid., p. 592; 1888 (313) xxii.

7. Ibid., p. 567; 1887 (260) xiii.

8. Ibid., p. 592; 1888 (313) xxii.

9. Ibid., p. 578.

10. Ibid., p. 567; 1887 (260) xiii.

11. Ibid., pp. 567–68.

12. Ibid., p. 593; 1888 (313) xxii.

Many estates, therefore, made it a practice to offer renewals to occupants well before the old leases fell in. The Foundling Hospital, for instance, was during the 1880s offering its tenants forty-year repairing leases five to fifteen years before the original building leases were to expire.[13] The Portland Marylebone estate ordinarily granted renewals during the last seven years of the lease, but "if a tenant, for some reason, wants to develop his business premises, or to build a billiard-room, or add another storey to his private residence," according to Edward Bailey, one of the two trustees of the estate, "we are ready to arrange . . . terms, by which we extend his term of years . . . although 20 or 30 years may have still to run."[14]

The agents of each of the London estates who were questioned by the Select Committee on Town Holdings reported that it was the invariable policy of their landlord to give the preference to the occupying tenant when a lease was to be renewed.[15] Edward Bailey, trustee of the Portland Marylebone estate, pointed out, however, that "the practice 30 years ago was different; but we thought that the middlemen might not deal so liberally with the occupying tenant as a large estate could afford to do, and we [now] always renew to the occupier . . ."[16] Most witnesses who were tenants confirmed the impression that landlords usually gave the preference to occupants. Brownlow D. Knox of Gloucester Place, whose evidence consisted mostly of complaints about the policies of the Portman estate and its surveyor, admitted "that it is Mr. Hunt's practice to deal exclusively with the occupiers of the premises, whether they hold the original Portman lease or whether they hold any sub-lease from middlemen . . ."[17]

On the other hand, more than one witness brought before the Royal Commission on the Housing of the Working Classes charged that the Northampton estate often refused renewals to occupying tenants, preferring to deal with middlemen. Samuel Brighty, a member of the Clerkenwell parish sanitary committee, reported that "in many of the houses the old tenants do not seem to get the offer of the houses, and that the rents are considerably increased. In consequence the old tenants have left the parish and gone into Highbury and round Finsbury Park, and the houses are let out in tenements . . . I am now referring," he insisted, "to the smaller houses in the parish where there have been in the

13. Ibid., pp. 173–74; 1887 (260) xiii.
14. Ibid., p. 450.
15. For the Norfolk estate see ibid., p. 614. For the Portman estate, see HWC, p. 204; 1884–85 (4402-I) xxx. TH, pp. 574–75; 1888 (313) xxii. For the Portland Marylebone estate see ibid., pp. 442–43; 1887 (260) xiii. For the Bedford estate see ibid., p. 567. For the Northampton estate see HWC, p. 53; 1884–85 (4402-I) xxx. For the Grosvenor estate see TH, p. 332; 1887 (260) xiii. For the Ecclesiastical Commissioners see HWC, p. 214; 1884–85 (4402-I) xxx.
16. TH, p. 442; 1887 (260) xiii.
17. Ibid., p. 485; 1888 (313) xxii.

past . . . men such as a postman . . . or a policeman . . . or small tradesmen, jewellers, and men of that class, who are responsible, respectable, and decent men." Instead house farmers would acquire the leases of as many as twenty houses, and proceed to raise the rents for the old tenants. "In some of the cases," Brighty asserted, the old tenants "have left altogether refusing to pay the increased rental, and then the houses have been let out by the house farmer in tenements, thus producing a higher return."[18] Benjamin Oswald Sharp, vicar of St. Paul's, Clerkenwell, confirmed Brighty's contention.[19]

Boodle vigorously denied the charges.[20] He pointed out, however, that he granted leases only to men whom he considered "substantial" enough to fulfill the responsibilities of the contract. "Those cases . . . of occupants being passed over I am clear must have been cases, if they existed at all, where, after inquiry, we found that the people were not in a position to undertake a lease, and because there were repairs required . . ." he explained. "We have had several cases where we have been disappointed in the tenant," he explained; "a man has undertaken to do the repairs, and he has broken down." The "insubstantial" tenant also was likely to let his rent get into arrear, "and under the present law you cannot eject without a great deal of trouble, and it is a very unpleasant thing to have to talk of ejectment; so that it is necessary to be particular as to whom one grants a lease to."[21] Despite Boodle's well-founded distrust of the middleman,[22] he seemed to regard a house jobber with capital as a lesser evil than a tenant without the means to maintain the property.

With respect to one class of premises, the ground landlords frequently departed from their customary rule of granting the first offer to the occupying tenant. This was the public house. In the late nineteenth century everyone, except presumably the publicans and their customers, agreed that London provided the lower orders with too many temptations to depart from the path of sobriety. Both the local licensing authorities and the ground landlords thought it their duty to reduce the number of public houses per square mile, thereby making it easier for the industrious artisan to arrive home with his pay intact. "No man can walk about London, though he be not a teetotaller, without thinking that the temptation places are too many," said Edward Bailey, of the Portland Marylebone estate. "If a man is walking," he continued, "and there are four houses that he has to pass, he is likely to go into one of them, whereas he may escape if there is only one."[23] Therefore the Portland estate saw to it

18. HWC, p. 108; 1884–85 (4402-I) xxx.
19. Ibid., p. 60.
20. Ibid., pp. 114–18. TH, p. 321; 1887 (260) xiii.
21. HWC, p. 117; 1884–85 (4402-I) xxx.
22. See above, pp. 104–05.
23. TH, p. 456; 1887 (260) xiii.

that no new public houses were established; it had already refused to renew the leases of six or eight existing ones, while about a dozen more were "doomed." Bailey pointed out that such a policy involved "a considerable pecuniary loss to the owners," since public houses "do bear a rather higher rent, even in our rent-roll, than others . . ."[24]

George B. Gregory, treasurer of the Foundling Hospital, suggested that leasehold enfranchisement would prove damaging to the cause of temperance: "There are six or seven public houses within a radius of 200 yards of our gates; you know that they have been so multiplied in London; and on the termination of the leases . . . we mean to reduce the number . . . by declining to renew the leases . . ." Should one of the bills for enfranchising leaseholds become law, "the brewers would take those houses out of our hands; they would turn round upon us the very next day, where the leases had 21 years to run, and purchase the fee. You know that the freehold of a public house sells at a fabulous price in London; they would not mind what they gave for it . . . and so it would be a public house forever."[25]

Boodle agreed that with leasehold enfranchisement "a ground landlord's good intentions on behalf of temperance would be frustrated." Both the Marquess of Northampton and the Duke of Westminster were eliminating public houses from their estates as the leases expired. "On the Duke of Westminster's estate more than 30 public houses have already been done away with during the last 10 or 12 years, not for the duke's profit, but at a great pecuniary loss to him."[26] Francis Edwards, surveyor of the Evelyn estate in Deptford, gave evidence that it was following a similar policy. There were very few pubs on the estate, and leases contained covenants against conversions for such a purpose. "There are many applications made for them," he remarked, "but they are universally refused."[27]

In his report for 1893, A. R. O. Stutfield of the Bedford estate wrote that for the past forty years the policy had been "to suppress as the lease fell in the license of every house that did not appear to be necessary to supply the requirements of the immediate neighborhood." As a result, the number of public houses and hotels on the estate fell from seventy-four in 1854 to fifty in 1869. By 1889 there were forty-one, and in 1893 only thirty-four. The steward predicted that three more would have ceased to exist by the end of 1894.[28] Such practices followed logically from the consistent desire to maintain Bloomsbury

24. Ibid., pp. 444–45.
25. Ibid., p. 183.
26. Ibid., p. 335. For the Northampton estate

see ibid., p. 369.
27. Ibid., p. 471.
28. 1893 Report, p. 107.

as an area of decency, uniformity, restraint, and above all of respectability.

The final volume of the 1902 edition of Charles Booth's *Life and Labour of the People in London* contains a detailed map of central London showing the location of all of its public houses. The three Bedford estates—Bloomsbury in particular—stand out as being noticeably less well supplied than their surrounding areas.

The terms of the new lease would vary according to the repairs which the lessee had agreed to perform, the size of the fine, if any, which he had paid, the rent, and the possibility that the site might be wanted later for redevelopment.

On the Bedford estate, Mr. Bourne reported that repairing leases varied "from 14 to 40 years, according to circumstances. The length of the term, and the amount of rent . . . [are] determined by the amount of outlay that the lessee is going to make in improvements."[29] The Portman estate was prepared to grant reversionary leases for forty years "where a tenant desires to make any material expenditure in the substantial enlargement and improvement of the premises," such as adding an extra story. Otherwise, a lease would be granted for twenty-five years on the payment of a fine"; but where [the tenant] neither wishes to make any improvement or pay a premium, the lease is usually for seven, fourteen, or twenty-one years. . . . determinable at the option of either party."[30] The Foundling estate was for a period in the 80s giving forty-year reversionary leases,[31] but later gave mostly twenty-one-year terms for renewals. The Evelyn estate in Deptford renewed for twenty-one years, probably the closest thing to a standard term for a repairing lease in the London area.[32]

Before it actually granted the lease, the estate would require the prospective lessee to carry out a number of repairs and improvements. In his report for 1870 Mr. Davison of the Bedford estate emphasized that the lessee's outlay on repairs was a matter entirely separate from any payment which he might have made for dilapidations under the old lease:

> There is a not uncommon idea more or less prevalent that a renewal of a lease upon terms involving an outlay for repairs is inconsistent with a claim for dilapidations under the expiring lease—and in such cases it is falsely assumed that the tenant pays twice for the repairs— vizt. once in money to the Duke and again in paying for the work. Upon every ground I regard it as most important in principle that there should be no confusion between the two sets of arrangements,

29. TH, p. 567; 1887 (260) xiii.
30. Ibid., p. 575; 1888 (313) xxii.
31. Ibid., pp. 173–74; 1887 (260) xiii.
32. Ibid., p. 472.

one following upon the other upon the renewal of a lease. Thus, if a fresh lease were made of the same premises to a new lessee the contract with such new lessee would be kept entirely distinct from the previous contract with the previous lessee—and I am quite convinced that it should be equally so in the case of a renewal of a lease to the previous lessee of the same premises—and that the effect of merging a claim for dilapidations in the arrangements for the renewed lease is sacrificing the lessor under both leases for the benefit of the lessee.

In such a case the lessee asks that the claim for dilapidations may be waived in consideration of repairs to be done as part of the new arrangement, ignoring the fact that the new rent is a lower one on account of the outlay for repairs.

There is no doubt that a great deal of temper and patience is and will for some time be necessary in the assertion of these principles, and a certain amount of desuetude in regard to the dilapidations question has been productive of irritation in some instances where the claim has attached—but at the same time I think the principles so essentially right in themselves, and so entirely founded on reason and justice that they will come to be accepted and recognized readily by the more intelligent, and eventually by all classes of the Duke's tenants—and with this view I am endeavoring to justify and explain them to all whom it is necessary to approach with any discussion of them.

I have heard it alleged that there is a custom upon the estate to take no account of dilapidations, and have always urged in reply that a custom can never control an express contract. At the same time there may have been in previous circumstances something suggesting for the present a tender and discretionary application of the principle of enforcing the claim.[33]

The repairs varied according to the condition and location of the house. The improvements might range in nature from a new marble chimneypiece to the installation of plate glass windows, from the addition of a bathroom to the rebuilding of the whole front of the house. In 1884 a lessee on the Portman estate was asked to do the following as a condition for a twenty-five-year lease:

> The premises are to be substantially repaired by the lessee, who is also to do the following additional works . . . thoroughly repair the roof and relay defective gutters with 6 lbs. lead; rebuild the upper part

33. London Reports, *1*, 70.

of back wall; and put proper Portland stone copings to all walls; reinstate flat over scullery with 6 lbs. lead; renew present internal partitions in stables and coachhouse, and re-arrange rooms over with new
partitions and ceilings; relay the drains with glazed stoneware socketed
pipes, if not already done, with proper surface gulleys for drainage of
yards and sinks, and disconnected from the main sewer and ventilated,
and also ventilate the soil pipes. The works are to be executed in accordance with drawings previously approved and signed by Viscount
Portman's surveyor, and completed to his entire satisfaction before
the 30th day of December 1888 . . . This proposal is to be subject to a
proper agreement being signed . . . The new lease is to contain all the
usual covenants now inserted in the leases granted on this estate for
private dwelling houses.[34]

The precise terms were a matter for negotiation; as a matter of fact the above
specifications were rejected by the tenant, and a new agreement with fewer requirements was eventually reached.

The form for renewed leases on the Northampton estate in effect in 1884 required the tenant "to repair, paint, paper, and cleanse the premises, both ex-
ternally and internally. To wash, color, and draw the external brick work,
including that of the chimney stacks, and to paint and repair the cement work.
To put the drainage into good order. If not already done, to ventilate the soil
pipes, and disconnect from the sewers and drains the waste pipes."[35] A landlord
could make fewer demands in Clerkenwell than in Marylebone, but the principle was the same.

If the repairs were heavy and the term of the new lease short, the landlord
might contribute to the cost of the alterations. Or he might compensate the
lessee by extending the term of the lease—giving him a longer period in which
to get back his investment—or by lowering the rent. The landlord could therefore argue that he himself paid, if indirectly, for the repairs. Edward Bailey, of
the Portland Marylebone estate, pointed out that demands for repair were not
made "capriciously . . . because for every outlay . . . [the tenant] makes he pays
us so much less rent. A small proprietor," he thought, "would very likely pass
over many things and say, 'Cobble it up, that will do; it will last your time;'
but on a large estate the owner wishes to have a good repute for the sanitary
condition of his estate and for its good appearance . . ."[36] He attributed the
demands for improvements not so much to economic motives as to "the pride

34. TH, pp. 485–86; 1888 (313) xxii.   36. TH, p. 452; 1887 (260) xiii.
35. HWC, pp. 41–42; 1884–85 (4402-I) xxx.

that a large proprietor has in his estate . . ." The Portland estate made a practice of requiring "not inevitably rebuilding, but a large rehabilitation, for sanitary improvements, modernising, putting in plate-glass windows, raising a story, and improving the property in that way."[37]

The popular notion of the renewal of a lease is of an occasion when the landlord can increase the rent to any figure he likes, adding immensely to his income. By the 1880s Londoners had added "unearned increment" to their vocabulary, whether or not they understood the full import of Henry George's theories. Frank Banfield could assert that with the expiration of a great many building leases on the Portman estate in 1888, "the process of drawing handsome premiums and of raising ground rents to seven and eightfold their original figure has been carried out on a wholesale scale, calculated to make the mouth of a Midas water, or to cause Croesus to turn in his grave for envy."[38] He later estimated "that 'unearned increment' on the Portman estate upon March 25, 1888, meant a million and a quarter of pounds sterling—not a penny less."[39]

Witnesses before the Town Holdings Committee and members of the committee sometimes asserted that on renewals a landlord invariably charged "the rack rent, that is to say, the highest rent that could be obtained . . . a starvation rent . . ."[40] Such definitions, with their emotional overtones, are of as little help in understanding what actually happened as the contrary assertions from the landlords' agents that "the rents are arranged at the amounts that we consider fair, and that the tenants do not object to."[41]

Henry Trelawny Boodle explained in this connection that "the Duke of Westminster's estate is managed by a board, and his Grace himself attends and presides. The estate surveyor, the agent who attends to the rents, and myself are there, and the estate surveyor reports to the board what per foot frontage should be charged, and who should be dealt with; and we act upon his report, or do not act upon his report, as the Duke decides."[42] Hunt, the surveyor of the Portman estate, said that he arrived at his valuation of premises to be renewed with "recourse to the parochial assessments, and correct this by my knowledge of recent underlettings, by lessees, and by sales at auction of adjacent property of a similar character." His valuation might sometimes exceed the parochial assessment, "but oftener it is less . . ."[43]

John Dunn, surveyor to the Duke of Norfolk, estimated that rents on his

---

37. Ibid., p. 450.
38. *The Great Landlords of London,* p. 34.
39. Ibid., p. 40.
40. TH, p. 379; 1887 (260) xiii.

41. Francis Edwards, surveyor of the Evelyn estate. Ibid., p. 472.
42. Ibid., p. 351.
43. Ibid., p. 575; 1888 (313) xxii.

estate averaged about 15 per cent lower than those on neighboring properties.[44] "The Duke's instructions to me are . . . to put the rents a little below the market value," with preference to be given to the occupying tenant.[45] He thought such a practice was not so much philanthropy as sound estate management: "I think that it has a better feeling; you get known in the neighborhood, and people know the property, and you always have it full. . . . I do not think it is the policy of a large estate to be exacting in rents."[46]

Bourne of the Bedford estate pointed out that "you seldom get two rents, even under adjoining repairing leases, identically the same, because the calculations are made on the basis of allowing a return to the tenant for any outlay that is going to be made in improvements."[47]

Sir John Ellis, a member of the Town Holdings Committee, concluded that "it is impossible to establish a principle" upon which rents are assessed. "Every house has its different value by reason of its present state, its construction, and suitability for any particular purpose that it may be applied to . . . And circumstances will render a fixed principle impossible."[48]

Still, no one denied that rents tended to rise considerably whenever a lease fell in, particularly when a long-term building lease was replaced by a repairing lease. To an age which retained its faith in the unchanging value of the pound, this was inevitably disturbing. Representatives of the estates pointed out that there was a real difference between a ground rent, which only paid for the building site, and an improved rent, which paid for both the site and the house on it. The second would naturally be much greater than the first. Furthermore, in most instances the actual tenant would be paying not the low ground rent but a rack rent to a middleman. If he was in a position to accept a new lease directly from the estate, he might well find that he was paying less rent than before.[49] F. W. Hunt said that on the Portman estate the new rent would be "certainly less than he has been paying" to the middleman.[50]

But the main cause of increased rents was, of course, the general rise in land values in central London for which neither landlord nor tenant was responsible. Sidney Webb estimated in 1890 that "during the last 20 years land in London has grown in annual value, after deducting all the annual value of buildings and of all structural alterations, at the rate of £300,000 a year."[51] The frequency

44. Ibid., p. 617; 1887 (260) xiii.

45. Ibid., p. 614.

46. Ibid., p. 624.

47. Ibid., p. 567.

48. Ibid., p. 355.

49. See, for instance, H. T. Boodle on the situation on the Northampton estate in HWC, p. 57; 1884–85 (4402-I) xxx.

50. Ibid., p. 205.

51. Town Holdings. Taxation of Ground Rents. Sel. Cttee. mins. of ev., pp. 21–22; 1890 (341) xviii.

with which ground landlords, on the expiration of leases, had the buildings demolished and the site relet to builders, would indicate that comparatively little of the increased value was due to the exertions of the old tenant.

Robert Vigers, surveyor to the Peabody Trustees, estimated that while the houses in Russell Square were then paying between twenty-five and fifty pounds annual ground rent, "every one of those is worth £100 a year; the bit of ground alone without the house is worth that."[52] For property in an "admirable situation" such as Oxford Street it was even more true "that the structure, the fabric, bears but a small proportion to the value of the right of occupancy."[53]

A recurring complaint was that tenants of shop property were forced, when renewing, to pay for the additional value created both by their own good will and by their structural improvements. Banfield was particularly eloquent on the subject:

> Allowing for the moment that the large freeholders should be left free to grant 99 years' leases and no more, I maintain that at the end of the term they should be allowed only to take back the land, and that for everything else which had been put there by the tenant, whether building or business connection, they should pay a fair valuation. It is of the nature of the shopkeeper's vocation as distinct from that of the wholesale merchant and manufacturer that his good will should be tied to the locality where it has been won.
>
> . . . The oppressor [the ground landlord] is bought off with the extortionate premium and the crushing tribute of the ground rent. No mogul monarch, no Persian satrap, was ever harder on a conquered people. They might go if they did not like the terms, it may be said. . . .
>
> But how is an old man of sixty or seventy to go and start in business elsewhere, and work up a circle of customers in a strange quarter of London? His apprehensions and his affections make him cling to the old spot. He will bleed through all his pores rather than be cut adrift. He may be buffeted about by the Viscount [i.e. Lord Portman] and the surveyor [Hunt]; but he will still hang on desperately, like the sailor to his last hope, the life buoy, flung to him amid the whirling surges of the sea. It seems to me that some impartial tribunal should step in between this old man and his master, and say, "No, you shall not trade on his fears so as to mulct him in these fearful financial penalties. The ground is yours, you say. Good; take it. It is in the bond, you affirm.

52. TH, p. 63; 1887 (260) xiii.   53. Edward Bailey, trustee of the Portland
                                                     Marylebone estate, ibid., p. 453.

But you may not, on that account, ruin him and drive him with his gray hairs to beggary in the cold streets, or to the harsh misery of the workhouse. English public opinion has so changed old feudal law, as to afford better protection than that to our citizens. You must compensate him handsomely for every penny he has laid out on that property of yours. Impartial valuers shall estimate it. You shall pay him the market value of that good-will of his, and give him an adequate solatium for the loss further accruing from his personal divorce from his property, and for the separation you have worked between him and his old home." This would be no plundering. It would take away from the landlord the guilt of the commission of it. The policy of confiscation has been the ground landlord's hitherto. We want him to cease from that, to be just, to be honest.[54]

Bailey of the Portland Marylebone estate and Boodle of the Grosvenor and Northampton estates both denied emphatically that good will entered into the calculation of the rent for the renewal of shop property.[55] Howard Martin, the surveyor, thought that ground landlords rarely raised the rent because of the tenant's good will. "I have no doubt," he admitted, "that in bargains of that kind people take advantage of each other sometimes, as they do in any bargain if they get the opportunity; but so far as my observation and experience go, it is not a usual thing that advantage should be taken of the lessee . . . under those circumstances. The usual course . . . is to charge . . . merely the fair rental value of the premises." He pointed out that "a good substantial tenant is much too valuable now . . . for a landlord to run any risk at all of driving him away by seeking to impose upon him excessive terms."[56]

As to whether compensation was paid, or ought to be paid, for tenants' improvements, the situation was less clear. Edward Yates, a builder in south London, said that he had "never known a case" himself where the landlord had made any allowance for unexhausted improvements on renewing a lease, and did not think that it was customary.[57] James Platt, house agent and woolen merchant, insisted that "the landlord makes no concession for any improvements made, but charges him [the tenant] for [them]."[58]

Agents of certain estates pointed out that alterations made by a tenant might not in fact be "improvements" from the point of view of the freeholder. "I have

54. Frank Banfield, *The Great Landlords of London*, pp. 106–08.
55. For Bailey, see TH, pp. 443, 453; 1887 (260) xiii. For Boodle, see ibid., p. 355.
56. Ibid., p. 86.
57. Ibid., p. 380.
58. Ibid., p. 264.

known many cases," recalled Boodle, "where a tenant thinks he has improved his house and the landlord would rather that he had not made the so-called improvements."[59] Bourne of the Bedford estate agreed: "The lessees are very fond of exercising their own good taste (as perhaps they may think it), in a way that does not in the least degree improve a property *qua* property, and for such an alteration . . . no one would dream of giving compensation or allowing it in rent."[60]

But where the tenants actually had increased the real value of their premises, the estates felt that some sort of compensation—perhaps a reduction of rent on the renewal—ought to be given. Edward Bailey said that on the Portland Marylebone estate, "If the tenant drew our attention to the fact that he had made some improvements within recent years, I do not mean fifty or forty years ago, but say within the last fifteen years or so . . . we certainly should not charge him anything in respect to that." On the contrary, "we should consider him an improving tenant and a man to be encouraged." He said that he had never come across an instance of another freeholder charging his tenants for their own good will, "and we have a pretty wide opportunity of learning . . . [about] other estates by the actual experience of our clients."[61]

Bourne said that lessees "invariably" had the value of improvements recognized when they settled terms with the Bedford Office.[62] Boodle thought that a landlord "ought to take into consideration the improvements in renewing the lease if they are really improvements." If, for example, "a man has added stories to his house in the last ten years, and if the landlord relets the house to that man and charges him the extra value on account of that improvement, it is very hard. This is never done," he insisted, "upon the estates that I have to deal with." He would have been "very glad if there were any alteration possible" in the law "that might fairly protect the tenant in such a case, except that would necessarily hamper the landlord in rebuilding. . . . For a landlord to be hampered by having to pay compensation to everybody who has improved a house, which then had to be pulled down for the purpose of . . . public improvements, would be a serious matter," he thought.[63]

On certain estates a tenant might be required to pay a lump sum called a fine, or premium, or consideration when he got his repairing lease, paying a proportionally smaller rent thereafter. The Foundling Hospital—except when renewing public-house leases—and the Evelyn and Northampton estates never took fines;

59. Ibid., p. 372.   62. Ibid., p. 570.
60. Ibid., p. 568.   63. Ibid., p. 372.
61. Ibid., pp. 443, 450.

the Bedford estate ended the practice in the 1820s.[64]

The Grosvenor estate always demanded fines, except for very short leases. Boodle described the system in this way:

> The fair annual value of a house (after making allowance for expenses, repairs, rates, taxes, and insurance, payable by the lessee) is ascertained, and a proportionate part, either about one-half or one-third of such net value, is capitalized by the 5 per cent table, and paid down on the granting of the lease as a fine or premium. By this means the lessee practically purchases the lease for a term certain at a reduced rent, and obtains 5 per cent compound interest for his money so applied.

Tenants, he thought, usually preferred the method, and it was advantageous to the estate "because, although the landlord receives a smaller rent than otherwise, he has a guarantee that the tenant has undertaken the responsibilities of a lease which he can fulfill."[65]

The Portland Marylebone estate, "with a view to the general welfare of the property," similarly thought "that the lessee should always have a substantial interest in keeping it in good order . . ." It therefore required him "to make an expenditure, either in a considerable outlay on the property or in a sum of money in the way of fine." Such a system "facilitates our collection of the rents," and also was "generally beneficial to the estate, because the lessees have a valuable interest up to the end of their term."[66] The Portman estate also required fines or extensive rebuilding for anything longer than a seven, fourteen, or twenty-one-year lease.[67]

Sometimes, when a block of leases fell in, an estate would use its powers not merely to maintain an existing level of respectability but to recapture a character which had been lost. The history of Gower Street in the late nineteenth century involves one such attempt by the Bedford estate.

To the Victorian with any pretensions at aesthetic discrimination Gower Street symbolized all that was deplorable in Georgian architecture. Dull, gloomy, and monotonous, the street inevitably suffered in the eyes of those who judged by the standards of Sloane Street and the Cromwell Road. Even the Georgians had their doubts about it. Edward Pugh, writing in 1805, chose Gower Street as an example of "that monotonous and never varying line now so much in vogue."[68] By 1839 another writer was describing it as "a street which

64. Ibid., pp. 349, 472.
65. Ibid., pp. 329–30.
66. Ibid., p. 443.

67. See above, p. 166.
68. David Hughson [Edward Pugh], *London* (6 vols., London, 1805–09), 2, 342.

scarcely exhibits any signs of its being an inhabited place. Here and there you
see a solitary pedestrian, or perchance a one-horse chaise. The stranger," he
wrote, "in passing along this street, feels an emotion of melancholy come over
him, caused by its dullness and unbroken monotony."[69] (See Figs. 24–26.)

The decline of the social character of Gower Street accompanied the decline
of its architectural reputation. By the late 1870s, when most of the original
leases were falling in, the older inhabitants had left the street, and "nearly every
house was occupied as a lodging or boarding house," according to the steward,
John Bourne. "In fact," he reported, "what may be termed the 'lodging house
dry rot' had entered the street, and unless this is eradicated the street must before very long lose its old standing and respectability." Out of thirty-four houses
in hand in 1880, only ten were still private residences. The estate decided to
restore the street to its old character by granting new leases only to private tenants and insisting on heavy repairs and alterations. "Even if the lodging house
element had been permitted, the outlay required," averaging £700 per house,
would, according to the steward, have made it impossible for them to obtain
new leases. Owing to the harsh conditions, the estate was able to let only six
of the thirty-four houses in 1880. Despite the discouraging beginning, Bourne
was confident that in the end "it will be found that a great and desirable improvement has been effected."[70]

But in his evidence before the Town Holdings Committee in July 1887,
Bourne said that several houses in Gower Street were still in hand, since he
would "not let them for any purpose except that of a gentleman's private residence." He thought such a policy justified "because the street, being a street
for private residences, and the houses built for that purpose, it is desirable to
preserve . . . that residential character." He said that he had "effectually stamped
out" the "lodging-house element." The new leases were for twenty-one-year and
thirty-year terms, "and in one or two instances for forty years, because in these
instances the houses had, for reasons that arise in the course of a century, gone
more out of repair, and needed a larger outlay . . ."[71]

His report the following December was pessimistic. Since "private occupying
investors" showed no interest in the houses, the steward was reluctantly negotiating with middlemen. The great number of leases falling in together had
produced "a 'glut' of houses, and consequent depreciation in the letting market
. . ." Even middlemen refused to take more than a few of them at any one time.[72]

69. Grant, *Sketches of London, 1*, 15.
70. 1880 Report, 2, 4–5.
71. TH, p. 569; 1887 (260) xiii.

72. London Reports, 2, 107 (14 December
1887).

The situation in Gower Street was not unique. There were at the time blocks of houses in Bloomsbury Square and Southampton Row to which occupying tenants were equally indifferent. In many instances, whether from the shortness of the term proposed or for other reasons, the steward explained, "a middleman is without inducement and a sitting tenant is not able or willing to meet an immediate outlay of capital, though ready to pay a rent."[73] He suggested that the estate depart from its usual policy and contribute toward the cost of repairs of such houses in order to facilitate their letting.

In October 1888 Bourne reluctantly recommended the granting of a lease of five houses in Gower Street to a middleman for thirty years, at £30 per annum for each house. Although he considered the rent far from adequate, the fact that the lessee would have to spend £5,000 on repairs made it impossible to ask more.[74]

Despite the endeavors of the Bedford Office, the lodging-house keeper began to return to Gower Street. In May 1889 A. R. O. Stutfield, the new steward, began a campaign to force a Mrs. Lawson to cease operating two lodging houses in the street. Pleas for leniency from her alternated with demands for action from the private residents in the street. By December 1890 Mrs. Lawson had given up one of the houses, but was still taking lodgers in the other. Observing that the estate had introduced especially strict covenants into the leases to attract a high class of tenant to Gower Street, Stutfield pointed out that "it was on the faith of the covenants being enforced that many private and professional gentlemen invested their money in the purchase of leases of houses in the street . . ." He concluded that there was "a moral—and I venture to think also a legal—obligation on the freeholder to enforce the covenants where the fact of a breach is clearly established."[75]

The efforts of the Bedford Office found recognition in Wheatley and Cunningham, *London Past and Present* (London, 1891). The entry for Gower Street describes it as "a dull, heavy street of commonplace houses, but as the leases fall in the houses are greatly improved, and in consequence the street wears a much brighter aspect."

The endeavors to maintain its bright aspect continued. In 1894 Stutfield was involved in a struggle with another tenant in the street, who was not only carrying on the business of a photographer but had built without authorization a series of one-story brick buildings over the garden of his house. The steward explained that when the original leases had expired, "the entire destruction and

73. Ibid., pp. 109–10 (31 May 1888).   75. Ibid., pp. 133–34 (11 December 1890).
74. Ibid., p. 116 (11 October 1888).

removal of all back buildings . . . [had been] rigidly insisted on, it being considered that all such additions to the structure tended in a remarkable degree to the deterioration of the whole street." The photographer's new buildings were, he thought, "merely a recrudescence of the old disease . . . It is obvious," he observed, "that there is a tendency to treat the contract (for such is a lease) as a one-sided one—to be neglected—and if this disposition should be encouraged by acts of condonement it will be well nigh impossible to maintain good management." He pointed out that the policy in reletting premises gave "special heed to provision for light and air—which can only be well safeguarded by insisting on sufficient open spaces at the backs of houses . . . but ground in London is so valuable that tenants unless watched are very prone (as in this case) to cover the reserves with low buildings . . ." In such a manner, he recalled, "Lord Northampton's Clerkenwell property gradually deteriorated—till it became such a slum and a scandal."[76]

In 1896 Stutfield advised the Duke to reduce by £20 per annum the rents of the block 1–15 Gower Street. The lessee believed "that if he were in a position to lower his rents by £20 per annum it might be possible to let these houses to private residents."[77]

In the long run the attempts to keep lodging houses out of Gower Street—or out of any part of Bloomsbury—were doomed to failure. The tenacity of the efforts of the Bedford Office to restore the Gentleman's Private Residence to Gower Street shows how seriously the great landlords tried to achieve their conception of town planning. The outcome shows how limited their powers were, even after the leases had expired.

One possible way for a landlord to intensify his control over the estate was not to grant new leases at all, but instead to retain the ownership of the leasehold interest. The only certain way to abolish the house farmer was for the ground landlord himself to become the middleman, take charge of the repairs, and let out the property directly on weekly or monthly tenancies. Such a policy would answer many of the objections of the Royal Commission on the Housing of the Working Classes to the system of great urban estates. Their report placed the responsibility for overcrowding not so much on the ground landlord himself as on the multiplicity of interests between the freeholder and the occupying tenant:

76. Ibid., pp. 471–72 (2 August 1894).   77. London Reports, 3, 56 (25 September 1896).

The freeholder of a building estate appears to be in practice not the responsible owner of the property for sanitary purposes. The terms of the leases provide that the tenant shall keep the house in repair, but the stringent conditions of the leases fall into disuse; the difficulty of personal supervision of the property is apt to grow greater, and the relations between the ground landlord and the tenant who occupies the house grow less and less. The multiplicity of interests involved in a single house and the number of hands through which the rent has to pass, causes the greatest doubt as to who is the person who ought to be called upon to execute repairs or to look after the condition of the premises.[78]

Because of such considerations, and because of their disillusioning experiences with their lessees, the Northampton estate began in 1884 a policy of retaining direct ownership of slum property when the leases expired. They were in part following the example of Lord Leigh's estate in Holborn. Lord William Compton told the Royal Commission on the Housing of the Working Classes of his interest in Lord Leigh's experiment:

. . . I have been over . . . [his property] very carefully to see what Lord Leigh has himself done. He has evidently taken the greatest interest in it; he has visited it frequently himself, and Lady Leigh too. In one part he almost rebuilt certain cottages, (there is very little but the original shell remaining,) and those he lets out at not excessive rents; although they are not very low rents, in my opinion. Lord Leigh kindly put me in communication with his agent, and he informed me that on the sum he spent he realized about 8 per cent, exclusive of everything else. But, I must add, that he picks his tenants, which always makes a great difference in that class of property.[79]

But the chief exponent of such a policy, and the main influence on the new practices of the Northampton estate, was Octavia Hill. This extraordinary woman (1838–1912) had since 1864 been buying up tenement houses, putting them into decent order, and managing them herself. The *Dictionary of National Biography* quotes her as listing the following principles, in 1899, as guiding her management: "Repairs promptly and efficiently attended to, references completely taken up, cleaning sedulously supervised, overcrowding put an end

78. Housing of the Working Classes. R. Com.   79. HWC, p. 35; 1884–85 (4402-I) xxx.
Rep., p. 21; 1884–85 (4402) xxx.

to, the blessing of ready-money payments enforced, accounts strictly kept, and, above all, tenants so sorted as to be helpful to one another." In 1884 the Ecclesiastical Commissioners appointed her to manage a great part of their property in Southwark.

Lord William Compton felt that a policy of letting directly to the occupants of tenements might well be desirable for all ground landlords holding lower-class property. "First of all," he remarked, "I should have thought that he would have made a much larger profit out of it if he did so."[80] The tenants would also benefit: "In all probability no diminution in the rents would result . . . in the large majority of cases; it would only be the philanthropist," he thought, "who would let his rooms at a small rent. But . . . it would be the interest of the ground landlord that it should be kept properly, because every month that it deteriorates it decreases in value; and every agent knows that or should know it."[81] Boodle was more optimistic about rents being lowered, despite the increased expense of repairs. "I do not think," he said, "that a landlord would exact every farthing of rent . . . out of the occupants like many middlemen do." Middlemen, he asserted, "enter into a speculation of that kind merely for profit, as a rule, and I do not think that that is the right way of approaching it."[82]

Three years later Boodle was able to describe some of the results of the new policy to the Town Holdings Committee. Since his questioning by the Royal Commission the estate had acquired the direct management of from forty to fifty houses, with a lady visitor, recommended by Octavia Hill, to collect the lodgers' rents. "This lady also looks round the other poor houses on the estate, and sends me reports as to defects, and I call upon the lessees to remedy them."[83] Since Miss Hill was opposed to the erection of special model lodging houses, Boodle was keeping the old buildings standing, putting them into proper repair, and improving the drainage and sanitation. Although no more than a start could be made with the new policy while most of the estate remained on the original building leases, he thought that there had been a noticeable improvement. Even the middlemen were better than they had been, because "they know there is more supervision than there was."[84]

80. Ibid., p. 36.
81. Ibid., p. 40.
82. Ibid., p. 57.

83. TH, p. 320; 1887 (260) xiii.
84. Ibid., pp. 338–39.

10 Redevelopment

A magistrate is said once to have asked, in a vague sort of way: "Where is the Act of Parliament under which the Duke of Westminster is proceeding in Grosvenor Place?" but the Duke disturbed, and beautified, and modified public rights of way as if he was monarch of all he surveyed.—Frank Banfield, The Great Landlords of London (1890)

Sometimes an estate would take advantage of the end of a lease to have the house taken down and to relet the site on a new building lease. The house might have grown too decayed to be worth repairing. Or it might, although itself in good condition, be part of a block of dilapidated buildings and be sacrificed in the cause of a general scheme of redevelopment. It might be too old fashioned in plan for the needs of the time. Or the character of the street might have changed so greatly as to require an entirely different sort of building.

The defenders of the London leasehold system thought that one of its great merits was that it facilitated programs of large-scale redevelopment. Edward Bailey, of the Portland Marylebone estate, argued that "the owners of large building estates are in a position to carry out many beneficial things which smaller owners neither have the power, nor from their lesser stake, can be expected to accomplish." Great landlords carried out improvements at their own expense which were "beneficial to the public, which could not have been carried out by isolated freeholders, and only by a public authority at great cost to the ratepayers."[1] Arthur Anthony Baumann, Conservative M.P. for Peckham and a member of the Town Holdings Committee, suggested that "under the leasehold system . . . as the leases fall in . . . slums are pulled down, whereas, if the property were freehold, they would probably continue to stand; in fact, they would be left until they were cleared away by a public authority at the public cost."[2] Robert Vigers, surveyor to the Peabody Trustees, said that in his experience, leasehold houses, when they "were getting old and out of date, and it was

1. TH, p. 444; 1887 (260) xiii. 2. Ibid., p. 85.

better to pull them down and build more convenient ones," generally were pulled down when their leases expired; comparable freehold houses were often allowed to deteriorate indefinitely.[3]

Opponents of the leasehold system admitted the frequency of rebuilding schemes, but attributed them to the bad state of the existing property, rather than to any philanthropic desire to provide metropolitan improvements or ameliorate housing conditions. Edward Yates, the builder, thought that such schemes stemmed from economic necessity only:

> The reason why a great many of the old buildings in London are pulled down is because they do not pay to keep them up any longer; it is a question which pays best, to pull them down and let the land for rebuilding, or to keep them up. Of course there may possibly be very wealthy people who are an exception, but as a rule it is simply a commercial question, which does it pay best to do; to patch the buildings up to keep them up a few years longer, or are we going to spend every penny we get in the way of rent in patching them up, and then get nothing at the end of the year. We should lay out . . . all our income in keeping them upon their legs. In most cases it is said these old buildings do not pay to keep up any longer; therefore clear the old rubbish away and let us let the land to build on.[4]

Such a decision, he thought, was ordinarily reached with the greatest of reluctance:

> Generally at the expiration of the lease it runs thus: the ground lease falls in, and of course there is no doubt the landowner imagines that he is going to have a very largely increased income of rack rental. The agent takes possession of the property, and he finds at the expiration of twelve months he has laid as much out on that property in repair as he has taken; and I should imagine when he makes his account up to send to his superior he feels in a very unpleasant position, because he begins to doubt whether his superior will not think he is managing that estate for his own advantage. The consequence is it is generally kept for eight, or ten, or twelve years, according to the status of it. At last they find that really the property is worn out; a natural state of decay has set in, and the best thing they can possibly do is to pull it

---

3. Ibid., p. 48.   4. Ibid., p. 377.

down, or rebuild it; and that is really about the history of a great deal of such property.[5]

Rational redevelopment for whatever motives was possible only if the leases of a number of adjacent houses fell in simultaneously, or nearly simultaneously. A well-managed estate had to think in terms not of individual houses but of blocks of houses. It was important that a street or square, when it was first laid out, be planned as a whole. It was equally important that at the time of its original planning provision be made so that it could at some future date be re-planned as a whole.

Edward Ryde, the surveyor, told the Town Holdings Committee that "on all well-managed estates, leases in different situations are made to expire at the same period." With such a policy, if "land which was suited for a small class of property at the beginning of the 99 years' term, should at the end of the . . . term, turn out to be better fitted for a greatly improved class of property, you would have an opportunity of clearing away all the smaller property and devoting the site to the improvement . . ."[6] Boodle reported that the renewals on the Northampton and Grosvenor estates were "nearly all made with the view to fitting in with the adjoining houses" in order to permit the landlord "ultimately to deal with the whole property in a comprehensive way . . ." The possibility of redevelopment was never forgotten: "Although there might be no question of rebuilding involved at the moment, there might be thereafter."[7]

As far back as the middle eighteenth century there were some streets on the Bedford estate in which all the leases were timed to expire together, although they were as yet the exception rather than the rule. Where such circumstances prevailed, conscious planning was certainly involved. Leases for adjacent houses reading respectively 21 years from Midsummer 1756, 14¾ years from Michaelmas 1762, and 30 years from Midsummer 1747—all expiring Midsummer 1777—cannot have happened by chance.

As early as 1730 the estate was engaged in rejuvenating both Covent Garden and Bloomsbury. In 1729/30 it granted fifteen building contracts calling for the demolition of houses on the north side of Henrietta Street, Covent Garden, and their replacement by a uniform row of second-rate houses. The buildings were to conform to a draft plan signed by the builders, and were to be "all of the same height so that the whole range of new houses to be erected . . . may appear regu-

5. Ibid., p. 381.
6. Ibid., pp. 309–10; 1886 (213) xii.

7. Ibid., p. 351; 1887 (260) xiii.

larly, uniformly, and handsomely built, the height of stories, windows, and doors to be of equal size." The builders agreed to share the expense of a "new common sewer of sufficient depth to drain the cellars and vaults of the said new houses, which said new sewer shall be of sufficient height and width and substantially built and arched with good sound bricks . . ." The new leases were to run for sixty-one years, the standard length for building leases at that time on the estate.[8] In the same month the estate granted building leases for four houses on the site of four old buildings in Hart Street, Bloomsbury.[9]

Similar small-scale schemes of redevelopment were continually going forward throughout the eighteenth and nineteenth centuries. In Bloomsbury, for example, Queen Street (now Museum Street), Peter Street, and Hyde Street were completely rebuilt between the 1730s and the 1760s. The whole of the north side of Little Russell Street was rebuilt during the 1730s, as was much of Hart Street in the 50s and 60s.[10]

The building of the Bedford estate never ceased. Out of forty-eight houses in Bloomsbury whose leases expired in 1745 and 1746, the estate had thirty-four pulled down and their sites let on building leases. Of the remaining houses, several were let on short-term repairing leases, designed to fall in at the same time as neighboring buildings, so that the whole block could be rebuilt together.[11]

Whenever leases fell in, the estate had a survey made to help determine its policy toward the buildings. A typical one was that made in August 1765 by John Gorham—who did a great deal of such work for the Bedford estate—of six houses in King Street, Bloomsbury. Gorham reported that although "the walls and timbers in general [are] very capable of standing a twenty-one-years' lease, some underpinnings are necessary. The houses," he wrote, "are thoroughly worn on the inside and will require £150 a house to put them into a proper repair; some regulation is necessary when they are repaired to make them alike in front . . ."[12] The following March, Gorham, together with William Lyster, submitted a report on seventeen other houses in King Street. Some of them they thought had such "bad plans" and were so thoroughly worn as to require complete rebuilding, "conformable to the houses on the opposite side of the way."[13]

The purchase in June 1763 of a piece of land to the west of Bloomsbury

8. Contract Book II for the Houses in and about Covent Garden from Lady Day 1730, pp. 9-10.

9. Contract Book for . . . Bloomsbury Commencing from Lady Day 1730, p. 53.

10. Bloomsbury Rental, 1770.

11. "An account of the houses in Bloomsbury and Covent Garden that the leases will expire in 1745 and 1746, and also of those that are in hand, and must be disposed of as soon as possible."

12. Mr. Gorham's survey of 6 houses on the east side of King Street, Bloomsbury, 15 August 1765.

13. Survey of several houses on the east side of King Street, Bloomsbury, 10 March 1766.

Square from the estate of the late Duke of Buckingham precipitated a large-scale program of demolition and reconstruction. The new property lay within the rectangle formed by Great Russell Street on the north, Duke Street (now Coptic Street) on the east, St. Giles's High Street on the south, and Dyott Street on the west. Bordering the Bedford estate on the north and east, it required extensive rehabilitation before it could become an integral part of the Bloomsbury estate, and worthy of its new landlord.[14] The estate proceeded to buy up the leasehold interests and have the houses either completely rebuilt or demolished and replaced by new buildings. It widened Castle Street and the northern part of Plumtree Street. It laid new sewers in Charlotte, Thorney, and Woburn streets. By 1770 it had spent £13,812 18s. 10d. on the property, of which £8,000 represented the purchase price.[15]

The estate continued to effect street improvements from time to time. In the early 1790s it again widened Castle Street.[16] In 1793 it extended Bow Street, Covent Garden northward, so that it ran into Long Acre.[17] In the middle of the next decade it widened a section of Southampton Row.[18]

The most far-reaching of all the schemes of redevelopment on the Bedford estate began with the reconstruction of Covent Garden Market in the late 1820s. Before it ended, the greater part of the Covent Garden estate had been transformed from a lower-class residential neighborhood into a prosperous mercantile quarter.

Until the 1820s the Duke had let the market to middlemen, who in turn collected the rents and tolls. The market was a steady source of income to the estate, without burdening it with the responsibilities of management. Yet the Bedford Office often felt the disadvantages of having no direct control over the central feature of its Covent Garden estate. The market proved a continual source of annoyance to the Duke's other tenants; even the customers and stall-renters of the market itself complained about its poor management.[19] James Malcolm described Covent Garden in 1807 as "a filthy scene, soiled by putrid refuse leaves of cabbages, shells of peas, and roots, the air of which is impreg-

---

14. "The price given by the Duke of Bedford for the waste ground in Bloomsbury, late the estate of Sheffield, Duke of Buckingham, containing about three acres and a half, was about 8,000 guineas; and until the ground about Marybone, and in the neighborhood of Cavendish Square, began to be built upon, was kept up at £12,000." *London Chronicle, 13* (28–30 June 1763), 624.

15. "Account of money paid for the ground purchased of the heirs of the late Duke of Buckingham . . . Lady Day 1770."

16. Bloomsbury Rental, 1791, p. 58.

17. D. McNamara to Daniel Beaumont, 9 August 1793.

18. Bloomsbury Account Book, 1806, p. 95.

19. See, for example, E. Foulkes to John Gotobed, 14 July 1803; Duke of Bedford to T. P. Brown, 25 November 1807, and 20 March 1824.

79. Taviton Street Gate, looking south into Gordon Square, in 1893

80. Tavistock Place North. Pulled down 1900–01

81. New Covent Garden Market.
Charles Fowler, 1830

82. Bury Street before being
widened in the 1870s, looking north
from site of Bloomsbury Market

83. Model lodging houses, St.
Giles's, 1850

nated with a stench that is wafted in every direction by the wind . . ."[20] In 1813 the Duke secured an Act of Parliament (53 Geo. III, cap. 71) for the better regulation of Covent Garden Market, but it failed to stop the nuisances.

The estate eventually decided that the best way to silence the complaints was to take over the management of the market itself. In his report for 1827 W. G. Adam explained that along with the necessity of removing "so great a nuisance, it seemed extremely likely that by improving the arrangement of the market an addition might be made to the income arising from the market." The sale to the Office of Woods and Forests of land it needed for the widening of the Strand would, he said, provide £28,993 toward the capital needed for the market improvements. In 1828 the Covent Garden Market Act (9 Geo. IV, cap. 113) authorized the Duke to take down the existing buildings, and replace them with others "suitable to the present improved and improving state of the metropolis . . ." The architect for the new buildings was Charles Fowler, but the Duke felt free to make alterations in his plans.[21] The total cost of the buildings— which still exist in an altered form—was nearly £61,000.[22] (See Fig. 81.)

The rebuilding of Covent Garden Market was a unique if momentous incident. Ordinarily the estate achieved its ends indirectly, by the power it exercised over its tenants when their leases were to be renewed. The rebuilding of the Hart Street schools in Covent Garden in the late 1830s is an instructive example.[23]

The steward's report for 1860, a typical year, indicates something of the scope of the civic improvements carried on under the direction of the Bedford Office. In that year the Duke spent over £15,000 on various improvements on his Middlesex estates. The estate had just taken down a group of houses in preparation for an extension of Burleigh Street northward into Covent Garden Market. It had dealt similarly with the houses on the west side of Upper King Street (now Southampton Row) in Bloomsbury. When rebuilt, the houses would be set back in order to widen Upper King Street, "and complete the elevation of that part

---

20. *Londinium Redivivum, 4,* 348–49.

21. "The enclosed is a sketch for altering the pavilions in the market. I wish you would show it to Fowler and tell him that the Duke thinks it is a great improvement. The square window in particular. I think it is a much handsomer front than Fowler's and the pillars are in character. . . . I think the great defect in Fowler's is that the Venetian doorway is too naked—a cornice or architrave would be a great improvement to his.

I think this better. I leave you to suggest these things to Fowler without wounding his *amour propre,* which I know you will contrive to do." (W. G. Adam to C. Haedy, 23 October 1828). Adam's letters to Haedy throughout 1828 are full of similar references to the market. See in particular those for 9 June, 26 September, and 31 October.

22. 1832 Report.

23. See Appendix III.

of the street erected by Mr. Cubitt in 1834." Mr. Parker, the steward, was planning to form a direct communication between Upper King Street and Theobald's Road as soon as the leases on the east side of the former street expired.

The estate intended the following year "to complete the continuation of Werrington Street through Crawley Mews into Crawley Street," in Bedford New Town. The project had been begun in 1856, but was discontinued, "on account of the opposition of several tenants, who have since either left the neighborhood or are now favorable to the plan."

"On the south side of Hart Street [now Floral Street], Covent Garden," Parker reported, "a large warehouse for agricultural and garden seeds has been completed, and on the adjoining site an agreement is made for building another large warehouse. As the leases fall in it is proposed to replace the buildings on this side of the street with warehouses for the same object." The steward hoped by such means to attract to Hart Street the seed merchants who were about to be displaced from Hungerford Market by the building of Charing Cross Station.

The report also referred to new mechanics' dwellings built in Little Russell Street, and improvements made to houses in Caroline Street. It contemplated the widening of the north end of Bury Street (now Bury Place) "to enlarge the access to the North Western Railway" at Euston Station, and improve the approach to the British Museum. New houses were to be built in both Bury and Museum Streets, of "an architectural appearance somewhat in accordance with the Museum . . ."[24]

Not every annual report described widespread and dramatic schemes of improvement, such as street extensions or the demolition of whole blocks of houses. But the cumulative effect of many smaller projects—whether carried out by the tenants or by the estate—was considerable. In 1862 alone tenants on the estate, under the supervision of the Bedford Office, rebuilt twenty-two houses at a cost of £34,000; other lessees carried out repairs and improvements in seventy-one old houses at a total cost of £18,765.[25]

In 1870, as a part of its program to improve conditions in the unsavory courts in Covent Garden, the estate determined to have four old houses in Broad Court and Cross Court pulled down, and their site let on an eighty-year building lease, "with liberty to the lessees to put shops in the frontage to Broad Court, the occupation of such shops being subject to approval." Mr. Davison, the steward, remarked that "perhaps a more profitable disposition of the ground would have been to have put five houses upon it, which would have afforded to each house

24. 1860 Report, pp. 1–7.   25. 1862 Report, p. 75.

the required statutory area of 100 superficial feet of open space, but having regard to the desire to make liberal provision in localities of this description for ventilation and sanitary requirements, it had been thought better to limit the number of houses to four, and consequently a lower ground rent may have to be accepted."[26]

In January 1872 the estate decided, in order to widen Maiden Lane, to take down a number of houses whose leases had expired. Recommending the program, the surveyor, W. S. Cross, cited "the decayed condition of the existing structures, their inconvenient and defective plans, inefficient drainage and ventilation, and the limited width of the cart and footways . . ." The widening of the roadway was particularly important, both "for improving the ventilation of the several premises, and forming a more convenient access thereto for business purposes . . ." As it was, "many branches of industry . . . [were] totally excluded from the street, owing to the difficulty of access and the impossibility of passage for the necessary vehicles."[27]

The middle 1870s saw the widening of Bury Street. (See Figure 82 for a view of Bury Street before the widening.) Although the Bury Street improvements had been contemplated at least as early as 1860, actual work did not begin until 1874, when the leases expired. The houses in the street were, according to the surveyor, "ill arranged, deficient in many particulars of salubrity and convenience," and so defective in structure "as to render rebuilding more economical than repair." The general rebuilding and the widening of the street would, the steward believed, "enhance the value of this side of the Bloomsbury estate by affording a better approach to it from Holborn and New Oxford Street."[28] The steward proposed that the estate take down the houses at its own expense, both in order "to accelerate the reletting of the ground," and to avoid the caretaking expenses for the old buildings.[29]

Probably the most interesting architectural event on the estate in the 1870s was the reconstruction of a portion of Inigo Jones's Piazza. In December 1873 Davison wrote that the main outer wall of the Piazza was at one point in a dangerous condition, and that the whole required rebuilding. "In a utilitarian and commercial point of view," he thought the reconstruction undesirable, but he was "not without misgivings that the destruction of any portion of this distinctive feature in Covent Garden architecture will provoke a considerable amount of unfavorable public criticism."[30] The Duke favored its retention,

26. London Reports, *1*, 53–54.

27. Ibid., pp. 129–30 (31 January 1872).

28. Ibid., pp. 282–83 (19 December 1873).

29. Ibid., p. 352 (26 October 1874).

30. Ibid., p. 277 (9 December 1873).

and at his suggestion the surveyor prepared a drawing of an elevation for the restored buildings in the block west of James Street. Davison suggested that the Piazza be extended along the south side of the market, as well as along the east side south of Russell Street (Figs. 7, 9–14).[31]

The surveyor's design evidently proved unsatisfactory, for shortly afterward the Duke commissioned Henry Clutton, the architect (1819–1893), to prepare designs for "rebuilding the three houses known as the Gordon Hotel lying between the west side of James Street and Evans Concert Room, with a view of reproducing in this block the Piazza as originally designed by Inigo Jones." Davison suggested that the estate entrust the actual building to a single firm "of high repute," preferably Cubitt's, "on account of the necessity for minute attention to artistic detail . . ." He reminded the Duke that "whatever is done in the reproduction or restoration of a work of this kind will probably be the subject of much public criticism and discussion."[32] A portion of Clutton's careful reproduction still stands at the northwest corner of the market.

The later years of the century saw a great deal of new building in Bloomsbury as the original building leases fell in. In 1880 the estate took down the block of houses between Store Street and Chenies Street, from the City of London's estate on the west to Chenies Mews on the east. The original leases had expired in 1874, and the houses were "thoroughly decayed and exhausted." The estate widened Chenies Mews and formed it into the present Ridgmount Street. It proposed to let most of the vacant ground for institutions or factories, as it did not think the location suitable for dwelling houses.[33]

There followed soon afterward a related scheme of redevelopment north of Chenies Street, from which the present buildings in Ridgmount Gardens and Huntley Street emerged.[34] Part of the area was devoted to ornamental gardens. The narrow strip of lawn running along the east side of Ridgmount Gardens was the first of a number of similar additions to the already numerous open spaces of Bloomsbury. In 1895 the Duke decided to turn the waste ground north of Tavistock Place North and behind the houses in Upper Woburn Place into a lawn tennis ground for "some of the tenants in the neighboring streets who had not the privilege of entrance to the Square gardens."[35] In 1898 and 1899 the estate demolished the whole of the stable premises in Southampton and Montague Mews (between Southampton Row, Bedford Place, and Montague Street) and had the sites landscaped. The Duke had similar plans for Tavistock and

31. Ibid., p. 434 (18 January 1876).
32. Ibid., pp. 455–56 (12 April 1876).
33. 1880 Report, 2, 1–2.

34. London Reports, 2, 68 (21 October 1886).
35. 1895 Report, p. 129.

Woburn Mews (east of Woburn Place) before he decided to sell the property to the London County Council for a housing scheme.[36]

Most of the estates whose representatives appeared before the Town Holdings Committee could point to similar projects of redevelopment and rehabilitation. The Portman estate had during the previous thirty-five years taken advantage of the expiration of leases to demolish tenement houses in Orchard Street, Lisson Grove, East Street, Seymour Place, York Street, and the Marylebone Road; most of the sites were let at artificially low rents for the building of model lodging houses. Granville Place and Stourcliffe Street were laid out on other sites, the upper part of Bryanston Street was widened, and Broadley Street and East Street were extended, the former in cooperation with the parish of St. Marylebone.[37]

On the neighboring Portland estate Edward Bailey could refer to an equally impressive list of recent improvements. His estate had in the past generation rebuilt and widened Woodstock Street, Paddington Street, the west end of Weymouth Street, the entrance to Beaumont Mews, Marylebone Court (renamed Wesley Street), Little (later New) Chesterfield Street, the north end of Westmoreland Street (formerly Woodstock Street), South Street, Chapel Court, Ogle Street, and Ogle Mews (formerly Upper Ogle Street). "I should mention," Bailey remarked, "that the estate was very well laid out originally. For instance, there are some very fine open streets; Portland Street, Harley Street, Wimpole Street, and Weymouth Street, were all parts of the original design . . ." In streets such as these, he said, "we have not had need to clear away rookeries; but wherever opportunity has occurred, we have done it; and done it all at our own cost."[38]

On the Grosvenor estate Mr. Boodle could cite recent instances of large-scale rebuilding in "Grosvenor Gardens, Hereford Gardens, half of Grosvenor Place, part of Grosvenor Crescent, nearly the whole of the Oxford Street frontage of the estate, besides the houses now being built in Mount Street, and in Duke Street, and isolated houses, and working-class dwellings." He thought Grosvenor Gardens a particularly good example of the public spirit of the Duke of Westminster. The building of Victoria Station and the Grosvenor Hotel in the 60s had "almost necessitated broad approaches . . . and the late Marquess readily agreed to take advantage of the expiration of the leases . . . in 1864, and to arrange for altering and widening the roads." The ground landlord paid all the

36. London Reports, 3, 96 (10 May 1897). For the LCC housing scheme, see above, p. 139.

37. TH, pp. 580–81; 1888 (313) xxii.

38. Ibid., p. 444; 1887 (260) xiii.

costs of the new roads and sewers, amounting to about £10,000. "He sacrificed also," Boodle pointed out, "some thousands a year [in rents] for the improvement, which sacrifice will continue until the building leases expire, and then the deferred benefit will accrue to the estate."[39]

Comprehensive rebuilding was not confined to central London, where land values were high. Howard Martin, the surveyor, was able to use the Rolls estate in Bermondsey, Southwark, Camberwell, and Newington as a further example of such practices. "The Old Kent Road in that district was at one time," he reminded the committee, "a suburb in which people of means lived. The houses were large, and had large gardens and stabling . . ." By the 80s, however, the old inhabitants had moved farther out, to Dulwich and beyond, leaving the Old Kent Road "occupied almost entirely by working people, and by the tradesmen who supply them." At first a situation not unlike that on the Northampton estate in Clerkenwell developed, but with the expiration of the leases the Rolls estate was able to rehabilitate the area:

> In many instances very miserable courts were built on the large gardens at the backs of those houses, which were held under loosely drawn old leases, but when the leases fell in all those slums and courts were cleared away, and the land was laid out properly, and proper dwellings for the working people who live in the district were built on the site. There is one case in the Old Kent Road where the gardens were 230 feet deep, and people had built little alleys and closes of cottages there, which were approached by the sides of those houses in front. When the leases fell in these were all cleared away, a new thoroughfare called Marcia Road was made, and the frontages thus created were let on building leases, and covered with houses, which were let on monthly tenancies to respectable mechanics.[40]

In 1887 the Norfolk estate, south of the Strand, was in the process of being completely rebuilt, for the first time since its original development two hundred years earlier. Except for the recently erected buildings, the whole of the property was in hand, or let out on yearly tenancies. For the new buildings, "first-class office property," the Duke was granting eighty-year leases; to facilitate the redevelopment he was advancing money to the builders, usually at 4 per cent interest. Most of the narrower streets on the estate, such as Essex and Surrey streets, were being widened.[41]

39. Ibid., p. 323.   41. Ibid., pp. 617–24. See also ibid., p. 242.
40. Ibid., p. 85.

In the second half of the nineteenth century much of the interest in urban renewal centered on the activities of the various companies which were erecting and operating model lodging houses. The first of them, the Society for Improving the Condition of the Labouring Classes, erected in 1845 in Clerkenwell, off the Gray's Inn Road, a group of two- and three-room houses, together with a thirty-room lodging house for single women. "In the arrangement of the buildings," according to a contemporary account, "the object has been to combine every point essential to the health, comfort, and moral habits of the inmates; reference being had to the recommendations of the Health of Towns Commission, particularly with respect to ventilation, drainage, and an ample supply of water."[42] Another notable early project was a four-story block in Streatham Street, Bloomsbury, which the Society erected in 1848–49.[43] The Duke of Bedford supplied the site at a nominal ground rent of 1½d. per foot.[44]

Beginning with the formation of the Metropolitan Association for Improving the Dwellings of the Industrious Classes in 1853, other bodies proceeded to build their own blocks of supervised dwellings, designed to provide cheap, decent housing for the poor and yet produce a reasonable return on investment. Interest of 7.5 per cent was neither uncommon nor regarded as incompatible with philanthropic intent.[45] "Prince Albert's Model Houses," erected in connection with the Great Exhibition of 1851, can be seen today in Kennington Park, while grim, solid structures—the Victorian ancestors of the twentieth-century Council flat—with inscriptions identifying their builders as the Peabody Trustees, the Improved Industrial Dwellings Company, or the Artizans' Labourers', and General Dwellings Company still loom above many a London street.[46] (For an early example, see Figure 83.)

The agents of the different estates invariably praised the activities of such companies, and usually indicated their willingness to grant them land to construct model dwellings at nominal ground rents, thereby combining philanthropy with the spirit of improvement. Bourne, for instance, had nothing but praise for the paternalism of the model dwelling companies:

---

42. *Illustrated London News*, 7 (1845), 244, quoted in Hitchcock, *Early Victorian Architecture*, *1*, 464–65.

43. Ibid., pp. 469–70.

44. TH, p. 581; 1887 (260) xiii. The date is erroneously given as 1858. In 1857 the Strand Buildings Society erected a large model lodging house on the Covent Garden estate in Eagle Court—which Christopher Haedy had in 1846 described as one of the three worst on the estate —on a building lease at £30 per annum. The Duke took ten £10 shares in the society. 1857 Report, p. 6.

45. Hitchcock, *Early Victorian Architecture*, *1*, 473.

46. See William Ashworth, *The Genesis of Modern British Town Planning*, pp. 82–87.

> It is found that the working classes can be better housed in large
> blocks of buildings where they can be brought together, and be under
> control and care, and management, and looked after. The very essence
> of it is their being looked after, and cared for, which secures for them
> the better dwellings.

He thought that it would be "generally found that all owners of a large estate
would aid in carrying out any scheme of that sort, partly on philanthropic
grounds, and partly on grounds of good management."[47]

Boodle agreed that enlightened self-interest would make the freeholder of
working-class property encourage the erection of model lodging houses. Referring to some recently built in Clerkenwell, he thought that "Lord Northampton himself is a gainer by the indirect benefit which his estate derives from
handsome buildings and the improved condition of the residents. Taking
purely a pecuniary view of the matter a landlord derives a great indirect benefit
from the prosperity of the residents on his estate." He did not think that such
buildings necessarily raised the class of the neighborhood, "and that is not our
object." What mattered was that a block of artisans' dwellings "sets a good example of cleanliness and decent behavior in the whole neighborhood. The very
last thing his Lordship wishes to do is to drive away the poor," he insisted; "and
I think these buildings, although they do not at present accommodate the very
poorest class by any means, still have a very good effect upon them."[48]

James Moore, secretary of the Improved Industrial Dwellings Company, had
taken leasehold property from several great landlords in London, including the
Duke of Westminster, the Marquess of Northampton, Baroness Burdett-Coutts,
and the Ecclesiastical Commissioners. He reported that large landowners had
dealt with the company "in a liberal spirit," asking less than commercial rents.[49]
Robert Elisha Farrant, deputy chairman and managing director of the Artizans',
Labourers', and General Dwellings Company, similarly had nothing but praise
for the policies of the Westminster, Portman, and Northampton estates, which
consistently let land for artisans' dwellings at much less than its market value.[50]

Boodle pointed out that he consistently made ground rents for such companies as low as possible, and thought that the freeholder "should take a broad
view of his leasing powers," and take less than the commercial rent from such
organizations.[51] Ralph Clutton, agent for the Ecclesiastical Commissioners, re-

---

47. TH, p. 581; 1887 (260) xiii.
48. HWC, p. 47; 1884–85 (4402-I) xxx.
49. TH, p. 461; 1887 (260) xiii.
50. Ibid., pp. 414–36.

51. HWC, p. 44; 1884–85 (4402-I) xxx. For an
account of workmen's dwellings erected on the
Grosvenor and Northampton estates, see TH, pp.
332–35; 1887 (260) xiii.

ported that that body made it a practice to rehouse in model dwellings the inhabitants displaced by demolitions of substandard property on their estates, which took place whenever the leases expired.[52]

Edward Bailey described in 1887 a slum clearance project which involved the erection of model dwellings by the Portland Marylebone estate itself:

> We have . . . very few rookeries, but there was one up near Paradise Street and Paddington Street. There was a disused burial ground there; a nest of courts . . . We have been studiously for the last three or four years refusing to renew the leases of a low class of houses. Of course they had got into a bad state. They were occupied by people who let their houses get into a bad state, and as we were not renewing the leases, and only two or three had to run out, we said we would re-lease the lessees from payment of further rent, and put a hoarding round until we had a sufficiently large site on which to build artisans' dwellings. The owners of the estate have furnished me with £10,000 for this purpose. It will not be a large undertaking, but with facility we are forming a company. We have got the rest of the necessary capital taken up, and directors appointed who will have the interest of the neighborhood at heart; and that scheme will be carried out, I hope, this summer. We have also told the architect to be kind enough not to renew the leases of an adjoining plot, as we wish to expand the undertaking.[53]

Practically every redevelopment scheme involved an immediate financial loss to the landlord. Boodle pointed out that "it would be to the pecuniary advantage of a tenant for life of an estate not to have rebuilding, but to renew the leases as long as ever the houses would stand. His income," he informed the committee, "suffers very considerably from the rebuilding, and it is only after two or three generations that the pecuniary advantage accrues." The ground rent for a new building would necessarily be less than the rack rent for the old one. "You may take it generally," Boodle estimated, "that rebuilding involves a loss of about two-thirds of the income."[54]

Obviously only a reasonably rich landowner with a reasonably big estate could be expected to sacrifice current income so that his descendants would have, eighty or more years in the future, a more valuable piece of property. Boodle suggested that some people thought that the Duke of Westminster "goes

52. HWC, pp. 206–09; 1884–85 (4402-I) xxx.   54. Ibid., pp. 322–23.
53. TH, p. 446; 1887 (260) xiii.

a little beyond what is necessary" in rebuilding on his estate. "For instance, the houses in Grosvenor Place, just by St. George's Hospital, would have stood for many years; they were very stoutly built, with very thick walls." On the other hand, "they were very ugly, and the servants' offices were not good . . . and they contained very bad rooms at the top." He thought that the motives of the Duke were "public spirit combined with [a sense of] what was due to the estate."[55]

But it is unnecessary to look for special motives to explain the frequency with which estates replanned, refurbished, and rebuilt themselves. The tenant for life who received the reversionary estate at the end of a building lease could be expected to regard the property much as his ancestor had when he granted the original lease: as a trust to be handed down to future generations preserved, and if possible enhanced, in value. To achieve such an end the original ground landlord insisted on the establishment of the best possible estate plan—open, airy, and impressive—and on the erection of the best and most substantial houses which speculative builders could be persuaded to put up. To achieve the same end, his descendant ninety-nine years later insisted on appropriate improvements in the estate plan, to make it even more open, airy, and impressive; and to require that houses be rebuilt, enlarged, and generally improved. Current income was always made subordinate to the creation of capital value in the long run. Such economic considerations in no way conflicted with a desire to make the estate an object of family or corporate pride, and to keep it so, or to make it contribute to the splendor and elegance of the town.

Once the leasehold interest had reverted to the ground landlord, there should have been little to prevent him from doing with it what he wanted to do. The intrinsic value of the property would then ordinarily be such that the occupying tenant would gladly carry out the repairs and improvements called for in order to get the new lease. If he would not, somebody else almost certainly would. If the estate decided on demolition and redevelopment, it would find it far easier to attract builders than had been the case when it was first being laid out. Building in Oxford Street in the 1880s was not the gamble that it had been in the 1780s. Even outside central London, the ground landlord of an established neighborhood was in a better position to bargain with a building contractor than one whose land was only just "ripe" for building. Since any financial loss brought about by a redevelopment scheme would be met by the freeholder rather than by the builder or tenant, the landowner could act with comparative freedom in imposing his conception of how best to adapt his town to the needs of the new age.

55. Ibid., p. 347.

This was only true if his conception of the needs of the new age corresponded with the views of existing or prospective tenants. The failure of the Bedford estate to convince the kind of tenant it wanted, to live in Gower Street, shows the limitations on the power of the ground landlord even when it seems the greatest. The Portman estate similarly found in the 1880s that a perceptible exodus from Marylebone was taking place at the same time that large blocks of leases were falling in. Such circumstances, whatever Frank Banfield might think, must inevitably have discouraged any possible impulse of the ground landlord to impose harsh or unusual terms.

The great London estates did not present Victorian England with many startling or revolutionary examples of urban renewal. Although they encouraged and subsidized the model lodging-house movement, they did not originate it. Their street-widening projects were for the most part simply an expansion of the ideas implicit in the original layout of the estates. Their architectural improvements reflected with hideous accuracy contemporary middlebrow taste. Yet any account of metropolitan improvements during the nineteenth century which concentrated solely on large-scale public projects such as Trafalgar Square, New Oxford Street, and the Victoria Embankment, would give an inadequate picture of the planned transformation of London from its Georgian self to what it had become by 1900. If less spectacular than the projects of the Metropolitan Board of Works and the London County Council, the systematic reconstruction of the big landed estates as their leases fell in did much to give London the shape it has today.

V *CONCLUSION*

11 Success and Failure

*I am quite satisfied that in the transition state of the Middlesex prop-
erty (and it is in such a state just now) we cannot adhere, in all cases, to
our old rules: We must give way to circumstances . . .—W. G. Adam to
C. Haedy,* 21 January 1836

A town plan is a work of art, and demands an artist with a vision to impose on
his material. His vision of the good society and the kind of environment in
which it can best flourish will determine the sort of town plan he will create.
But his scheme will have little value unless he can put it into effect. Here the
town planner suffers in comparison with other artists. The poet, the painter,
the sculptor, the musician can create his own world, impose his own vision of
the beautiful on his material, irrespective of what the public may want, or
think it wants. Even the architect, if he can find a patron, can afford to ignore
majority tastes and the inertia of vested interest. But the town planner can only
achieve his vision by influencing the actions of the individual property owners
of the community. In a democratic and capitalistic society he is usually confined to a restrictive role, telling the property owner what he may not do. Only
if the planner has the support of an absolute despot or the owner of an extensive
tract of land can he perform a more active role in shaping or reshaping the
town. If he is to impose his vision for more than his own lifetime, he must
establish a tradition of planning and ensure that the power to control the subsequent development of the town be as great as that which first determined its
shape and character.

The great landed estates of London from the seventeenth to the nineteenth
centuries fulfilled such conditions, combining the will to plan with the power
to do so. Whatever the virtues of the different estate plans, there is no question
that there were plans, that they were put into effect, that measures were taken
to maintain them, and that from time to time they were either modified or re-

placed by new ones. The wording of building agreements, leases, and licenses gives the impression that the ground landlord had the power to make his estate anything he wanted to make it, and keep it that way until he decided to change it into something else. No governmental authority even today has anything like the control over architecture, street plans, or zoning that the Bedford, Portland, or Portman estate offices had in the nineteenth century.

Frank Banfield could compare the ground landlords of the metropolis with "an old Rhine baron of the Dark Ages,"[1] the Pharaohs of Egypt, the "Oriental monarchs of the past,"[2] and Charles I.[3] "No Mogul Monarch, no Persian Satrap, was ever harder on a conquered people" than was Lord Portman when the time came for leases to be renewed.[4] The agents of the landlords themselves could speak complacently of "enlightened despotism."[5] Yet although the estate offices had a clear conception of the sort of town planning they wanted, and consistently invoked their powers in order to achieve it, the ordinary educated Englishman persists in his belief that despite such efforts, despite Regent's Park and Carlton House Terrace and Belgravia, London is an unplanned city. Why does he believe this? Is he entirely mistaken?

More fundamentally, are the goals of town planners attainable in a more than temporary or superficial sense in our society? A town plan cannot be judged a success until it has shown its ability to adapt itself to changing circumstances, changing technological and functional requirements, changing aesthetic values, changing kinds of life desired by its inhabitants. Admittedly many town plans of the past command admiration today from their very refusal or inability to change with the times. Venice and Bath and Kyoto survive as proud anachronisms, teaching humility to those who would provide aesthetic delight for the twentieth century. But London is not a museum to be preserved unchanged for the instruction and pleasure of foreign tourists. It was the poverty of Dublin after 1800 and Charleston after 1865 that preserved their architectural purity: one would not wish the same fate for London. Nor would one for the New Towns of our own century. Yet however admirable Crawley or the rebuilt center of Coventry or the satellite communities around Stockholm may seem today, they have yet to prove themselves capable of meeting the test of time. The town plans of Stuart, Georgian, and Victorian London have faced such a test. How well have they met it?

No one could call Oxford Street or northern Mayfair or the area west of

1. *The Great Landlords of London*, p. 76.
2. Ibid., p. 72.
3. Ibid., pp. 53–54.

4. Ibid.; p. 107.
5. See, for instance, John R. Bourne's 1877 Report to the Duke of Bedford, 2, 3.

Kingsway architecturally pleasing. Even in the more attractive parts of Chelsea or Marylebone or Bloomsbury there is much from which to avert the eye. Yet all these areas are, or were until recently, on enlightened, well-managed estates. One might argue that the parts of London that do not belong to one or another of the great estates are even more ugly than those that do, but this is at best a dubious compliment.

Essentially the question is this: if the Dukes of Bedford and Portland and Westminster and their fellow landlords had so much power and the will to use it, why isn't London the earthly paradise instead of the lovable mess that it is?

One answer is that London's difficulty lies not in having no plan but in having had too many little plans. Each landlord's power was confined to his own estate, and no centralized authority existed to coordinate the individual plans. Each estate was dealt with as if it were an autonomous village. What was good for Bloomsbury might well be good for the rest of London, but not necessarily.

Even if judged in isolation, the estates leave something to be desired. Aesthetically, the great difficulty was the decline of faith in the values of classicism and the failure of successive architectural fashions to provide any satisfactory alternative. Had the ground landlords single-mindedly resisted the changing standards of beauty that have succeeded in making hideous the nineteenth and twentieth centuries, all might have been well. It is tempting to speculate on a Bayswater and a Hammersmith and a Croydon covered with a succession of Bedford Squares and Portland Places, punctuated with Baroque churches and Regency shopping arcades, against which Pugin and Ruskin might fulminate in vain. But it is hardly fair to blame the ground landlords for not holding out completely against contemporary architectural theory. As it was, the conservatism of landlord and builder alike kept producing squares and terraces in at least a debased classical tradition for several decades after it had ceased to be intellectually respectable.

But the degree to which the great estates have not only permitted but encouraged the destruction of good architecture from the past is less excusable. For while it is possible to forgive Wimbledon for not being another Belgravia, it is hard to forgive Bloomsbury and Mayfair for willfully discarding so much of their original Georgian dress. The improvements and rebuilding schemes to which the Victorian landlords pointed with such pride are precisely what the modern architectural critic finds hardest to accept. The rebuilding, at vast expense, of street after street between Berkeley Square and Oxford Street in terra cotta, the Imperial and Russell hotels, the Senate House of the University of London—all are products of the vaunted flexibility and comprehensive redevelopment possible under the leasehold system. Whatever the improvements in sanitation and convenience, it is hard to rejoice with the Duke of Norfolk over the systematic destruction of quantities of large seventeenth-century houses south of the Strand in the 1880s.

Yet the very nature of town planning often requires architectural crime. As London must now come to terms with the glass and concrete of the mid-twentieth century, so the Duke of Westminster came to terms with the terra cotta of the late-nineteenth. As it must in the twentieth century come to terms with the motor car, so in the nineteenth it came to terms with the railway. Yet in pursuing such functional ends, the town planner, however conscientious, cannot avoid doing violence to the aesthetic aims of his calling. Buildings and street plans can never be as flexible and adaptable to changing needs as town planning itself must be.

Sir John Summerson has wisely stressed the eminently functional character of eighteenth-century domestic architecture:

> It is all devised for the conduct of an elaborate social parade, a parade which was felt to be the necessary accompaniment of active and responsible living. These houses of [Robert] Adam's . . . were not built for domestic but for public life—a life of continual entertaining in drawing-rooms and ante-rooms and "eating-rooms" . . .
>
> Adam's letters and sketches show how fully he appreciated for what kind of life he was planning. He ponders the assembly of guests, the conversation before dinner, the procession to the dining-room; he considers where the upper servants shall stand, how the under servants shall perform their duties without being noticed; and behind the parade he plans for the dignified, easy privacy of lord and lady, with study, dressing-rooms, closets, and bed-chambers.[6]

Not only the individual house, but the structure of the eighteenth-century urban neighborhood was designed to facilitate a particular way of living. When that way of living ceased, the environment which had been created for it lost its reason for existence:

> The real glory of the Adam houses died with the life for which they were built. When they became "mixed" clubs, council rooms for distillers, and seminaries for the University of London, it is no longer easy to see what underlies the Pompeian lace and the Etruscan colouring or to give back to each room the measure of emphasis or reticence

6. *Georgian London*, pp. 144–45.

which it had when the regulated tide of eighteenth-century society flowed through it. Adam houses are always pretty but in their origin they were something more.[7]

Bloomsbury was built for a less exalted kind of life than were the Adam houses in Mayfair and Marylebone, but that life, too, came to an end. When the English middle classes stopped being able or willing to lead the kind of life which Bloomsbury and Bayswater and Kensington were made to house, their town houses were converted into private hotels, solicitors' offices, student hostels, and self-contained flats. The square gardens are either beautiful but unused—like Bedford Square—or, like Bloomsbury and Russell squares, turned into public "amenities," parodies of their original selves. The Georgian and Victorian estates of London are today neither what their planners intended them to be nor wholly satisfactory environments for life in the 1960s. The street pattern is ill suited to modern traffic, the houses are ill suited to an age without servants.

But if Bedford Square and its successors have become uneasy anachronisms, unsuited to the needs of the twentieth century, one might well say, so much the worse for the twentieth century. If they fail wholly to satisfy our physical wants, they compensate by delighting our aesthetic sensibilities. If they do not fulfill the practical requirements of our own age, they at least fulfilled the requirements of the age for which they were designed, which is more than can be said for most twentieth-century building in London.

"It is a mistake in aesthetic theory," writes Lewis Mumford, "to assume that the demands of vision and economy, of aesthetic pleasure and bodily comfort, always coincide."[8] The bitter cold and the foul odors of Versailles and the leaking roofs of the buildings of Frank Lloyd Wright come to mind as examples of men consciously preferring aesthetic luxury to physical comfort. And those of us who would gladly undergo any amount of inconvenience rather than see any Georgian building whatsoever demolished are in no position to reproach Louis XIV for not building instead a centrally heated bungalow. The provision of visual delight is as functional an end as the provision of water, gas, and electricity. But we must on occasion be prepared to give up the one in order to have the other.

The flexibility which the London leasehold system made possible essentially meant that outmoded buildings could be demolished and replaced by ones better suited to the demands of the time. The spectacle of mid-town Manhattan

7. Ibid., p. 145.   8. *City Development*, p. 71.

rebuilding itself once a generation shows that redevelopment schemes are as compatible with freehold tenure as with leasehold. But the extent of some of the London estates and the practice of making adjacent leases expire simultaneously facilitated such schemes, without making it necessary for the local political authority to intervene. Unfortunately redevelopment could destroy the precious and the beautiful as easily as the squalid and the ugly.

Each generation has had its own conception of what constituted desirable metropolitan improvements. If London could have been remade entirely every fifty years or so, the antiquary and the art lover might have protested, but the practical town planner would have rejoiced. In fact, what has happened is a succession of attempts to modernize an older fabric: a Palladian façade for old St. Paul's, a new street to cut through the rookery of St. Giles's, the conversion of town houses into flats, the insertion of plate glass shop windows into Georgian buildings. There has been neither a policy of uncompromising modernism nor consistent preservation, but an uneasy compromise between the two, satisfying nobody. The characteristically English attempt to unite the past with the present has succeeded less well in architecture and town planning than it has in political and social institutions.

The big London estates did not pretend to lead architectural taste but at best to maintain currently accepted aesthetic standards. Yet even if the success of their policies is to be judged purely by what they were consciously trying to achieve, it is obvious that something went wrong. They did, for instance, really try to maintain decent sanitary standards and to prevent the spread of slums. Yet here, too, despite efforts which were at times heroic, they failed. Slums did grow up both on and off the great estates, and no landlord could have read the Report of the Royal Commission on the Housing of the Working Classes with complacency.

One could justly reply to the account of the squalid conditions on the Northampton estate by pointing to the excellent conditions on the Bedford or Foundling estate, and argue that what mattered was not the system of landownership but how well a particular estate was managed. Slums could develop anywhere, on leasehold land as on freehold, but an energetic landlord, acting on the principles of enlightened self-interest, could do much to inhibit their growth on his own estate. By laying out the property in a generous fashion, putting stringent covenants in his leases, and rigorously enforcing them, he could usually keep his estate from falling below a reasonable level of decency. If, through neglect, property did sink to slum standards, there was always the possibility of pulling it down when the leases expired and replacing it with something better. Every established estate could point to improvement schemes of this nature.

While the Select Committee on Town Holdings was debating the connection between systems of land tenure and the growth of slums, Charles Booth was gathering evidence for his monumental *Life and Labour of the People of London* (London, 1892). The collection of maps in volume 10 supports the assertion made by the great landlords of the metropolis that careful management had kept the condition of their estates better than would have been the case had the land been freehold. The maps, dated 1889, classify by colors all the streets of central London according to the economic status of their inhabitants. Booth uses seven colors, each of which represents a grade of society, ranging from the wealthy (yellow) to the criminal poor (black). On his map the three Bedford estates and the Foundling estate stand out with particular clarity against their surroundings. The estate boundaries and the boundaries separating decency from poverty roughly coincide.

A surprisingly large portion of the Bedford estate in Bloomsbury is colored yellow: Booth classified the whole of Bedford, Gordon, and Tavistock squares, Gordon, Taviton, Endsleigh, and Upper Montague streets, Byng and Upper Woburn places, and all but a corner of Russell Square as "wealthy." Most of Bloomsbury is colored red, the highest grade except for yellow, indicating well-to-do "middle-class families who keep one or two servants." Most of the streets, together with Woburn and Torrington squares—composed as they were chiefly of second-rate houses—appear red on the map.

The next lowest rank is pink, representing "working-class comfort." Families living in pink streets did not ordinarily keep servants. In such a category were Chenies, Francis, and Ridgmount streets, and much of the property south of Great Russell Street—such as Little Russell, Silver, Dyott, and Museum streets. All of the mews property on the Bedford estate is colored pink.

With one small exception Booth's four lowest classifications, purple ("Mixed. Some comfortable, others poor"), light blue ("Standard poverty"), dark blue ("Very poor . . . inhabited principally by casual laborers and others living from hand to mouth"), and black ("The lowest grade . . . occasional laborers, loafers, and semi-criminals—the elements of disorder"), are not found on the Duke's Bloomsbury property.[9]

It is hardly necessary to say that there are no yellow patches in either Covent

9. The one exception is the area behind Woburn Place and Russell Square, adjoining the Foundling estate. There, Little Guilford Street is light blue, and the Colonnade is dark blue lined with black. Little Coram Street and its adjacent courts are all pink.

Garden or Bedford New Town. Both of these are predominantly red, comfortably middle-class. In Figs Mead, Oakley, Ampthill, and Harrington squares, Crowndale and Hampstead roads, Houghton and Lidlington places, and Bedford Street are all red. Goldington Crescent, Seymour Street, and most of Werrington Street are pink. Only Stibbington Street and one side of Crawley Mews, which are purple, had crossed the poverty line by 1889. There are no light or dark blues or blacks in Bedford New Town, although they become common as soon as the Duke's boundaries are crossed. Most of Somers Town, for example, is purple, while many of its streets are blue.

Much of Covent Garden, having by 1889 ceased to be residential, is uncolored. The principal streets, where colored at all, are respectably red. Pink is practically nonexistent, except for the more prosperous parts of Crown, Broad, and Bedford courts. There is a fair amount of purple in the courts between Drury Lane and Bow Street. A tiny area of light blue lies south of Drury Lane Theater. A section of White Hart Street—notoriously the worst part of the whole estate—is dark blue, indicating extreme poverty. There are no black patches on the Covent Garden estate, although there are several just to the east, across Drury Lane.

The Foundling estate, if socially inferior to the adjacent Bedford estate, contrasted favorably with the neighborhoods to the north, east, and south. If it had no wealthy yellow streets, it was well supplied with middle-class red ones. Brunswick and Mecklenburgh squares, together with Bernard, Great Coram, Grenville, and Doughty streets and Lansdowne, Caroline, and Tavistock places, were all safely red. Guilford, Millman, Hunter, and Heathcote streets were partly red and partly pink. Parts of Marchmont and Kenton streets, and the whole of Little Coram and Compton streets, together with much of the mews property, were pink. Beneath the poverty line was Handel (formerly Henrietta) Street, which was purple, as was part of Marchmont Street. Worse still were Little Guilford Street and part of Kenton Street, which were light blue. The Colonnade was dark blue edged with black, while the notorious Compton Place was wholly black.

The picture—particularly on the Foundling estate—was not in itself a wholly satisfactory one, at least on the assumption that the chief function of estate management was to attract the wealthy and discourage the poor. It is only when the streets on the two estates are contrasted with streets in surrounding areas that the full significance of the labors of the estate offices becomes apparent. Booth's map shows street after street of purple, blue, and black just over the borders of the Bedford and Foundling estates. There is no reason to suppose that Bloomsbury would not have sunk to the level of Soho or Clerkenwell, that Bedford New Town would have been at all superior to Somers Town, if the Foundling Hospital and Bedford Office had not consistently exercised their prerogatives from the beginning.

The Westminster, Portland, and Portman estates are, as one would expect, similarly striking for their abundance of yellow and red streets. The better-known, at least, of the West End estates succeeded in maintaining a higher social character within their boundaries than would have been possible without centralized ownership and management. Certainly on the Bedford and Found-ling estates, and probably on the others, the increasing value of the land was due at least as much to the policies of the ground landlord as to the actions of the tenants. From the economic standpoint the function of the landlord was often to prevent the tenant from sacrificing the value of the whole neighbor-hood to his own immediate advantage.

Booth's maps show, of course, that the London leasehold system did not al-ways produce such results. The existence of extensive slums on some of the great estates in London—such as the Northampton property in Clerkenwell, and the Somers estate in St. Pancras—shows that leasehold tenure in itself did not ensure respectability and decency. It merely made it possible for an energetic landowner to practice town planning within certain limits. Whatever virtues the system of great urban estates may have had depended entirely on the way in which such estates were managed, on how enlightened and how despotic the ground landlord was.

The experience of London shows that leasehold tenure does not necessarily create slums. It is evident that energetic management on many estates suc-ceeded fairly well in keeping slums from establishing themselves within their boundaries, and in maintaining a reasonably high standard of repair and occu-pation even in neighborhoods which were the reverse of fashionable.

Some critics of the leasehold system admitted that the policies of certain estates did discourage slums and promote periodic rebuilding, but questioned the validity of the assumptions on which such policies were based. They sug-gested that the street-widening programs, and the demolitions of rookeries, and the model lodging houses might not be the unmixed blessings which the land-lords took for granted they were.

H. L. W. Lawson, one of the founders of the Leaseholds Enfranchisement Society, asked the Town Holdings Committee, "Has it not happened frequently in London of late, and I have the Cadogan estate in my mind's eye, that the working class property is not replaced by better working class property, but is pulled down to make room for residential property of a higher class?" The improvement schemes of which the great landlords were so proud simply meant, he suggested, "that the landlord thinks by clearing his property of small tenants to increase its value to himself."[10]

The Royal Commission on the Housing of the Working Classes went so far as to suggest that all slum clearance projects contributed to the general overcrowding of London, creating worse slums than they demolished:

> It may be asserted, without denying the consideration which some property owners have shown for the welfare of the inhabitants, that demolitions made by owners have for their main purpose the improvement of the value of the property, whether these "owners" be landlords whose leases are falling in, or those who purchase property for commercial purposes. . . . Rookeries are destroyed, greatly to the sanitary and social benefit of the neighborhood, but no kind of habitation for the poor has been substituted. This is the extreme instance of everything being sacrificed to the improvement of the property. There are also cases where the landlord, on the leases falling in and the property coming into his own hands, removes the unsatisfactory houses and builds a better class of dwellings. The consequence of such a proceeding is that the unhoused population crowd into the neighboring streets and courts when the demolitions commence, and when the new dwellings are completed little is done to relieve this increased pressure, as the tenants are not the identical persons displaced; they are now picked and chosen, and those whose need is the greatest suffer most acutely.[11]

The Commissioners did not regard the ground landlords as the only guilty parties, but pointed to similar displacements caused by railway extensions, and most particularly by the street improvements of the Metropolitan Board of Works and the slum clearances carried out by the various local authorities.

Even so, their criticism struck at the heart of the system of values on which the operation of the great estates was based. Most of the attacks on the estates had been for not doing well enough what they were trying to do: establish and maintain wide, airy streets and squares, and substantial, well-built houses; pro-

10. TH, p. 259; 1887 (260) xiii.

11. Housing of the Working Classes. R. Com. Rep., pp. 19–20; 1884–85 (4402) xxx. A similar connection is being noticed today (1964) between the massive slum clearances in Harlem and the West Side of Manhattan and the creation of new slums in what were luxury flats along Riverside Drive.

mote good architecture, suppress nuisances, and provide a decent and respectable environment for decent and respectable people. Now it was suggested that this was not enough, that the older conception of town planning was in itself inadequate.

Probably the very excellence of the town planning on the great estates was indirectly responsible for aggravating the overcrowding of the poor. By insisting on high standards of construction and maintenance, by encouraging the building of first and second-rate houses rather than smaller dwellings, by prohibiting subletting and the conversion of town houses into tenements, as well as by demolishing slums and redeveloping their sites for commercial purposes, the well-managed estates forced the lower classes to live elsewhere, on poorly managed estates or on freehold land where conditions might be even worse. The larger the area of the Bedford, Westminster, and Portman properties devoted to garden squares and wide, salubrious streets, the more stringent the building agreements and restrictive covenants, the greater the proportion of the population of London that had to live away from the protection of the benevolent ground landlords.

"I cannot conceive," wrote the Duke of Bedford in 1844, "what becomes of all the poor people who are compelled to leave their houses and lodgings for the improvements of the town."[12] The following month he wrote to ask his steward if the "poorer class of mechanics" had increased in numbers on the Covent Garden estate "since the Metropolitan improvements were commenced."[13] And yet the policies of his own estate resulted for the most part in a level of rents too high for the very poor to afford.

The tendency, noticeable in Charles Booth's maps, for pockets of extreme poverty to exist along the borders of well-managed estates, was often mentioned at the hearings of the Town Holdings Committee. In 1859 Charles Parker, in his report to the Duke of Bedford, remarked that "the dedication of such large estates as your Grace's to the erection of superior dwellings exclusively . . . [tended] to attract and concentrate at the outskirts the poorer classes."[14] Two years later John Hollingshead wrote, "From Belgravia to Bloomsbury—from St. Pancras to Bayswater—there is hardly a settlement of leading residences that has not its particular colony of ill-housed poor hanging on to its skirts."[15] To Frank Banfield, naturally, the situation resulted essentially from the greed and

12. Duke of Bedford to C. Haedy, 12 December 1844. He was no doubt thinking in particular of the building of New Oxford Street, which involved the destruction of the notorious rookeries of St. Giles's.

13. Duke of Bedford to C. Haedy, 27 January 1845.
14. 1859 Report, p. 6.
15. *Ragged London* (London, 1861), p. 143.

depravity of the landowners. He defined the problem in the course of an extended indictment of the policies of the Bedford estate:

> There is no slum in Bloomsbury because His Grace's forbears, in their own interest, laid out the place in big squares, and arranged for the building of houses whose rentals would necessarily keep the poor away. . . . The poor, it is to be assumed, must live somewhere. If one ground landlord edges them off his estate, they must crowd in on some other estate—on the Marquess of Northampton's for example. But if there is one ground landlord for the whole kingdom, and this sort of superior management was universal, the indigent members of the State would be compelled to take up their abodes on the seashore, between high and low water mark, where the waves of oblivion would at once pass over them, and the next morrow's sun would rise and shine upon an England of unmitigated respectability—a Bournian paradise.
>
> The poor of London would have been indeed in a bad way if they had been left to the tender mercies of the ground landlords. Happily the agents of a large-hearted and large-headed charity like the Peabody trustees, have stepped in to remedy some of the horrors of over-crowding, due directly, as we know, and on good authority, to the leasehold tenure. The working population has been tossed about from pillar to post to suit aristocratic caprices, and if there is a promise of better days now, it is clear that it does not come from Mr. Bourne and his colleagues.[16]

But to blame the landowner because the poor lacked decent housing is like blaming the farmer because they did not have enough to eat. The basic difficulty was that they couldn't afford to pay for any better housing than they had. A few shillings increase in the minimum weekly wage would have enabled the poor to afford decent lodgings in central London or the added cost of a railway journey to the suburbs, where housing was better and rents lower. The subsidized housing estates of the LCC, a greatly increased and more equitably distributed national income, the development of today's extensive London Transport network, and the proliferation of private motor vehicles have transformed the green fields of the Home Counties into Subtopia; they have also made the conditions described before the Royal Commission on the Housing of the Working Classes a thing of the past.

The question remains, however, to what extent the practices of the great

16. *The Great Landlords of London,* pp. 110–11.

landowners can be held responsible for the wretched living conditions of the lower classes in Victorian London. Certainly the absence of any coordination between the estate plans was particularly unfortunate in this respect. But it is hard to imagine what sort of policy toward lower-class dwellings could have been evolved in an age dominated by theories of laissez-faire, the sanctity of property rights, and the pauperizing effects of charity. Some of the most vehement attacks on the great landed estates came from their departure from such principles. Town planning itself is incompatible with a laissez-faire economy. Perhaps it can exist comfortably only in the environment of a welfare state.

The individual tenant on the Bedford or Foundling estates enjoyed few of the conditions of a laissez-faire society. At every turn his economic individualism was thwarted. He could not put his property to the most profitable use, but only to the use sanctioned by the terms of his lease, or by a subsequent license from the ground landlord. If he neglected its repair and upkeep, he might find himself facing an action of ejectment. He could introduce no structural alterations without permission from above. It is understandable, therefore, that many of the attacks on the leasehold system were made in the name of economic liberalism. The charge that the great landlords tyrannized over the small shopkeepers and thwarted individual enterprise anticipates the criticism which would later be made against socialism and a planned economy. As miniature "welfare states" in the midst of a comparatively free, competitive economy, the landed estates of London denied the basic assumptions of traditional liberalism.

Charles Harrison, for example, told the Town Holdings Committee that all specific restrictions in leases were injurious and "ought not to be inserted." Covenants restricting the use to which premises might be put interfered with the free working of natural economic laws: "I do not think that there ought to be those restrictions allowed, and for this reason, that you will find that persons who are the occupiers of the property will not establish any objectionable trade or any objectionable business or profession in a place where it is not wanted, and if it is wanted they ought to be allowed to do it." The Invisible Hand could be trusted to manage any zoning regulations: "It takes care of itself and cures itself."[17]

To Frank Banfield, as might have been expected, improvement schemes even in middle-class and upper-class neighborhoods were essentially diabolical means whereby the landlord could further tyrannize over the tenant. The rebuilding which was going on in the 1880s on the Grosvenor estate struck him as being

17. TH, pp. 345–46; 1886 (213) xii.

especially outrageous. "I like fine streets as much as any one," he protested, "but I object to see numbers of Englishmen forced to tax their capital so heavily and perilously merely to suit the dictatorial architectural caprices of a millionaire Duke."[18] Although he might reluctantly admire the "Queen Anne" buildings then going up in and around Mount Street, all the enchantment of "Pont Street Dutch" at its most splendid could not make him forget their ducal origins:

> On the . . . northeastern end of Mount Street, there is a ghastly gap where houses have come down and the builder has not yet had time to replace them. On . . . the southern side, stretches for a considerable distance a massive pile of dwellings, rich in all the ornament which the artistic skill of Messrs. Doulton can command. The ground floors are handsome shops, and above rise five or six storeys of such height and general dimensions that one immediately comes to the correct conclusion that they are not adapted to be abodes for the tradesmen who carry on business below, but must be meant for letting in residential flats. This side of the street now presents a very fine appearance, and there can be no question that when the architectural schemes have been carried out to completion, Mount Street will be one of the most striking thoroughfares in the metropolis. "Very noble and public-spirited of the Duke," it may be observed. Just so, but then these grand edifices were not raised at his cost, but by the present tenants out of their hard-earned savings, on the commercial credit they possess, and on pain of having to wander forth. They constructed this massive pile no more willingly than the children of Israel, some thousands of years ago, expended their energies in deference to the task-masters of Pharaoh.
>
> Each of these new houses cost, on an average, seven thousand pounds to build, and, in certain instances, the occupier has found his outlay run up to nine thousand pounds, and has had no choice in the matter. He has been obliged to follow the Duke's plans, and his liberty has been further fettered in that he has had to accept the Duke's architects. A list of them has been given him, and from this list he has been obliged to choose. If he consents to build in this way he is granted a lease, the ground rent varying from £3 to £6 a foot, and as much as £6 10s. a foot has been asked. . . . Of course, where the tenant may be

18. *The Great Landlords of London*, p. 68.

lucky enough to let the superimposed flats at a good rent, he may survive the ordeal through which he has been forced to pass; but this is
a speculative matter, and we may venture to inquire what moral
right the Duke of Westminster has to compel old tenants of fifty years'
standing to go to an enormous expense, at grave risk to themselves, to
launch out in such an experiment.[19]

In summarizing his objections, Banfield made the rebuilding schemes of the
Duke of Westminster symbolize the tyranny which a great landlord could exercise over his tenants in order to gratify his own pride:

> He makes the tenants impoverish themselves to build too costly
> structures, because he has them by the throat, and can kick them out
> of their livelihood, if they do not erect enormous piles, for his grand-
> sons to annex one day altogether. . . . As for the new avenues built by
> the Duke at other people's expense, forced by a cruel, mercilessly ex-
> ploited terror, which tells them they must do it or starve—well, I pre-
> fer the more modest, but still handsome thoroughfares where free men
> dwell. Admiration of the great architectural remains of Oriental mon-
> archs of the past is tempered by the reflection that those huge piles of
> bricks and mortar represent not only the pride of one, but the groans,
> the tears, the life-long misery of millions. So it is with the Duke of
> Westminster's achievements in street reconstruction. And this is to be
> deplored—that the terrible anxiety of the many, and their attachment
> to home, should minister to the triumph of an autocratic whim. Phar-
> aoh and his prerogatives are an anachronism in modern London.[20]

Although they attacked the restrictions placed on the urban tenant by the
private landlord in the name of economic individualism, opponents of the
leasehold system were willing to contemplate similar restrictions if imposed by
political authorities. The bills before Parliament in the 80s which provided for
compulsory leasehold enfranchisement included provisions which would have
kept the covenants in operation even after the leasehold had been converted to
a freehold; the local authority would have the power of enforcement. Frank
Banfield dismissed the argument that civic decay would result from the breakup
of the estates by insisting that the local authorities would enforce the covenants
at least as efficiently as the ground landlords had: "We no longer need the great

19. Ibid., pp. 57–59. From the vantage point
of the 1960s it is hard to sympathize with down-
trodden tenants forced to invest seven or nine
thousand pounds in blocks of luxury flats in Mayfair.

20. Ibid., pp. 71–72.

feudal lord to protect us from each other," he exclaimed. "Are there not municipal authorities and sanitary authorities? If they did not exist, would it not be possible to erect a council which should have power to keep the freeholder within the limits required by the need of the community?"[21] It is significant that even the opponents of the leasehold system recognized the political nature of many of the activities of the great estates.

But although the scope of the activities of a London estate office was far greater than is often realized, it is an unwarranted anachronism to regard Belgravia and Bloomsbury as miniature welfare states, for they were not, any more than they were arenas of unrestricted economic freedom or the oriental despotisms of Mr. Banfield. Nor were they paternalistic planned communities comparable to New Lanark or Port Sunlight or even Pullman, for London's landlords were not also the employers of their tenants. Still less could there be anything remotely comparable to the personal relationship between landlord and tenant such as might exist on a country estate. What paternalism existed was necessarily impersonal and institutionalized—more like that of a government department than that of a Lady Bountiful.

However extensive the powers of a landlord might seem from the wording of a lease, there was in practice one consideration which prevented him from fully exercising his authority: he could not force anybody to live on his estate. He could not force builders to build in the first place or tenants to move into the houses in the second. Once there, they were under no obligation to remain. No London landlord had anything like a monopoly of land or houses, and therefore no landlord could afford to acquire a reputation for harshness or rigor.

"Any attempt," said John Bourne, "to impose an unusual term, either as to the amount of rent or restrictive conditions, or outlay by the tenant, or anything of that class, would simply result in having the property empty; no one would take it."[22] He had himself earlier found that the attempt, seemingly quite reasonable, to preserve Gower Street for the use of private families only resulted in practice in the houses remaining empty. The recurring conflict between the governors of the Foundling Hospital and their surveyors during the building on their estate was one between ground landlords wishing to exercise their theoretical powers and men of practical building experience who knew that it could not be done. The subsequent history of the estate could have been designed as an object lesson in the difference between the theoretical and actual powers which a building lease gives to a ground landlord.

21. *The Great Landlords of London*, p. 100.   22. TH, p. 569; 1887 (260) xiii.

For all its minor triumphs, the history of the great London estates remains one of partial victories and strategic retreats. The governors of the Foundling Hospital could not force James Burton to use the quality of building materials stipulated in his contracts. The Duke of Bedford could not force Thomas Lewis to put up bigger houses in Keppel Street than he wanted to erect. The Foundling estate could not, without recourse to extraordinary measures, turn Compton Place from a slum into a decent place to live. The Bedford estate could not in the long run keep boarding houses away from the best streets in Bloomsbury.

The experience of other estates reinforces the impression that Banfield's Mogul Monarchs and Persian Satraps were in fact nearly as much at the mercy of anonymous economic and social forces as were their cringing tenants. Rather than an absolute despot, shaping and reshaping the fabric of London to suit his whims and desires, the ground landlord was only one of the many agents whose varied and conflicting actions have made the metropolis what it is.

Town planning in England has until recently been a private concern, the duty of the great landowners, not of the political authorities. Now the state has taken over the responsibility, leaving the landlords with comparatively little scope for initiative. It remains to be seen whether the Ministry of Town and Country Planning will be more successful in achieving its aims than was the great landlord of eighteenth- and nineteenth-century London.

APPENDICES

APPENDIX I LANDED INCOME

Whether or not the great landlords of London managed their properties on "strictly commercial principles," there is no doubt that their estates have provided them over the centuries with a substantial and steadily growing income. Whether more enlightened or more ruthless policies would have increased the figures is another question. Yet if the town planning of the estate offices were to be judged solely by the growing income from ground rents, improved rents, and fines, no one could suggest that it has proved other than enormously successful.

"From the time of the third Earl [of Bedford]," wrote the eleventh Duke in 1897, "the Russells have identified themselves with the improvement of the soil. Landscape gardening, reclamation of fen land, arboriculture, high farming and stock breeding, housing of agricultural laborers, education of the rural population, and experimental farms form the history of the race in connection with the lands they owned."[1] He might have added that the enlightened practices on the country estates were made more feasible by the profits from the London properties.

The steadily rising income from Bloomsbury and Covent Garden, particularly in the nineteenth century, helped to enable successive Dukes of Bedford to lavish money on their country holdings, developing them as model estates, where they could follow humanitarian principles as much as commercial ones. Without a substantial and steady income from ground and house rents in London, the Russell family could not have fulfilled as they did their obligations toward the welfare of their country tenantry. The great houses of Russell

1. [Herbrand, 11th] Duke of Bedford, *A Great Agricultural Estate* (London, 1897), pp. 12–13.

Square and the warehouses of Covent Garden paid for the schools and churches of Tavistock and Thorney. The tolls and rents from Covent Garden Market paid for the model cottages at Woburn and Chenies. The importance of landed income in maintaining the political predominance of the fourth Duke of Bedford is obvious; the Bloomsbury Gang would have played a smaller part in the Parliamentary history of the 1760s had they not been supported by Bloomsbury ground rents.

The Russell family did not, of course, rely as heavily on urban rents in the 1660s as they did in the 1890s. In the 1650s, for example, the ground rents from the Covent Garden estate amounted to little more than £1,500 per annum.[2] In 1668, the year before Lady Rachel Vaughan married William Russell, Bloomsbury produced only slightly more than £1,200 in ground rents. In addition, the market in Bloomsbury brought in around £340, while not quite £400 came from that part of the Middlesex estate which was still let for farming purposes.[3]

By 1700 the ground rents from the Bloomsbury estate had risen to over £2,000 annually.[4] Including the grazing rents, the total Bloomsbury rental at Lady Day 1733 was £4,517.[5] In the same year the Covent Garden rental was £7,094, including £1,000 from the market. This figure probably does not include fines, which were an important source of income during the middle years of the eighteenth century. On the Covent Garden estate nineteen fines paid between September 1729 and February 1730/31 amounted to no less than £2,935. Where fines were paid, rents had of course to be reduced proportionally.

At the accession of the fourth Duke in 1732 the total rental from all his estates was £32,545, of which nearly a third came from Bloomsbury and Covent Garden. The total expenditure on all the estates at that time, including taxes, came to about £6,700.[6] In the years that followed, the income from the London estates steadily grew. The gross Bloomsbury rental exceeded £5,700 at Lady Day 1739; twelve years later it was £7,187. The Covent Garden rental in 1759 was £10,356.

In December 1760 the Duke settled on his eldest son, the Marquess of Tavistock, properties in London and elsewhere with an annual value of £8,272.[7]

2. Gladys Scott Thomson, *Life in a Noble Household* (London, Cape, 1937), p. 79.

3. Scott Thomson, *The Russells in Bloomsbury*, p. 58.

4. Ibid., p. 186.

5. 1733 Rental. Unless otherwise indicated, all information as to estate income (calculated to the nearest pound) comes from the annual rentals and account books in the Bedford Office. The figures are not the actual receipts—which often fluctuated greatly from year to year—but the amount owed by the lessees.

6. Scott Thomson, *The Russells in Bloomsbury*, p. 301.

7. Abstracts of leases on estate of the Marquess of Tavistock, 1760–1786, pp. 6–7.

The settlement included a sizable portion of the Covent Garden estate. Lord Tavistock died in 1767, leaving a son as heir to the dukedom. For purposes of accounting the late Marquess' estate was kept separate until 1855. Beginning in 1819, however, the rents from his estate were included in the regular Covent Garden rental.[8]

At Lady Day 1763 the rental of the Marquess of Tavistock's estate in Covent Garden was £3,043. On the Duke's Covent Garden estate the rental totaled £7,916. Neither of the totals includes fines. In 1765 the Bloomsbury rental was £7,832. The actual gross income was usually somewhat less than the rental would indicate, due to non-payment of rent. Marginal comments such as "insolvent," "run away," and even "these premises can't be found," occur frequently in the volumes of the rentals.

The total rental at Lady Day 1775 for London and Middlesex was £21,109, including £164 from property in the City of London. The largest increase came from the Bloomsbury estate, which by then produced £9,055. Ten years later the total rental had grown to £23,653, most of the increase again coming from Bloomsbury, on which a great new building program was going forward on the fields north of Great Russell Street. Fines were a negligible factor, as they had been since the 1760s.

In 1805, just before the ground rents from the new streets on the site of the grounds of Bedford House started to come in, the Bloomsbury rental came to slightly less than £13,800. The following year it jumped to £17,242. In 1811 it reached £20,273, and by 1816 was close to £25,000.

By 1819 the London rental equaled that of all of the other Bedford estates, and from then on increasingly surpassed the country receipts. In the year ending Lady Day 1819 the London steward paid into Child's Bank a total of £48,413 which he had received as rent; all the country estates together produced £48,605 over the same year. The following year the total payments into Child's had risen to £101,259. The increase came chiefly from the Covent Garden estate; excluding the Marquess of Tavistock's property, the income had grown from £18,548 to £22,500 during the year.[9]

During the next few years fines became an important source of income for

---

8. The Marquess of Tavistock's estate lay wholly within the parish of St. Martin-in-the-Fields. It included property in Bow Street, Broad Court, Bridges Court, Cross Court, Chapel Court. Duke's Court, Drury Lane, Hart Street, Jackson's Alley, Long Acre, Marquess Court, New and Old Crown courts, Phoenix Alley, Russell Street, Russell Court, St. Martin's Lane, St. John's Court, and White Hart Yard.

9. W. G. Adam, Annual Statements, 1815–29, fols. 59, 71. The figures all represent net income, hence are not strictly comparable with the gross rentals listed in earlier paragraphs.

the first time since the 1760s. In Bloomsbury alone, casual profits—mostly fines —from 29 June 1820 to 15 November 1821 came to more than £8,500. The reason for the sudden resort to fines was the fear on the part of the Duke's auditor that deflation might make it impossible for houses to "sustain an increase of annual rent if the times should alter; and that therefore it was prudent to secure their present value by partial fines."[10] By the end of the decade the practice had ceased. From that time the estate took fines only when granting new leases of public houses. In 1870 it ceased to take fines even on such occasions.

Despite the anxiety of the auditor, the yearly rentals of the London estate grew steadily during the post-Napoleonic period, counteracting the fall in agricultural rents. In 1822 the rental from the two Covent Garden estates was £23,526. Ten years later it was £26,138. The Bloomsbury rental for the year ending Lady Day 1824 was £31,218. In 1830 it had reached £40,357.

The estate took over the management of Covent Garden Market in 1830. At first the income from market tolls and stall rents was added to the Covent Garden rental, but by 1837 the market receipts were being recorded separately. In that year the gross receipts were £8,972, and the net produce £5,913. The lessees of the market had in the first two decades of the century paid a rent of only £2,900 to the Duke. Since that time, however, the Duke had spent close to £61,000 in rebuilding the market.[11] Net market receipts fluctuated, but generally rose during the remaining years of the century. In 1897 gross market receipts totaled £54,142, and the net income exceeded £32,700.

The growth in ground rents and house rents over the same period was less spectacular but equally satisfying. At Lady Day 1844 the total Middlesex rental, excluding market receipts, was £75,837. Bloomsbury contributed more than half, or £40,468. In 1865 the Middlesex rents, again excluding Covent Garden Market, came to £73,061. Expenditure on the estate during the year amounted to £14,617. Gross receipts from all the Duke's estates in 1865 came to £273,200.

At Michaelmas 1880 the Middlesex rental totaled £104,880, reflecting in part the building leases in the Bedford Square area which had recently fallen in. Of the total, ground rents from Bedford New Town accounted for £3,958. Bloomsbury provided £65,791, while Covent Garden rents came to £35,131. In 1897 the gross annual rental of the London estates was £115,593. The net income was £100,837. To this must be added the more than £32,000 of net income from Covent Garden Market. And since the ninety-nine-year leases of the greater part of Bloomsbury—roughly covering the area north of Great Russell Street and

10. Ibid., fol. 85.   11. 1832 Report.

east of Gower Street—would expire in the next generation, there was every reason to expect a considerable increase in rentals in the near future.

Although smaller than the neighboring Bedford estate, the Foundling estate provided a comfortable income for the Hospital. The ground rents from the original building development amounted to £5,500.[12] By 1897 enough of the original ground rents had risen to house rents to increase the income to over £18,930. Improved rents—that is, rents representing the full value of the buildings as well as the ground they occupied—accounted for more than £15,000 of the total.

In 1926 the Hospital sold the whole of its property in London for £1,650,000 and moved to a new site in Berkhamstead. At the time of the sale, practically all the original leases had expired, and the income from the estate had risen to £42,000 annually.[13]

12. Information as to income all comes from the annual accounts included in the volumes of minutes of the General Court.

13. Nichols and Wray, *The History of the Foundling Hospital,* p. 284.

APPENDIX II KEPPEL STREET, BLOOMSBURY

Thomas Lewis to Thomas Pearce Brown, 8 June 1807:

> I cannot help expressing my wish that you will reconsider the subject.
> The houses in Keppel Street, although smaller than intended, will I
> am sure be found to be as well built, as far as they have proceeded, as
> any upon the estate; and in respect to the others, any alteration will
> be made that you may be pleased to direct; and although I am unfor-
> tunate in losing your approbation on this occasion, I am sure you will
> not involve the other persons (who are building, and are innocent) in
> the resentment reserved for me . . .
>
> I have taken the liberty to send the plans and elevations designed
> for the present buildings, and shall be happy to wait upon you to ren-
> der any explanation you may require . . .

Draft of a letter from T. P. Brown to a builder in Keppel Street, 25 June 1807:

> To my astonishment I learn that you have begun to put bricks on the
> ground in Keppel Street without having made any agreement for it,
> and with an evident intention of erecting houses of a description
> never intended to be built there. As it becomes necessary that the
> agents for his Grace should have some control over his property, I
> think it my duty to acquaint Mr. Adam [the chief agent] of the cir-
> cumstances, and to submit to him that you should not have the
> ground, and you will accordingly desist from proceeding any further
> till his pleasure on the subject shall be known.

Thomas Lewis to T. P. Brown, 25 June 1807:

> With deep concern I have perused the letter you did me the honor to address to me on the subject of the ground in Keppel Street. I will not exasperate the transgression by attempting a defense of my proceedings after the decided opinion you have expressed upon them. With submission however I beg to state that I understood for some months past that I should have the remaining ground in Keppel Street, at a rent to be approved of by Mr. Adam; and week after week attended at the Office to sign any paper you thought proper on the subject, conceiving that a difference of two or three shillings a foot for so small a quantity and for so important an object as to complete the street ought not to weigh with me against it. Undoubtedly I have acted under this impression, or I should not have done anything upon that part of the estate, and most certainly I have thought myself furthering your views by the expedition with which the buildings are commenced. In respect to the size of the houses, allow me, Sir, to say that I have most innocently offended in that respect, as I had ascertained by measurement that out of twenty-four houses in Keppel Street fourteen are smaller than those proposed by me, and the persons building will vouch for it that I advised them to make them smaller than they had intended, knowing that in these times many genteel families will give more for a small house in a good situation than for a large one; and having a concern for their success, it was my advice to them. Mr. Gubbins saw the foundations laid, and excepting the projected houses in Torrington Street gave his sanction to them, as my people have informed me. If I had not understood it so, they should not have proceeded after Wednesday the 14th inst.
>
> Upon such an occasion as this it does not become me to go into a longer explanation, for I am not justifying myself; I must however say that so far from any sentiment of disrespect ever actuating my mind towards the Duke of Bedford or his agents, in the humble path it is my province to tread in life, no man can be [mo]re sincere in his attachment to the August House of Russell, or better acquainted with the honor, talents, and integrity of those who administer his affairs.

T. P. Brown to [Thomas Lewis], draft copy, 27 June 1807:

> In answer to your last letter, I beg leave to say that at the very last meeting I had with you respecting the ground in Keppel Street the

matter was left thus: you disapproved of the plan which had been laid
before Mr. Adam, and on which alone he had given any opinion as to
the quantum of rent, etc., and you proposed to produce a new plan.
This you have never done, and for the best reasons: because you was
conscious that the plan on which you have begun to build would not
be approved of. The size of any houses which may have been built in
a street is not in all cases to regulate the whole line, and houses which
might be proper towards the west end of Keppel Street might not be
deemed so at the end next the square [i.e. Russell Square]. You mention that Mr. Gubbins saw the foundations of the houses laying in
Keppel Street, but you are aware that neither Mr. G. or any other person than Mr. Adam can give any consent to the building on any part
of his Grace's property.

You cannot have forgot that you took possession of the ground on
the south side of Keppel Street without any agreement with the agents
of his Grace as to rent, the styles of building, or otherwise, and what
you have done on this ground by no means adds to the beauty of the
estate, or have the buildings anything to boast of on the head of
stability.

Thomas Lewis to T. P. Brown, 22 July 1807:

[Lewis begins with a complaint about the terms which the Bedford Office had imposed for granting leases for four houses on the south
side of Keppel Street, which he had disposed of more than six months
before, and which terms he describes as incompatible with an earlier
verbal understanding he had from the Bedford Office.]

. . . I beg to assure you I have suffered much inconvenience for
want of two of those leases, the regular forms having been gone
through by your surveyor, and a promise given for the execution of
them at the Office some months ago. In respect to what has taken place
since, on which account you are pleased to say the previous arrangements cannot be complied with, I beg to observe that you cannot have
been *rightly informed* of those proceedings, and determine as you are
said to have done in this instance; because I know that *next to your duty*
to his Grace the Duke of Bedford, you have avowed yourself the pro-
moter of the interests of those who (allow me to say) sacrifice *every
instant of private comfort,* and put to risk their all; and it may be a considerable stake too; and for what is in *better times* a reasonable *pros-*

pect of remuneration; but at all times, and under all circumstances the certain benefit and improvement to his Grace's estate. It is not for me, especially under the misfortune of having incurred your displeasure, to set up any pretensions to extraordinary notice in the improvements on this part of the Bedford estate; but I must in justice to that honorable frankness of disposition so characteristic of your nature insist upon it; that I have your own testimony through different channels of communication for more than becomes me to say on the occasion. Arithmetic however *demonstrates* to me that I have given currency to upwards of seventy thousand pounds upon your buildings, and I challenge those who have attempted to depreciate any of them to detect a *material* defect, particularly in the external brickwork, so essential to the stability of a building, whilst they themselves have not equaled them in those they have erected upon the estate.

. . . I certainly thought, and allow me to say I still think the houses erecting in Keppel Street best adapted for the situation and the times. The persons building with my assistance after many months negotiating would have embarked upon another estate, as they told me, if they were not permitted to proceed at the time. . . . It will . . . when you see it completed form a consistent finishing to the street without encroaching too much upon the large houses in the square, which deeper houses would have done, and in respect to the houses in Torrington Street, they shall be erected according to the alterations proposed. . . .

Messrs. Brown and Gotobed, solicitors, to [Mr. Minot, builder in Keppel Street], copy, 26 August 1808:

Complaint having been made at Bedford Office that you were erecting a building contrary to the covenants of your lease, and which would prove a serious inconvenience to your neighbors, we directed the Duke's surveyor to view the premises and make his report thereon. He has done so, and his report confirms the statement of the complaint; he also mentioned to us that he had given orders to your workmen not to proceed; it is therefore with some concern that we learn you continue to go on with the work, as unless the terms of the lease are complied with, and any nuisance occasioned to the neighbors is removed, we must be under the necessity of proceeding to vacate the lease.

APPENDIX III HART STREET SCHOOLS, COVENT GARDEN

Christopher Haedy to T. Moseley, 6 November 1837:

Herewith I send you the draft proposals and the draft lease referred to in them, relative to the Hart Street schools.

The matter, as I believe you know stands thus—we say, and the trustees are aware, that the Duke's tenants *must* be protected from annoyance, and if when the building is erected, the annoyance should (notwithstanding the care, by double windows, etc., taken to prevent it) still be felt, *that the schools must cease to be carried on in the building.*

It is impossible for us beforehand to tell whether the means proposed to be taken to prevent the annoyance will really prevent it: and it is for the trustees well to consider, before they incur the cost of building the schoolhouse, whether after it is built the annoyance will with certainty be abated; for, if it should not be, it must be distinctly understood that the covenants to be inserted in the lease relative to the annoyance will be rigidly enforced, and that the Duke of Bedford's agents cannot and will not allow his Grace's tenants to be continued to be annoyed.

Another point too which it will be proper for the trustees seriously to consider is whether it will be possible for so many persons as will be assembled in the schools to breathe in rooms in three sides of which there will be no openings for air; for as no openings can be made to admit air which would not also allow the escape of sound, it must also be distinctly understood that no openings in the back, front, or sides of the building will be allowed to be made, either in the first erection of the building or at any time afterwards.

If the treaty should proceed, it must likewise be distinctly understood that the entire responsibility of expending the funds of the school upon a building in which (in case of failure of the means resorted to to abate the annoyance to the Duke of Bedford's tenants, or the impossibility of using it for a school, for want of proper ventilation) the schools cannot be continued to be carried on will rest exclusively on the trustees, and in no degree upon his Grace or his agents.

Christopher Haedy to W. G. Adam, 8 December 1837:

Whilst I was with you today a deputation headed by the Rev. Mr. Bowers, without making any appointment or informing me that they were coming, called here to confer with me on the subject of the Hart Street (Covent Garden) Infant etc. schools, a subject I mentioned to you a year or two ago. Great complaint was made of them by the Duke's tenants in King Street. The children chant their lessons, and they play in a garden behind, making altogether a noise which was, beyond all doubt, a very great nuisance and a positive injury to such of the tenants in King Street as let lodgings, and to the grand hotel. I went to hear it, and I was quite satisfied that it was not a thing that we ought to allow to continue, and the tenants in King Street were promised that on the expiration of the lease at Midsummer 1838 the nuisance should be abated. His Grace was written to on the subject by the trustees of the schools, and he expressed his hope that we should be able to reconcile the interest of his tenants in King Street with the continuance of the schools, on account of their great use to the neighborhood in keeping so many children out of the streets, as well as from the interest his Grace takes in the spread of education.

In two or three interviews I have lately had with the trustees I informed them that if they could so rebuild their schools as effectually to put a stop to the nuisance, we would treat with them for a lease of the premises; but that it could only be on the condition of the Duke's tenants being protected by the strongest covenants against a continuance or renewal of the annoyance. This was before I went to Brighton this year. Had they not applied till my return, I should have hesitated to let the ground to them on any terms—for, whilst there, I was (with reference to this question) to see some similar schools there. The roar of the ocean was nothing to the ear-tearing noise of those schools.

Mr. Brown, the architect of the trustees, said he could so build the schools as to throw all the noise into Hart Street; and on the condition of our approving the designs, and of their having no windows (except with double and unopening sashes) at the back, and not using the yard as a playground, we consented to treat with them for a lease, with covenants strong enough to protect the Duke's tenants in King Street.

Accordingly the designs were presented, and with a few alterations were approved of, and I prepared the accompanying drafts, proposals, and lease, and I sent them to Mr. Moseley . . . with the accompanying letter dated 6 November 1837. He altered them, striking out the special covenants, and returned them to me. I then sent him the letter dated 29 November.

I have since (a day or two ago) seen Mr. Brown, their surveyor, and he thinks, with what I have since struck out, they will be content to take the lease as originally drawn, but he said he had no authority for saying so.

The covenants are certainly strong—I knew whom I had to deal with, and I made them as strong as I could—but no stronger than I think they ought to be. If they (as they say they wish) make no noise and do not annoy the Duke's tenants, then, strict as the covenants are, they will be a dead letter. If they do make a noise and disturb the Duke's tenants, then we shall want these covenants to force them to put a stop to the annoyance. . . .

The covenant beginning (in fol. 6) "and also that if at any time or times" I introduced to avoid the risk of a jury's not finding that the noise proved was an annoyance or a breach of the covenant. In all matters of the kind (matters of opinion what a thing is) there is always uncertainty as to what a jury may think. It is not like a simple matter of fact, as to whether rent is due or a window blocked up. If a coppersmith or other person carrying on a very noisy business, or a person living in a street through which the omnibuses thunder and where hardly any noise can be heard should be on the jury, it would be difficult to convince such a juryman that the screaming of children was an annoyance. To make our remedy (if it should be necessary to use it) as certain as possible, I thought and think that covenant should be retained—for we shall do the greatest possible injustice to the Duke's tenants in King

Street if we do not reserve the most ample power to protect them—and they are persons paying to the Duke from five to six hundred pounds a year in rent.

The estate and the trustees eventually reached agreement, and the Duke granted a new sixty-year lease, at £20 per annum. On 26 October 1838 the trustees wrote to the Duke, informing him that the schools had been rebuilt according to the agreement, to the satisfaction of the tenants in the neighborhood. They went on to ask that the Duke become the patron of their institution, which they described as being "calculated to effect so much good to the children of your Grace's tenantry, and the neighborhood in a locality where your Grace's influence is so extensively felt, and so highly appreciated." The Duke consented to become the patron, and gave a sum of £50 to the building fund. From the Annual Report for 1859, p. 5:

Covent Garden. Hart Street Schools.

On the representation of the Rev. Henry Hutton that the school premises had long been in a very unsatisfactory condition, Mr. Parker viewed and reported on them, and having suggested various alterations which would remedy objections and accommodate one hundred additional children, the school committee applied to your Grace through Mr. Hutton to undertake the work, which you consented to do. Plans have accordingly been prepared by Mr. Searle, the architect, and the contract has been let to Mr. Howard for £1,787.

BIBLIOGRAPHY

The literature on urban estate management is meager. Many books deal with the growth of London, but few of them do so with reference to its landed estates. Two general works on London which recognize the important part played by the great landowners in its history are Sir John Summerson, *Georgian London* (Baltimore, 1962), and S. E. Rasmussen, *London: The Unique City* (London, 1948). The two are essentially architectural studies, but both deal at length with questions of town planning and the economic bases of urban growth. Both are indispensable for an understanding of how London has become what it is. William Ashworth, *The Genesis of Modern British Town Planning* (London, 1954), also describes the planning of the estates in the metropolis. H. J. Dyos, *Victorian Suburb* (Leicester, 1961), a model of detailed analysis, shows how the landowners and speculative builders of Camberwell went about turning that parish into a dormitory suburb.

The many topographical studies of other districts of London contain little of importance about the estates or their management. Exceptions are Charles T. Gatty, *Mary Davies and the Manor of Ebury* (2 vols. London, 1921), which includes a history of the Grosvenor estate down to the early eighteenth century, and B. H. Johnson, *Berkeley Square to Bond Street* (London, 1952), which has a useful account of the building history of the Berkeley estate in Mayfair.

The thirty-two volumes of the *Survey of London,* which the London County Council has so far published occupy a unique position in the literature on the metropolis. When completed it will be the definitive work on London's topographical history. Volumes 5 and 21 include information on parts of the Bedford estate in Bloomsbury, while Volume 24 covers the Foundling estate.

An unpublished thesis by K. Melville Poole, "Portman Estate: A Study in Private Planning" (1952), a copy of which is deposited in the Marylebone Public Library, is an appraisal of the original development and subsequent history of the Portman estate from the standpoint of modern principles of town planning.

The best published accounts of the actual management of the great London estates are to be found in the minutes of evidence of the Royal Commission on the Housing of the Working Classes (London, 1884–85), and the Select Committee on Town Holdings (London, 1886–90) in the Parliamentary Papers. Reasoned attacks on the long-leasehold system can be found in *The Land*, Vol. 2, *Urban* (London, 1914), published by the Land Enquiry Committee, and S. Vere Pearson, *London's Overgrowth and the Causes of Swollen Towns* (London, 1939). Charles Henry Sargant, *Ground-Rents and Building Leases* (London, 1886) describes in an elementary fashion the long-leasehold system in London.

The Bedford and Foundling estates are more fully dealt with in published monographs than are most estates in London. In addition to the relevant volumes of the *Survey of London*, R. H. Nichols and F. A. Wray, *The History of the Foundling Hospital* (London, 1935) deals briefly with the history of the Foundling estate. Gladys Scott Thomson has written the history of the first century of the Bedford estate in Bloomsbury in *The Russells in Bloomsbury 1669–1771* (London, 1940). Her earlier *Life in a Noble Household 1641–1700* (London, 1937) has some information about the Covent Garden estate. Eliza Jeffries Davis, "The University Site, Bloomsbury," *London Topographical Record, 17* (1936), 19–139, recounts in some detail the history of the part of the Bedford estate which the University of London purchased in the late 1920s. Rowland Dobie, *History of the United Parishes of St. Giles-in-the-Fields and St. George Bloomsbury* (London, 1834) includes much first-hand information about James Burton and the building developments on the Bedford and Foundling estates after 1800.

Three excellent studies of English landed estates and their management appeared in 1963; although they deal for the most part with agricultural policy. they help to put urban estates in their economic context. F. M. L. Thompson, *English Landed Society in the Nineteenth Century* (London, 1963) has more information on the specific practices of individual estates than has G. E. Mingay, *English Landed Society in the Eighteenth Century* (London, 1963). David Spring, *The English Landed Estate in the Nineteenth Century: Its Administration* (Baltimore, 1963) deals at some length with the estates of the Duke of Bedford.

Apart from the abundant material in the above-mentioned volumes of Parliamentary Papers, the bulk of this work is based on manuscript sources in the Bedford Office in London, and the records of the Foundling Hospital (now the Captain Coram Foundation) both at its offices in Brunswick Square and, on deposit, in the London County Record Office at County Hall.

The records of the Foundling Hospital are unusually complete and extensive. The minute books of the General Court and general committee are to be found in Brunswick Square. During the 1840s and 1850s the surveyor's quarterly reports are included in the volumes of the General Court minutes, but at other times they are useful chiefly for their information on the annual income from the estate and the granting of new leases. The general committee, meeting at weekly intervals or oftener, handled the day-to-day management of the estate.

There are five volumes of minutes of the building committee, from 1790 to the completion of its labors in 1826. For the years after, the volumes of the Estate Committee continue the account of the further management of the property. An estate book lists the original building leases granted down to 1826. These volumes are at County Hall, together with the records of the Foundling Estate Paving Commission.

From the Bedford Office I have used rentals, account books, the volumes of annual reports and letters to and from the agent-in-chief, London steward, and solicitor, together with leases and building agreements. The latter were particularly useful, since they often include drawings and elevations of the buildings agreed to be erected, along with plans of the sites. During the two decades after 1893 the estate made a policy of photographing all of its buildings which were about to be torn down or altered. The resulting pictures, some of which are here reproduced, provide an incomparable record of what Bloomsbury and Covent Garden used to look like.

INDEX